HELPING PEOPLE
WITH EATING
DISORDERS

HELPING PEOPLE WITH EATING DISORDERS

A Clinical Guide to Assessment and Treatment

Robert Palmer
University of Leicester, UK

JOHN WILEY & SONS, LTD
Chichester · New York · Weinheim · Brisbane · Singapore · Toronto

Other Wiley Editorial Offices

John Wiley & Sons, Inc., 605 Third Avenue,
New York NY 10158-0012, USA

WILEY-VCH Verlag GmbH, Pappelallee 3, D-69469 Weinheim, Germany

Jacaranda Wiley Ltd, 33 Park Road, Milton,
Queensland 4064, Australia

John Wiley & Sons (Asia) Pte Ltd, 2 Clementi Loop #02-01,
Jin Xing Distripark, Singapore 129809

John Wiley & Sons (Canada) Ltd, 22 Worcester Road,
Rexdale, Ontario M9W 1L1, Canada

Library of Congress Cataloging-in-Publication Data

Palmer, Robert L.
  Helping people with eating disorders: a clinical guide to assessment and treatment / Robert Palmer.
    p. cm.
  Includes bibliographical references and index.
  ISBN 0-471-98647-X
    1. Eating disorders. I. Title.

RC552.E18 P35 2000
616.85'26—dc21

                                        99-089738

British Library Cataloguing in Publication Data

A catalogue record for this book is available from the British Library

ISBN 0-471-98647-X

Typeset in 10/12pt Palatino by Saxon Graphics Limited, Derby
Printed and bound in Great Britain by Antony Rowe, Chippenham, Wilts
This book is printed on acid-free paper responsibly manufactured from sustainable forestry, in which at least two trees are planted for each one used for paper production.

CONTENTS

ABOUT THE AUTHOR

Bob Palmer is Senior Lecturer in Psychiatry at the University of Leicester and Honorary Consultant Psychiatrist at the Leicestershire and Rutland Healthcare NHS Trust, Brandon Mental Health Unit, Leicester General Hospital. He is Clinical Director of the Leicestershire Eating Disorders Service. He has written books and papers on the subject of eating disorders and is the Editor of the *European Eating Disorders Review*.

PREFACE

I have written this book to provide an introduction for clinicians to the eating disorders, anorexia nervosa and bulimia nervosa – conditions that have become increasingly salient over recent years. More and more people working in various health professions have been confronted with the need to try to help sufferers to escape from what can be miserable and life-blighting disorders. Some professionals find themselves with the additional task of organising services for people with eating disorders, and in doing so they may get caught up with the ambivalence of the general public who often seem to hold contrasting attitudes to the eating disorders, viewing them at times as the trivial fads of silly young women and at other times as mysterious and deadly diseases lurking in their midst and picking off young people at the threshold of promising lives. Those who plan and fund health care may share these extreme views – albeit less openly – but almost everywhere provision is patchy and often inadequate.

Those who would seek to do better face a variety of obstacles. Not least amongst these is the wide range of advice and opinion about the nature of these disorders. There is a lot to sift through and at times it seems that there is a more dirt than gold. This book is designed to do some of that sifting and sorting for the reader. I hope that it may be useful to have some help from someone who has been panning this particular stream for many years. However, I would warn you that although I have tried to give a balanced account, I can present things only as they appear to me. Even an experienced eye may miss what is important or be sometimes misled by 'fool's gold'. The enthusiasm that we all need in clinical practice may at times distort judgement. It is important to be confident about what we do and for that confidence to rest on as sure a foundation as possible. Where possible I have tried to include discussion of, or reference to, the sources of the views that I put forward. However, in the end you must judge for yourself – and for the people whom you are trying to help.

I have tried to make the book practical in orientation. It is about trying to help people with eating disorders. Whenever I was faced with a decision as to whether to include something or leave it out, I decided on the basis of clinical utility. Consequently some topics which might have made the book more interesting may have been omitted in favour of some which are less fascinating but more useful clinically. This book does not set out to be a theoretical treatise upon the nature or wider significance of eating disorders. Such books can be of great interest and may even be important but something different is required to support the professional confronted by a sufferer asking for help as the professional needs to be able to put the person seeking help into wider context, to assess her problems, to know what others have found useful to offer and to avoid making things worse. Most of all the professional needs a measure of confidence. Of course, such competence and confidence cannot come just from a book, but the right kind of book could help, and I have tried to write such a book. I cannot be the judge of how useful it will be in practice. Only time, and those who read the book, will tell.

I shall, of course, be delighted if as many people as possible read – and buy – this book. These might include the student, the sufferer, perhaps the families of sufferers and even that fabled figure 'the interested general reader'. However, it is not written with them in mind. I have written this book for people who have chosen – or find themselves chosen – to offer help to those suffering from clinical eating disorders. My guess is that they may come from a variety of the so-called 'helping professions', mainly but not exclusively those relating to mental health. Their background – and perhaps their professional qualification – may be in nursing, psychology, occupational therapy, social work, counselling or one of the medical specialities, especially psychiatry. Or sometimes in none of these. Nevertheless, I have assumed some basic clinical knowledge and vocabulary. I have sometimes used terms such as 'major depression' or 'electrolytes' or 'obsessive compulsive disorder' without definition, confident that most readers will know what I mean, or at least can easily find out. More importantly, I have assumed that most readers will have that less definable characteristic – clinical nous. They may or may not have had much experience of being with people suffering from eating disorders but they will know what it is like to be in a professional 'helping relationship' with people who are ill or in distress. I hope that this description fits you or, if it does not, that you will understand for whom the book is mainly intended.

The subject of helping people with clinical eating disorders is a large one. This book is not. This means that the overview of these disorders which the book provides may be fairly comprehensive but often not detailed. Where appropriate I have added references at the end of chapters to books and journal articles that discuss the topics in greater depth. Furthermore, I am the sole author of the book although, of course, I am largely passing on what I have learnt from others. This means that it surveys the field from my viewpoint. I have alluded above to the need to be wary of the results of lacunae in my vision which may distort the picture. I guess that I am unaware of most of these; however, one issue of which I am aware is that my clinical experience is that of an adult psychiatrist. I have almost no experience of trying to help sufferers who are under the age of 16. Many issues involved in dealing with children and early teenagers are the same as those encountered with late teenagers and adults, but many are not. The younger the sufferers, the more 'special' are their needs although even the use of this word reveals the perspective from which I am viewing things. Any account given in this book of the particular characteristics and needs of the youngest sufferers is second hand. I have tried to discuss them somewhat but I am aware that the emphasis throughout the book is on older sufferers. The recommended further reading is especially important for this topic.

Another important limitation of this book is that it deals with obesity only as a close neighbour of the eating disorders and as an association in some cases. Again this is for practical reasons as the book needed to be fairly short. Obesity is a big topic and I am not myself greatly experienced in that field. My practice reflects the view of many, perhaps most, clinicians working with eating disorders, in that people suffering from obesity without definite eating disorder are usually considered to be outside the remit of the clinical service in which we work. That is the way things are. Whether it is the way things should be is another question. Over the last few years there has been a welcome coming together of people with a research interest in the eating disorders and in obesity. Perhaps clinical practice will follow. This might have real advantages. (As I write this I am pondering the question of whether or not to start an obesity clinic as part of our service.) However, for the present, I have followed what may become the old-fashioned path of focusing upon anorexia nervosa and bulimia nervosa and leaving obesity at the margin.

Throughout the main text of the book, I have chosen to use what might be called the 'scientific passive voice'. I dithered somewhat about this but decided in the end that it was best. By contrast, I have used the device of notes at the end of the chapter whenever I wanted to add a more personal or idiosyncratic comment or indeed anything additional to the main text that seemed worth including, but not at the expense of interrupting the flow. For these notes, I have used the first person.

Another point of language concerns the potentially touchy matter of gender. Most of those suffering from eating disorders are female. Certainly this is the case for most people who seek help. I have therefore chosen in general to use the female gender – she, her and so on – when discussing sufferers rather than resorting to the clumsy 'she or he', the unpronounceable s/he or the complications associated with the unnecessary plural 'they'. When talking of those who seek to help I have tried to avoid gender words but where this has not been easy I have used the male 'he', even though in most contexts the majority of helpers are female. This is less of a distortion than making the sufferers male and tends to clarify the text. I realise that such clarification may be at the expense of aligning the gender split in the text and what may often be thought of as the overt power dynamic of the therapeutic relationship thus described with that which has been traditional in the wider society.

The book is divided into two parts. The first, from Chapter1 to Chapter 5, describes and attempts to explain the eating disorders. This is a prelude to the rest of the book which is more directly concerned with the practical matter of trying to help people who suffer from these disorders. This second part begins by discussing assessment and the treatment of anorexia nervosa and bulimia nervosa. The next chapters discuss the management of atypical cases and of situations where things go wrong – as, of course, they always will from time to time. It is important that the book avoids giving the impression that helping people with eating disorders is a matter of following a 'cookbook' approach – that all will be well if the correct recipe is followed. Of course, sometimes it may be a good idea to follow a particular plan – for instance, by using one of the manualised treatments – but even the best plans will not cope with every situation. Even an approach that gives a central place to clinical research and the evidence which it generates can do no more than inform the clinician what *may* be the best thing to do. If effective, this book may play a part in that process of informing clinicians, but it is not a 'what to do next' instruction book. At best, it may simply help the reader to prepare for a better informed clinical practice including, where appropriate, the use of manualised and other treatments which require particular training. Such treatments and training will be discussed in the book but – to state the obvious – a book such as this cannot provide such training of itself. Individuals and services need to organise appropriate training and the final chapter discusses issues of service organisation and provision within which the issues of training and supervision are of central importance.

Part I

1

WHAT ARE THE EATING DISORDERS?

It is safe to assume that most people starting to read this book will already know a fair amount about what the eating disorders are and about how they affect those who suffer from them. Indeed, a majority of the public at large have heard of both anorexia nervosa and bulimia nervosa and know something about them. However, this was not the case until fairly recently. Before 1979, the term bulimia nervosa had not been coined and very few people were aware of the condition it names. Anorexia nervosa had been described for well over a century, but until the 1960s it was thought of as a rarity. However, what had, until the 1960s and 1970s, been the subject of brief entries in medical textbooks has now become the stuff of countless articles in magazines and newspapers. The increased prominence – and probably the increased prevalence – of the eating disorders was a phenomenon of the late twentieth century.

This chapter will outline briefly the history of the development of the modern concept of the eating disorders and will then describe the key features of these disorders. There will be discussion of the way in which these features have been wrapped up into formal sets of diagnostic criteria and the advantages and difficulties of doing so. This chapter will be long on description and short on attempts at explanation or understanding. That will come later. 'What' comes before 'why'.

A BRIEF HISTORY

What follows is a sketch of the history of the concept of the eating disorders. It is mainly about how people – until recently, mainly doctors – have *thought* about such problems rather than about the problems themselves. This emphasis is for two good reasons. Firstly, we may still be influenced by the history of the ideas that we use today. Secondly, the writings of clinicians who have dealt with problems of eating in the past may tell us a good deal about their observations and opinions of the few people whom they had treated, but little about the many people who were not patients. There was little systematic research until relatively recently, so we can study only the opinions of clinicians as revealed in their writings.

It seems likely that there have been some people throughout history who have got into difficulties with what, for most people, is the straightforward matter of eating and maintaining a healthy body weight. Indeed, perhaps it is incorrect to describe these matters as straightforward; they are after all so important that they almost universally accrue a great deal of social and cultural meaning. However, most people do not and have not become ill or disordered in relation to these issues. Of the few who became so disordered before the last four decades or so we can catch only glimpses. However, such glimpses, although doubtless unrepresentative, can often be fascinating.

Over the centuries there have been people who have starved themselves. Some could be interpreted from a modern perspective as having had anorexia nervosa, or something akin to it. However, anorexia nervosa is a state with psychological aspects which cannot easily be detected in the minds of those who are long dead unless they have themselves written about their inner lives and done so in a way that can be translated into modern terms. That, however, is rarely the case and we are left to make rather tenuous inferences about these early 'cases' (Habermas, 1989, 1992; Parry-Jones, 1991; Parry-Jones & Parry-Jones, 1995). It is thus difficult to make knowledgeable judgements of the fasting saints and people – interestingly often young women – who were held up and sometimes exploited because of their apparent ability to live without eating (Vanderycken & van Deth, 1994). Likewise, there must remain a deal of uncertainty about the nature of the maladies in the very earliest clinical descriptions, such as the famous and often quoted 'nervous consumption' described by Thomas Morton in 1689 (Silverman, 1995). Different times may construe similar states in different ways (Brumberg, 1988).

The earliest 'modern' accounts of what came to be called anorexia nervosa were made more or less simultaneously – although independently – by Charles Lasegue in France (1874) and Sir William Gull (1874) in England. Both accounts are worth reading although they are different in style.[1] Gull's paper is straightforward and descriptive. Lasegue is more concerned with the psychological aspects of the patients he describes.

He invoked the then prominent but protean concept of hysteria and called the illness *anorexie hysterique* – hysterical anorexia. It was Gull who invented the name that was to stick, anorexia nervosa.

There was a steady trickle of publications on anorexia nervosa in the last decades of the nineteenth century and the first half of the twentieth (Mount Sinai, 1965; Silverman, 1997). There was debate as to its nature. It is said that there was a degree of muddling of the anorexia nervosa and hypopituitarism (Simmond's disease) after that disorder was described in 1913. Furthermore, even when anorexia nervosa was construed as a psychiatric disorder, there was continuing debate as to whether it was better thought of as an entity of itself or merely as a variant of some other condition such as obsessional neurosis or schizophrenia (Bliss & Branch, 1960). Debates about the relationship of the eating disorders to other psychiatric disorders continue in more muted form to this day.

From the 1960s onwards the utility of assigning anorexia nervosa to a diagnostic category all of its own became increasingly established. The modern concept of anorexia nervosa had reached maturity (Crisp, 1967; Russell, 1970; Bruch, 1973) However, as sometimes happens to people, no sooner had a measure of maturity been achieved than things began to fall apart. Anorexia nervosa started to undergo a form of nosological mid-life crisis.

Firstly, there were attempts to produce a useful subcategorisation of the disorder. The most significant split was that between sufferers who maintained a low weight solely by restraining their eating and those who resorted to vomiting (Beumont, George & Smart, 1976). Many, but not all, of the latter also showed bingeing behaviour (Casper, Eckert, Halmi, Goldberg & Davis, 1980). The two groups were shown to differ on a number of characteristics of their background and current clinical picture, the latter seeming to be on average more likely to show a wider variety of troubled or troubling behaviour.

Secondly, a group of people was recognised as suffering from eating disorders which closely resembled this second bingeing and vomiting group of anorexia nervosa sufferers except that they were of normal or high body weight (Vanderycken, 1994; Russell, 1997). With the publication of Gerald Russell's classic paper (1979), bulimia nervosa had emerged. The wider concept of 'bulimia' was included in the DSM III (APA, 1980) but Russell's term and, broadly speaking, his concept came to be included in later revisions of the main classificatory systems. The broad outline of the syndrome seems to have unequivocal utility, although there is still room for doubt about the detailed criteria (Sullivan, Bulik & Kendler, 1998).

At the time of publication, the current formal systems are the fourth revision of the *Diagnostic and Statistical Manual of the American Psychiatric Association* – DSM-IV (APA, 1994) and the tenth Edition of the *International Classification of Diseases* – ICD-10 (WHO, 1992). The DSM-IV system is arguably superior for the eating disorders because it provides rational subcategories as well as the additional category of binge eating disorder. It will be used as the basis for discussion in this book unless otherwise stated. However, the criteria for the main eating disorders within these two systems are similar. The following sections will describe and discuss the broad features of anorexia nervosa and bulimia nervosa which are common to all modern definitions of the disorders. These will be in the main familiar, but they are so basic that they are worthy of discussion. Each disorder will be illustrated briefly by a case history.[2] There will also be a brief discussion of binge eating disorder and of obesity.

THE FEATURES OF ANOREXIA NERVOSA

The most prominent feature of anorexia nervosa is **low weight**. This is almost always the result of **weight loss**. (The exception is when a child comes to be at a lower than average weight because he or she has failed to gain weight in the expected way.) In general, it is best to discuss body weight using an index which takes height into account, for instance the Body Mass Index or BMI.[3] Some sets of diagnostic criteria specify a level below which a low body weight is thought to be significant. For example, ICD-10 requires a BMI of less than 17.5 whilst DSM-IV suggests but does not seem to require a body weight less than 85% of what would be expected. Clearly weight is a continuous variable and the level of body weight or amount of weight loss taken as counting for the diagnosis is somewhat arbitrary; a line is being drawn in order to define a category for practical use.

The weight loss of anorexia nervosa is attained and maintained by inadequate eating. Typically this is because of **motivated eating restraint** rather than loss of appetite or of any reduction in the drive to eat. Indeed, the sufferer may feel that her urge to eat is very strong and potentially out of control. She nevertheless attempts to eat little – less than she would normally do and less than is required to maintain a normal weight. She sits on top of her hunger. Of course, for many sufferers the issue of their drive to eat is a touchy topic and their account of it to others – perhaps even to themselves – is variable and may be evasive. Some will acknowledge an urge to eat but will deny being hungry because that word has too positive a connotation for them. Other sufferers will deny having any drive to eat at all. However, whilst it is possible that a few sufferers do come to experience true anorexia in the sense of loss of appetite, this is certainly not the case for the majority. Of course, 'anorexia' means lack of appetite and the inclusion of the word in the name anorexia nervosa is strictly a misnomer. However, after well over a century of use, it is probably too late to change it now.

Some sufferers will give in to their urge to eat more than they intend and may then seek to thwart the effects of this by use of **abnormal weight control methods** such as inducing vomiting or taking laxatives or diuretics. Sometimes, sufferers will **exercise** excessively. This may be directly motivated by beliefs about 'burning off calories' although there also seems to be some biologically driven connection between food deprivation and overactivity.

Some anorexia sufferers will truly binge – they will show the **symptom of bulimia**. (The issues involved in what this means will be discussed below in the section on bulimia nervosa.) More often, the person will *feel* that she has binged even though objectively she has eaten only a little. She feels that she has binged because she has transgressed her own personal rules by having given in to her urge to eat. The DSM-IV classification divides anorexia nervosa into a restricting type and a binge-eating/purging type (see Box 1.1).

The motivation for the eating restraint of anorexia nervosa typically has something to do with the sufferer's wish to keep her weight low. Indeed variants of this particular motivation are specified in most sets of diagnostic criteria. They set out attitudes and beliefs which are said to constitute the **specific psychopathology** of anorexia nervosa. The words used to capture these include 'intense fear of gaining weight or becoming fat' (DSM-IV) or 'a dread of fatness' (ICD-10). Of course, such motivation resembles that which underpins much 'normal' slimming although the anorexia sufferer continues with her motivated eating restraint to a point way beyond that to which the typical slimmer aspires. The sufferer may have started out with similar ideas but she takes them to the extreme. She neither gives up in the face of the negative consequences of eating restraint (not least hunger) nor does she do so when she reaches the body weight that was her original aim. By the time that she fulfils criteria for anorexia nervosa, ideas about body weight and its control have become unusually important for her. Typically she will have become preoccupied with food – reading about it, often cooking it for others but not eating what she cooks. She will fear loss of control of her weight or eating or both. She may feel that if she allows her weight to rise just a little, she will 'lose it', become fat and be unable to regain control. In truth, of course, it is her control that is out of control. The whole thing becomes charged with emotion and meaning, *letting go* being followed by guilt and self-recrimination and *holding on* being associated with a fragile satisfaction.

The person who develops anorexia nervosa will typically show other characteristic features, both psychological and physical. Prominent amongst the former is the phenomenon known as **body image disturbance**. This has become well known and it is one of the clichés of illustrators to depict the emaciated young woman standing before a mirror in which she sees herself reflected as grossly obese. Perhaps something like this is experienced by some sufferers. However, for most, body image disturbance is less stark and more complex. The usual experience seems to be one involving knowing that the body is thin *and* having a variable

---

Box 1.1   DSM-IV Criteria for Anorexia Nervosa

A. Refusal to maintain body weight at or above a minimally normal weight for age and height (e.g. weight loss leading to maintenance of body weight less than 85% of that expected; or failure to make expected weight gain during period of growth, leading to body weight less than 85% of that expected).

B. Intense fear of gaining weight or becoming fat, even though underweight.

C. Disturbance in the way in which one's body weight or shape is experienced, undue influence of body weight or shape on self-evaluation, or denial of the seriousness of the current low body weight.

D. In postmenarchal females, amenorrhoea, i.e. the absence of at least three consecutive menstrual cycles. (A woman is considered to have amenorrhoea if her periods occur only following hormone, e.g. oestrogen, administration).

Types
Restricting Type: During the current episode of anorexia nervosa, the person has not regularly engaged in binge-eating or purging behaviour (i.e. self-induced vomiting or the misuse of laxatives, diuretics or enemas).

Binge-Eating/Purging Type: During the current episode of anorexia nervosa, the person has regularly engaged in binge-eating or purging behaviour (i.e. self-induced vomiting or the misuse of laxatives, diuretics, or enemas).

---

feeling of fatness that exists alongside. The contrast is broadly that between thinking one thing and feeling another although each, of course, influences the other. The concept of body image is itself far from being simple (Smeets, 1997). Nevertheless, simply stated, body image disturbance is included as a criterion in most diagnostic systems.

Another feature which is usually included amongst diagnostic criteria, is the physical symptom of **amenorrhoea** (lack of menstruation) in females. In most cases amenorrhoea is secondary in the sense that periods have been present in the past but have now stopped. In a few cases of early onset, amenorrhoea may be primary. Underlying the lack of menstruation is a change in function of the axis of neuro-endocrine control which involves the brain (mainly the hypothalamus), the pituitary gland and the ovaries. In an anorexia sufferer aged 19, the function of this system, as reflected in levels of the relevant hormones, resembles closely that which might be expected in a girl of 9. The system is effectively switched off and this switch off tends to be reflected in the experience of a lack of libido as well in a diminution of acne and adolescent angst. Sometimes the changes which accompany the loss, then recovery, and then loss again of hypo-thalamic–pituitary–gonadal function in someone repeatedly regaining and losing a normal body weight can be striking for the observer. The person seems to change in all sorts of ways from child to teenager and back in just a few weeks. The experience for the sufferer must be extraor-dinary and profoundly unsettling. This may also be the case for those who are emotionally involved with the person and the process – notably the family. In male sufferers, the parallel system is likewise switched off. For men, the symptomatic effects are confined to the more general changes – for instance, loss of sexual drive – since there is no precise physical equiv-alent of the cessation of menstruation. In practice, even in the female, there may be some problems in judging whether to count amenorrhoea as being present. This is not only because the symptom is usually elicited purely by self-report but also because the issue is complicated by the widespread use of hormonal drugs, most notably the various oral contra-ceptive pills. What might be called 'pill periods' tend to continue to occur at a much lower body weight than that which would sustain normal menstruation. However, pill periods also tend to stop if the weight is low enough. Another difficulty is that, on recovery of normal body weight, the return of menstruation is sometimes delayed in a way that is not well understood.

In addition to the diagnostically relevant features outlined above, people suffering from anorexia nervosa typically experience **many less specific symptoms**. Physically, they may complain of bloating and other gastrointestinal symptoms. They often feel weak, tired and cold but may nevertheless push themselves to be active in their everyday lives and, as mentioned above, sometimes undertake programmes of special exercise in the belief that it may help to control their weight. Sleep is often disturbed and commonly has an early morning waking pattern which is akin to that in depressive illness. Indeed, in both states it may be driven by undereating. Psychologically, they often experience **depression of mood, anxiety and obsessional symptoms**. Sometimes such additional symptoms are of such a degree and pattern as to fulfil criteria for comorbid major depression or other syndromes. More generally, anorexia nervosa sufferers typically have a poor view of themselves and a **low self-esteem,** except perhaps in the matter of their eating habits which may sometimes be a source of perverse satisfaction. But mostly they are unhappy and, furthermore, feel trapped because of the fear that things would get even worse in nameless ways if they were to change.

These then are the core features of anorexia nervosa. More will be said about many of them later in the book as part of the discussion of possible processes which may bring the disorder about or perpetuate it. Furthermore, later chapters will contain accounts of the main complications which may arise in some but not all sufferers.

Faith: a Story of Anorexia Nervosa

Faith was the younger daughter of two schoolteachers. Her earlier childhood was settled and happy but things began to go wrong when she was 14 and her sister Fiona was 16. Their father, who was then aged 46, had a major heart attack. This came out of the blue and was a shock and surprise to the whole family. It also changed a lot. He had continuing angina and other problems. By-pass surgery did not seem to help much. He had to stop work and give up his ambition to become a headmaster. He became prone to bouts of depression. He was touchy and irritable, especially with Fiona. Over the next two years, rows between the two of them dominated the household. Faith tended to keep quiet and try to not get involved. However, she felt upset and torn between the two of them.

Much to her parents' disapproval, Fiona left school at 17 and got a job in a local record shop. At 18 she became pregnant and left home to live with her boyfriend. Her father was devastated and said that he would have nothing more to do with her. Her mother and Faith continued to visit her secretly. When Fiona's baby was born there was some reconciliation but her father continued to be low spirited and upset. He often complained of chest pain. Sometimes he said that Fiona had ruined his life. Faith's mother struggled to hold things together, working hard at her job, acting as go between and looking after her sick and troubled husband.

Meanwhile, Faith was doing well at school. Her parents were delighted when her teachers suggested she try for a place at Oxford or Cambridge. She was studying modern languages, her father's subject, and he coached her in the evenings. He described himself as her 'trainer' and Oxbridge entrance as the 'Olympics'. He also encouraged her to go jogging, making pronouncements about a healthy mind in a healthy body. As his disappointment with Fiona became more open, his involvement with Faith became more intense. She valued her father's interest but was increasingly aware of the extent of his expectation. She began to fear letting him down.

Faith began going out with a boy called Andrew who had been at the same school. It was her first real boyfriend. However, she soon came to feel a sense of conflict between her wish to spend time with Andrew and her wish to devote herself to her studies. She also felt that her father disapproved of her new relationship and feared that she would 'end up like Fiona'. One weekend she stayed out late and worried her parents. Her father had a bad angina attack and her mother reminded Faith how important it was that her father should not be upset. She began to make excuses not to meet Andrew and before long he left her for another girl. Faith felt heartbroken and secretly angry that her father seemed so pleased about the ending of the relationship. She felt upset and uncertain but resolved to pull herself together. She decided to apply for Oxford and dreamed of being a success there. She would wait for her reward. In the meantime she would work hard, save money, get fit and even lose a little weight as she had been promising herself for months that she would do.

At first things went well. Faith worked hard. Her father was delighted. Her mother seemed more relaxed and even Fiona began to visit more often. Faith produced a timetable for her studies and her father helped to plan it all out. She lost a few pounds by taking up running and following what her mother called a 'sensible diet'.

Faith felt good for much of the time but sometimes when studying her mind would wander. She would chide herself for wasting time daydreaming. She worried what would happen if she did not do well. She felt bad one evening when she found that she had eaten a whole packet of biscuits whilst at her studies. She weighed herself and found that she had regained three pounds. She felt that somehow she must get back on track. She produced a new timetable and this time it covered not only her school work but all of her activities, including running and eating. She rationed the times when she would allow herself to have a cup of coffee and just one biscuit. Soon she cut out the biscuit altogether.

As the weeks went by, Faith lost more weight. At 16 she had weighed about nine stones (58 kg.). A year later she weighed just six and half stones (42 kg.) and her periods had stopped. She was by now preoccupied by just two things – succeeding at her studies and controlling her weight. She feared that she would fail at both. By now she was studying so much that even her father advised her to ease off. Her mother was worried about her eating but Faith would lie and say that she had eaten at school when she had not. She wore baggy clothes and avoided letting anyone see her undressed. She knew that she looked thin but often felt fat. She thought about food a lot but distracted herself by studying even more. Once she got up in the middle of the night and ate two packets of biscuits and a tub of ice-cream. She then tried to make herself vomit but did not manage it. This reinforced her feeling that if she allowed herself to eat freely, everything would get out of control.

That autumn Faith was rejected by Oxford. By now it was evident that she was very thin. At Christmas her behaviour led to major rows and upsets. Early in the New Year, her mother persuaded her to see the family doctor. When weighed she was just under six stones (37 kg.). It was now clear that she was suffering from anorexia nervosa.

BULIMIA NERVOSA

The core-defining symptom of bulimia nervosa is frequent **binge eating**. However, in everyday talk the term 'binge' is imprecise. Many of us would admit to enjoying a belt-loosening blow-out on occasion and we might well call it a binge. Those who are especially concerned about their weight may judge themselves harshly in this respect and describe thus any mild indulgence. Such subjective binges may occur in dieters and even more in those suffering from anorexia nervosa, as was mentioned above. However, the kind of binge that really counts as such for the diagnosis of bulimia nervosa has two other crucial characteristics. Firstly, the binge should be accompanied by a subjective sense of loss of control. Secondly, it should involve eating an amount of food which would be unusual in the prevailing circumstance. Sometimes the amount eaten may be extraordinarily large and reports of binges in excess of 10,000 kcals are not unusual. Some sets of criteria also emphasise the idea that a binge should be a discrete episode of eating in this way rather than a long drawn-out excessive graze. (DSM-IV suggests that a binge should last for 'a discrete period of time' for example a 'two-hour period'. Whether specifying such a time limit really captures some important characteristic is rather unclear.) Such binge eating is usually secret and occurs when the person is alone. To count for full syndrome bulimia nervosa within the DSM-IV classification, bingeing must occur on average at least twice per week for three months.

Loss of control and excessive intake taken together are valuable in separating off 'true' binge eating from the what might be called normal indulgence. However, they are not without problems. For instance, many people with bulimia nervosa at times plan their binges and deliberately shop for the binge foods that they eat. Such behaviour complicates the meaning of what it is for a binge to involve loss of control. The idea may still be valid but clearly cannot mean that the binge is carried out impulsively and on the spur of the moment. The loss of control is perhaps more like that of the drug addict who finds himself grappling with a continuing additional drive which motivates him to behave regularly in ways which the non-drug dependent person does not. It is part of him, but a part which he would rather not own and against which he sometimes struggles but often succumbs and at times even enjoys. Certainly details of the experiences of bulimic bingers seem to vary widely between and within episodes of bingeing. Sometimes the associated affect is of miserable failure and guilt throughout. Sometimes the experience is of catharsis and release of tension. All sorts of feelings are reported.

As with anorexia nervosa, bulimia nervosa characteristically arises against a background of attempted eating restraint. Furthermore, the motivation for such eating restraint usually resembles that of the anorexia sufferer and thus bulimia nervosa has a similar **specific psychopathology**. This is described in DSM-IV (Box 1.2) as involving self-evaluation which is 'unduly influenced by body weight and shape' and other criteria use such terms as 'morbid dread of fatness' (ICD-10). Much has been written about the way in which the ideas of bulimia nervosa sufferers may differ from those with anorexia nervosa. However, the words used in the criteria to describe these matters are remarkably similar. Furthermore, of course,

---

Box 1.2 DSM-IV Criteria for Bulimia Nervosa

A. Recurrent episodes of binge eating. An episode of binge eating is characterised by both of the following:

   (1) Eating, in a discrete period of time (e.g. within any 2-hour period), an amount of food that is definitely larger than most people would eat during a similar period of time and similar circumstances.

   (2) A sense of lack of control over eating during the episode (e.g. a feeling that one cannot stop eating or control what or how much one is eating)

B. Recurrent inappropriate compensatory behaviour in order to prevent weight gain, such as self-induced vomiting; misuse of laxatives, diuretics, enemas, or other medications; fasting; or excessive exercise.

C. The binge eating and inappropriate compensatory behaviour both occur, on average, at least twice a week for 3 months.

D. Self-evaluation is unduly influenced by body shape and weight.

E. The disturbance does not occur exclusively during episodes of anorexia nervosa.

Types
Purging Type: During the current episode of bulimia nervosa the person has regularly engaged in self-induced vomiting or the misuse of laxatives, diuretics, or enemas.

Non-purging Type: During the current episode of bulimia nervosa, the person has used other inappropriate compensatory behaviours, such as fasting or excessive exercise, but has not regularly engaged in self-induced vomiting or the misuse of laxatives, diuretics, or enemas.

many people move from one disorder to the other and it is not clear that this coincides with a change in their thinking as well as in their behaviour. It may be best to construe the two 'specific psychopathologies' essentially as variants of a similar way of thinking occurring within different contexts and histories. When bingeing occurs, the individuals will usually reverse the dictates of their dieting and eat the very kind of foods that they do not allow themselves within their non-binge thinking.

The person who 'dreads fatness' but who finds herself breaking out of her attempted eating restraint into bingeing will tend to adopt **various compensatory behaviours** to try to thwart the effects of the excessive eating upon her weight. Their use is a necessary part of the diagnostic criteria for bulimia nervosa. The most common of these compensatory behaviours is **self-induced vomiting**. Most sufferers do this by putting their fingers down their throat.[4] However, some discover or develop a facility for vomiting without any such mechanical stimulation. Vomiting is effective at getting food out of the body although many sufferers have an exaggerated idea of its efficiency. Some food is left down and absorbed. Some people elaborate the process of vomiting, for instance, by eating marker foods first in the naïve belief that when the marker appears everything has been brought up. Others engage in the potentially dangerous practice of drinking and then vomiting large quantities of water to wash themselves out. Any vomiting can lead to potentially hazardous electrolyte disturbance. **Laxative abuse** is another method of trying to get rid of binged food. This, too, can be dangerous and furthermore is rather ineffective. (Occasionally enemas may be used.) The main result of taking even very large quantities of laxatives – over fifty senna tablets would not be unusual – is to cause loss of fluid and electrolytes from the large bowel rather than to reduce absorption of food (Lacey & Gibson, 1985). However, the sensation of painfully won emptiness perhaps accompanied by feelings of 'cleanliness' may itself be rewarding for the guilt-ridden binger. The **abuse of diuretics** (water tablets) is even less rational as a way of losing fat or other body substance but, nonetheless, may be adopted because of its immediate if essentially illusory effect upon apparent body weight. As with the other methods, the abuse of diuretics can cause major disruption in body chemistry.

Other methods may be employed by the bulimia sufferer to try to compensate for her overeating.[5] The most common of these are **fasting** and **excessive exercise**. Both of these are included in the DSM-IV criteria but neither is easy to define. When does eating restraint become fasting and when does exercise become definably excessive? These difficulties make these two compensatory mechanisms the 'soft' end of the definition of bulimia nervosa. DSM-IV divides bulimia nervosa into two subtypes characterised by the presence or absence of 'purging' behaviour, namely 'vomiting or the misuse of laxatives, diuretics or enemas'.

As with anorexia nervosa, the syndrome of bulimia nervosa is often accompanied by many **symptoms of wider physical or psychological discomfort and distress**. Depressive symptoms are common and comorbid major depression or a history of such disorder occurs in as many as a half of sufferers from bulimia nervosa (Cooper & Fairburn, 1986; Cooper, 1995)

Rachel: a Story of Bulimia Nervosa

Rachel was the elder child and only daughter of a policeman and a nurse. When she was aged 11 her father left his family to live with another woman. Rachel was upset and angry and had almost no contact with her father for the next eight years. She tried to comfort and support her mother. They became very close. Her mother tended to confide in her to an unusual degree and together they looked after Rachel's brother, Sean, who had been only six when his father left.

Rachel has no major regrets when her parents were finally divorced two years later. However, she was not sure how she felt when a little later her mother started going out with John, a colleague from work, and within six months announced that they were to marry. Rachel was just 15 when her mother married John and he moved in. She told herself that she was pleased for her mother but she missed their former closeness. Furthermore, she did not feel comfortable with John. He tried hard to be friendly but tended to tease her about going out on dates, her taste in clothes and about her worry about her appearance. He also teased her about the way in which she was always going on and off slimming diets which lasted for just a day or two.

Over the next year or so, Rachel felt more and more isolated and unhappy at home. She tried to spend as little time there as possible. She went out almost every evening and often ended up drinking a lot. This added to her difficulties at home. She greatly resented it when John started to behave like a strict father. There were many rows between them. That summer she took her GCSE examinations but the results were disappointing. She was unsure what to do but she decided to leave school. She signed up for a course at the local college.

When Rachel was 17 she met a professional footballer called Mark, who was seven years her senior. From the start it was a difficult relationship because, although Mark was lively and glamorous, he also seemed rather unreliable. Just before Christmas, as she was wondering whether to finish with him, Rachel discovered that she was pregnant. To her surprise, Mark seemed pleased at the prospect of becoming a father and they decided to live together. Her mother and stepfather protested that she was 'too young' but Rachel suspected that they were secretly relieved that she was leaving home. At Easter she dropped out of her college course and in July gave birth to a baby boy, Rory.

Rachel loved her new baby but found motherhood overwhelming. She felt mixed up and uncertain about herself. Furthermore, she had put on a lot of weight during her pregnancy and felt fat and unattractive. She wanted to lose weight but found it difficult. Sometimes she was uninterested in food but at others ate more than she intended. She became miserable and mildly depressed. With the start of the football season, Mark was often away and seemed less interested in the baby. As the months went by the couple had more and more rows. Rachel worried that Mark would meet other women on his trips away from home. And he became more and more jealous and possessive, objecting even when she went out with her old girlfriends. She became increasingly unhappy and isolated just as she had done a year or so before. This time, however, there was no obvious escape route open to her. She certainly did not want to go back to her mother's house. She also regretted having given up her education. However, when she talked to Mark about going back to college he accused her of wanting to meet other men. In the midst of one row, he called her fat, ugly and boring. He said that she had 'let herself go'. She was angry and upset but secretly these were the very things that she had been thinking about herself.

Rachel made another resolution to lose weight. She started by going on a crash diet. She was pleased to lose some weight quickly but felt unhappy, hungry, preoccupied with food and irritable. One evening Mark telephoned yet again to say that he would not be home. She felt angry, upset and out of control. She stuffed herself with food until she could physically eat no more. Then she felt guilty and in a panic. She made herself vomit by putting her fingers down her throat. The next day she resolved to eat even less but a week later she binged again. Much as she tried to stop, she felt caught up in a pattern and soon she was bingeing and vomiting several times each week. Although her eating was now wildly erratic her weight stayed much the same.

Rachel left Mark shortly after Rory's first birthday. The final break had come when Mark had hit her in an outburst of jealousy. Rachel had recently re-established some contact with her father and when he heard about Mark's violence he had threatened to come around and 'sort out' Mark if she stayed. So she left. At first, Rachel moved back to her mother's house but after a few weeks she moved into a flat of her own with Rory. Soon, in some ways, things began to look up for her although she still felt lonely and unsure of herself. Indeed at times in the first weeks she felt quite desperate and even thought of trying to kill herself. However, she resolved to rebuild her life. She resumed some contact with Mark, but just as friends. She went out occasionally with her old friends and attended an aerobics class. She started a new course at the local college and talked of eventually going on to university. To other people it looked as though things were going well but secretly her life revolved around a battle with bingeing and vomiting. She was stuck within bulimia nervosa.

Although most sufferers from bulimia nervosa are attempting eating restraint and, furthermore, seem to have developed their disorder in the context of such restraint, a minority offer a history in which bingeing ante-dates restraint or in which restraint is largely absent (Mussell *et al.*, 1997).

They may not restrain because they are relatively less weight concerned. When such people do not purge, they may hover at the edges of the definition of bulimia nervosa or even fall outside of it. They may nevertheless have a significant eating disorder. The earliest American classification which considered bingeing – the DSM-III of 1980 – wrapped up all such states, together with those now called bulimia nervosa, into a widely defined disorder which was called simply 'Bulimia'. Subsequent classifications have used narrower definitions for bulimia nervosa as described above, but DSM-IV has included, albeit provisionally, a new category called 'Binge Eating Disorder' to try to capture some of those states that have been excluded by this process of nosological refinement.

BINGE EATING DISORDER

The concept of a third eating disorder has been defined only recently. It arose from an awareness that many people have highly problematic binge eating without fulfilling criteria for bulimia nervosa. Most of these fail to qualify for that diagnosis because they do not show the characteristic attempts to thwart the effects of binge eating upon their weight such as vomiting, abusing laxatives and so on. Furthermore, for some the bingeing does not seem to have arisen following attempts to restrain their eating in the way that would be characteristic of most bulimia nervosa sufferers (Mussell et al., 1995). Many, but not all, people in this category are obese. Binge eating in obese people had, of course, been well recognised for years (Stunkard, 1993) although its close definition and study tended to be hampered by erroneous beliefs about the ubiquity amongst the obese of 'bingeing' in the widest sense of any overeating. Clearly, there is a sense in which those who are obese must have 'over-eaten' relative to some standard of intake which might have kept them at an average weight. However, it is not the case that most obese people binge in any useful sense of the word and certainly not in the sense defined in the diagnostic criteria for bulimia nervosa or binge eating disorder.

The idea that this pattern of binge eating without compensation warranted the creation of a new diagnostic category was championed by Spitzer and colleagues who conducted field trials of diagnostic criteria (Spitzer et al., 1992, 1993). The new category, binge eating disorder (BED), was included in the appendix of DSM-IV as a 'provisional diagnosis worthy of further study' (see Box 1.3). This phrase accurately reflects the current status of binge eating disorder. The concept seems to capture and place into the classificatory canon part of the elusive lay concept of 'compulsive eating'. However, there are some who doubt its validity and consider the creation of a third syndrome premature (Fairburn, Welch &

Hay, 1993). Nevertheless, it has stimulated a good deal of interest and some useful research (de Zwaan, 1997).

There are some difficulties inherent in defining binge eating disorder. These include the question of how to define a binge. In purging bulimia nervosa the issue is to a degree made easier by the relative ease with which vomiting or purging, which are discrete behaviours, can be defined and counted. However, overeating is different. Furthermore, although the suggested criteria for BED include the idea that the binge eating should occur in discrete episodes as in bulimia nervosa, there is some evidence that much problematic overeating in the obese has different character-istics, including what might be called all-day binges (Marcus, Smith, Santelli & Kaye, 1992).

The suggested criteria contain little in the way of necessary psycho-logical characteristics. In particular, the attitudes towards weight and shape which are required for bulimia nervosa and anorexia nervosa are omitted, as is any hint of the attempted eating restraint for which they may provide the motivation. (Indeed, such attempted restraint does often seem to be absent.) A person who would fit the bill for binge eating disorder but has unusually strong concerns about weight and shape might well fulfil criteria for bulimia nervosa non-purging type. The boundary and rela-tionship between the two disorders is not entirely clear in practice (Santonaso, Ferrara & Favaro, 1999).

Binge eating disorder occurs in a substantial proportion of obese people presenting at weight reduction clinics and services, but in a lower proportion of the obese in the community at large. Reported percentages range from 30% for the former to 5% or so for the latter, although these figures may be overestimates (Marcus, 1995). Furthermore, in at least one wider community survey less than a quarter of women with binge eating disorder were obese (Fairburn et al., 1998). Nevertheless, the disorder has mainly been studied in people who are overweight. The 'further study' envisaged by DSM-IV is certainly required. However, it does seem likely that the category of binge eating disorder or something like it will continue to be useful and necessary.

OBESITY

Obesity is variously defined but a person with a BMI of over 30 would usually be thought to be appropriately described as obese and a BMI of over 40 warrants the term severe obesity. Some people with eating disorders are obese, but only a minority of obese people have a definable eating disorder. As was stated in the introduction, for better or worse, this book will consider obesity only as a background factor or comorbidity for some eating disorder sufferers rather than as a topic in its own right.

BOX 1.3 DSM-IV Criteria for Binge Eating Disorder

A. Recurrent episodes of binge eating. An episode of binge eating is characterised by both of the following:

1. Eating, in a discrete period of time (e.g. within any 2-hour period), an amount of food that is definitely larger than most people would eat in a similar period of time under similar circumstances.
2. A sense of lack of control during the episodes (e.g. a feeling that one cannot stop eating or control what or how much one is eating).

B. The binge-eating episodes are associated with at least three or more of the following:

1. Eating much more rapidly than normal.
2. Eating until feeling uncomfortably full.
3. Eating large amounts of food when not physically hungry.
4. Eating alone because of being embarrassed by how much one is eating.
5. Feeling disgusted with oneself, depressed or feeling very guilty after eating.

C. Marked distress regarding binge eating is present.

D. The binge eating occurs on average, at least 2 days a week for 6 months.

E. The binge eating is not associated with the regular use of inappropriate compensatory behaviours (e.g. purging, fasting, excessive exercise) and does not occur exclusively during the course of anorexia nervosa or bulimia nervosa.

What part 'overeating' in each of its several senses plays in the genesis of obesity is unclear. Indeed, it is not at all clear in general how best to think about the originating and perpetuating factors in most cases of obesity. What are certainly not justified are simplistic explanations which suggest or imply that obesity is to be thought of as the result of greedy overindulgence with or without the addition of the noxious influence of deep and dark emotional forces. However, such ideas seem to be at the root of much popular thinking about obesity and underpin the stigma that surrounds it.

Such ideas should be opposed, although unfortunately more rational accounts of the origins of obesity are neither simple nor certain. Genetic influences are undoubtedly important but not all-important as developmental and environmental factors play their part. Some factors are best construed in psychological terms. However, to say all that amounts to very little. Such bland generalisations hide a deal of ignorance.

DIAGNOSTIC CRITERIA AND ATYPICAL DISORDERS

This chapter has been concerned with defining and describing the main eating disorders. This exercise has been addressed in relation to one of the formal systems of diagnostic criteria, namely DSM-IV, and it has been helpful to have such formal definitions as an anchor to the discussion. However, it is important to remember that even the broad diagnostic categories, such as anorexia nervosa, are themselves best thought of a conceptual tools. They have value and are 'true' inasmuch as they are useful in organising our thinking and clinical practice, but they are inventions and should be thought of as provisional. Only if they were to survive criticism and be bolstered by more and more evidence of their utility, integrity and mechanism should they be accorded the kind of status enjoyed by a disease like syphilis where symptoms, signs, aetiology and pathogenesis can all be wrapped up together into some kind of convincing whole. Indeed, there would be those who would suggest that finding such a disease concept is unlikely when considering a psychological disorder or, perhaps, that the very idea is incoherent even as a goal.

In practice with the eating disorders, such theoretical considerations are hardly an issue since the present entities are so clearly provisional and the subject of much tinkering. Furthermore, it is a fact that an important proportion of people presenting to clinicians with significant eating and weight problems do not have disorders which fulfil criteria for any of the main syndromes. Some suffer states which resemble such syndromes closely, but others seem to be importantly different and yet still invite a mainly psychological explanation. Most diagnostic systems have a residual 'rag bag' category to cater for these diagnostic non-conformists. In DSM-IV, it is called Eating Disorder Not Otherwise Specified, an inelegant term which inevitably gets shortened to EDNOS. The capital letters are best preserved in writing to indicate that the word is an acronym. In speech however, 'EDNOS' has come to have some currency as a word pronounced phonetically with two syllables rather than as five letters spoken separately. It is now part of the jargon of eating disorders, although it denotes more of a problem for consideration than a classificatory solution. The issue of EDNOS will appear again throughout this book.

Another issue which should be flagged at this stage and revisited later is that of *comorbidity*. By this is meant the coexistence of two or more diagnosable disorders in one person at the same time – for instance, bulimia nervosa and major depression. Here again, the need to make such dual diagnoses – especially if they are common pairings such as this – should make us aware of the shaky conceptual rigging that holds up many of our cherished diagnostic concepts.

This chapter has been concerned mainly with definition. The next will look at the results of taking these definitions out into the world and counting and describing the kind of people to whom they apply.

NOTES

1. Both of these papers can be found in the original volumes but both are reprinted in a book called *'Evolution of Psychosomatic Concepts – Anorexia Nervosa: a paradigm'* which was published in 1965. This is now itself of historical interest. It contains several other reprints of papers about anorexia nervosa from the early twentieth century. It is included in the reference list under Mount Sinai (1965). A commentary and additional translation of Lasegue's account may be found in a paper by Vanderycken and van Deth in the *British Journal of Psychiatry* (1990) 157, 902–908.

2. The case histories used in this book are fictitious. I have concocted them to avoid problems of confidentiality. Also, invented stories can be fine tuned to illustrate certain points. They are, of course, merely illustrations – cartoons even – and not evidence. It should be kept in mind that the use of such stories can make things seem too clear and reinforce stereotypes. Real people are less neat.

3. The Body Mass Index or Quetelet's Index is calculated by dividing the weight in kilograms by the square of the height in metres. It is used as a way of trying to remove the issue of height when comparing degrees of thinness or obesity. People with the same BMI have broadly similar degrees of plumpness whatever their height, even though their crude weight may differ markedly. A normal healthy BMI range is usually taken to be that between about 19 and 25. As an example, for a person who is 1.76 metres tall, this range would coincide with body weights between 57 and 75 kg. BMI is not a perfect index but it is much superior to weight alone.

4. Regular induction of vomiting by this method may lead to one of the few physical signs of psychiatry, Russell's sign. This is a callous on the back of the hand which has been caused by the repeated impact of the teeth on the skin when sticking fingers down the throat. The sign was

described and illustrated in Gerald Russell's classic paper which first defined and named bulimia nervosa (Russell, 1979). Russell's sign is not common. However, its recognition can cause a glow in the bosom of the psychiatrist with a nostalgia for physical medicine with its abundance of eponymous signs.

5. I guess that most eating disorder buffs have their stories about people who have demonstrated their combination of desperation and ingenuity by trying to adopt extreme or unusual methods of weight control. Using enemas or claiming to have taken a drug overdose in order to gain a stomach washout are not that rare. Inducing vomiting by the use of the emetic drug ipecac was not uncommon for a time in North America although it was never popular in Europe. It caused cardiomyopathy. One of the more unusual stories in my experience was that of a young woman who observed that horses lost condition and weight when infected by the larvae of the bot fly. She decided to eat bot fly eggs in the hope that they would hatch out within her and help her to use up her binged food. Unfortunately for her plan, although fortunately for her health, the bot fly is a discriminating little creature and lays eggs which hatch out happily in the innards of a horse but not in those of a human. Nothing happened.

FURTHER READING

APA (1994) *Diagnostic and Statistical Manual* (fourth edition) (DSM-IV) American Psychiatric Association: Washington, DC.

Walsh, B. T. & Garner, D. M. (1997) Diagnostic issues. In: Garner, D M & Garfinkel, P E (editors) *Handbook of Treatment for Eating Disorders* (second edition) The Guilford Press, New York, London.

WHO (1992) *The ICD-10 Classification of Mental and Behavioural Disorders: Clinical Descriptions and Diagnostic Guidelines*. World Health Organisation, Geneva.

2

WHO SUFFERS FROM EATING DISORDERS? WHO ASKS FOR HELP?

Only a small minority of people suffer from eating disorders. Furthermore, eating disorders are not spread evenly through any population. Some groups of people seem to be at much greater risk than others. Epidemiology is the science which studies the distribution of diseases and disorders in populations. Its findings can give important clues about their likely causes and their usual course and outcome. Furthermore, epidemiology may provide estimates of the possible levels of need and demand for treatment or other kinds of help. This chapter will give a brief account of findings relevant to each of these broad issues. It will provide a background to the wider discussion of the aetiology of the eating disorders in the next two chapters and to that of treatment and services which fills the rest of the book.

EPIDEMIOLOGICAL RESEARCH

The core method of epidemiological research is dazzlingly simple in principle but often complicated in practice – just like assembling do-it-yourself flat pack furniture. The instructions seem to be straightforward but when you try to follow them you often get into a mess.

The simple bit is that epidemiologists like to construct fractions with the following general form:

$$\text{Rate} = \frac{\text{Number of people with the condition}}{\text{Number of people in the population at risk}}$$

People with the condition being studied are called 'cases'. Rates may be expressed as incidence (new cases arising in a time period) or prevalence (total cases existing at a point or in a period in time). Incidence rates tend to be more difficult to estimate but give a better indication of differential risk and clues as to causation. However, for other purposes, such as planning service provision, prevalence may be more relevant. If rate fractions differ markedly between populations or subgroups in a population, then this suggests that there is something about the group with the higher rate that makes them more vulnerable.

Epidemiological study can give important clues about aetiology. The role of smoking in the aetiology of lung cancer was a classic discovery of epidemiology. The rate of lung cancer in that subgroup of the population who smoked cigarettes was found to be much higher than that in the population as a whole and, in particular, that in the subgroup who did not and had never smoked. In this case increasingly refined epidemiological research clarified the link and it was confirmed by other kinds of research. But it all started with the comparison of rates.

The problems in practice arise for a number of reasons. On the top of the rate fraction, there may be problems in deciding what counts as a case. Differences in definition or in the application of criteria may lead to false inferences. Likewise, it may be difficult to be sure that all cases have been detected and counted, or, in comparing two rates, that the definition and efficiency of detection have been the same in both instances. On the bottom of the fraction, there may be similar problems in defining and counting the relevant population at risk. Furthermore, because it is usually not possible to study a complete population, there may be all sorts of difficulties in choosing a sample to study which is both practical and representative of the whole. Too often samples are chosen for study because they are handy rather than representative.

Epidemiology may tell us a lot that is useful about the eating disorders. However, the available evidence is far from being comprehensive. Much of the research on anorexia nervosa concerns the incidence of presentation to services, whereas that for bulimia nervosa arises from community surveys. Each of these methods has limitations. In reviewing the findings mentioned in this and subsequent chapters, it is important to keep in mind some of the potential difficulties and sources of error, otherwise it is easy to jump to premature conclusions or get the wrong end of the stick.

WHO SUFFERS FROM EATING DISORDERS?

Some things are clear. Most sufferers are female and most are young – either late adolescent girls or young adult women. These broad statements are supported by the plentiful evidence from reports of the kind of people who come along to professional services and by the more limited evidence of community surveys (van Hoeken, Lucas & Hoek, 1998). Most clinical series report a ratio of at least ten females to each male. Sometimes males form an even smaller proportion. Ignoring the fine details of diagnosis, just under 5% of a series of over 1,000 recent referrals to our Eating Disorders Service in Leicester, were male, and such a skew is not unusual. Of course, it could be the case that males suffering from what are thought of as female disorders may tend to go undetected or may perhaps be especially reluctant to seek help. However, it seems unlikely that this effect is sufficient to distort the picture so greatly. Indeed, it is also plausible that clinicians may find male cases especially 'interesting' and so be more likely refer them to specialists, which would tend to exaggerate the apparent rate of the disorder in men. However, evidence from the few community surveys which have studied both sexes confirms the general preponderance of female sufferers (Hoek *et al.*, 1995; Turnbull, Ward, Treasure, Jick & Derby, 1996). There may be two exceptions to this rule. The very youngest cases of anorexia nervosa – say, those with an age of onset of 14 or less – include a much more substantial minority of boys, perhaps around a quarter of cases (Fosson, Knibbs, Bryant-Waugh & Lask, 1987; Higgs, Goodyer & Birch, 1989). The same seems to be the case for binge-eating disorder where perhaps a third of sufferers are male (de Zwaan, 1997).

The typical age of onset of anorexia nervosa is in the mid to late teenage years. In most clinical series the presentation is two or three years later. However, onset may less commonly occur in early teenage or before. Cases have been reported in children as young as 8 (Bryant-Waugh & Kaminski, 1993). Certainly it may start in girls before the menarche. However, there is a widely held view that anorexia nervosa does not occur before the onset of puberty, although dating the earliest flicker of that prolonged process is not an exact science. As will be discussed later, some theorists construe anorexia nervosa as essentially a disorder of adolescence – the process of psychosocial change around growing up (Crisp, 1980). Sometimes such a formulation may demand stretching the concept of adolescence to embrace processes that may still be going on even in chronological middle age since, occasionally, onset is delayed until then. In attempting to understand something of the nature of the disorder, such a view may be useful since we can often see in our older patients – and indeed in ourselves – experiences and processes which are closely akin to those of adolescence. However, to talk of these still as 'adolescent' issues may muddle language too much.

Bulimia nervosa is rare before the age of 14 and has a typical age of onset from mid teenage to early twenties, perhaps a little later on average than that of anorexia nervosa (Fairburn, Welch, Doll, Davies & O'Connor, 1997). The data on binge eating disorder is less clear: there seems to be evidence that bingeing starts early – in mid teenage – but that the full syndrome may not be present until several years later (Raymond *et al.*, 1995; Fairburn *et al.*, 1998).

Most sufferers from the two main disorders report that eating restraint – usually as 'slimming' – preceded the onset. (This does not seem to be the case in a minority of cases of bulimia nervosa and perhaps in most cases of binge eating disorder. Likewise, some cases of anorexia nervosa may report other difficulties in eating rather than typical restraint. The possible significance of these findings will be discussed below.) It seems that such restraint increases the vulnerability of individuals (Hsu, 1997) and a number of studies have produced prospective evidence that eating restraint is indeed a risk factor for later eating disorder (Patton, Johnson-Sabine, Wood, Mann & Wakeling, 1990; Killen et al., 1994; Patton, Selzer, Coffey, Carlin & White, 1999).

So the broad response to the question 'Who gets eating disorders?' is adolescent girls and young women who try to lose weight. Most sufferers will fit this description and people who fall into the category thus defined are at greater risk than those who do not. Nevertheless, epidemiological and other research has suggested many other possible risk factors for one or both of the eating disorders, and these will be discussed below. However, none is as robust or as widespread across different populations as age, sex and eating restraint.

EATING DISORDERS ACROSS TIME

Most people would say that both of the main eating disorders are phenomena of the late twentieth century and that they have notably increased in incidence and prevalence over the last few decades. However, there is room for debate about this. The evidence is contradictory and incomplete. Furthermore, it is different for the two disorders.

The best conclusion may be that anorexia nervosa has increased somewhat in incidence over the last 50 years or so but not as dramatically as many people would guess. The problem is that such judgements have to be based almost entirely on data relating to presentation to services, and even those data are limited in both extent and quality (van Hoeken, Lucas & Hoek, 1998). Thus, whilst some studies show some increase, others show little. Furthermore, because of the limitations of the data, the findings which suggest an increase can always be explained away and the null hypothesis of no change cannot be entirely refuted (Fombonne, 1995; Williams & King, 1987). However, there is an increase in demand for services for anorexia nervosa (van Hoeken, Lucas & Hoek, 1998).

The picture for bulimia nervosa is of a big increase in recognition and evident demand for services over the 1980s (Soundy, Lucas, Suman & Melton, 1995; Turnbull et al., 1996). However, the syndrome did not have a name before the late 1970s and such anonymity is a real impediment to adequate research. A study which looked backwards and attempted retrospective diagnosis with cohorts of women of various ages found that those born before 1950 had a substantially lower age-corrected risk of apparent bulimia nervosa than women born in the 1950s and 1960s (Kendler *et al.*, 1991). Although other explanations are possible, it seems likely that bulimia nervosa did indeed become much more common in the early 1980s or thereabouts. Why this should be remains a mystery although there are speculative answers (Russell, 1995; Palmer, 1998).

These tentative conclusions are relevant mainly to North America and Europe. The picture about change over time in other countries and cultures is even less clear. Indeed, there must be real uncertainty even about the present prevalence of eating disorders in much of the world.

EATING DISORDERS ACROSS COUNTRIES, CLASSES, CULTURES AND SUBCULTURES

It is important to remember that rates of presentation to services may or may not reflect rates of a disorder in the community. For most kinds of illness, there are forces at work and obstacles on the way to services which may change markedly the proportion of sufferers who get through to, and hence get counted by, various kinds of studies. For the eating disorders, and especially for bulimia nervosa, it is likely that only a minority of all sufferers are in touch with professional help of any kind, even where this is fairly readily available. Where services are scarce, estimates of rates could be seriously misleading.

Most clinical accounts and research concerning anorexia nervosa and bulimia nervosa come from Europe, North America and Australiasia. These parts of the world are variously described as 'western', 'first world' or 'developed'. Put bluntly, they are the parts of the world with populations that are predominantly 'white' and relatively affluent. Until recent decades they have, in many cases, been the colonial dominators of much of the rest of the world and still often exert dominating economic power. Of course, they also tend to be the parts of the world with relatively more developed health services and so they have more clinicians and researchers to write about eating disorders. It is in these countries that both anorexia nervosa and bulimia nervosa seem to be most prevalent. There are relatively few systematic studies from other places and so it is just about possible that eating disorders are as prevalent elsewhere, but the best guess is that this is not so – or perhaps that it has not been so until recently (Nasser, 1997).

This 'western' pattern of eating disorders – where both anorexia nervosa and bulimia nervosa are reported in substantial numbers – seems to go along with a particular culture which is perhaps not difficult to recognise but is also not easy to define. This culture is associated with free market economies, access to global media, a degree of affluence and a particular idea of 'modernity' – or 'post-modernity'. More concretely it goes along with cars, cola, pop music, fast food, advertising and designer clothes. It seems that wherever these things are available – or sought after – the 'western' pattern of eating disorders is to be found. This 'western' culture is characterised also by the valuing of slimness in women and the association of such slimness with a range of other valued attributes such as beauty, youth, competence and, perhaps more ambiguously, autonomy. For this culture to be influential, young women must be free, at least to some degree, to pursue these valued attributes, including slimness, without undue hindrance from contrary social prescriptions or proscriptions. Such circumstances occur throughout the world. This 'western' culture, in the relevant sense, is therefore not in general geographically or ethnically constrained although strong prevailing local or religious cultures may mute its influence. In most of Europe and North America it is the dominant culture at least for the age group at risk. It is – or in some cases seems to be becoming – the similarly dominant culture in those parts of Eastern Europe which were previously part of the Soviet bloc and in certain 'non-white' countries such as Japan. In most other countries it is an important subculture for many of those who are most affluent. Increasingly it is becoming the culture of most people in many countries and of the rich in most countries (Nasser, 1997). However, even in countries where this culture is in general dominant there are likely to be groups of people who do not conform to it either for personal reasons or because they subscribe to a subculture with other imperatives.

Interestingly even in the most 'western' countries, eating disorders – and especially anorexia nervosa – have often been thought of as disorders of the well-off and sometimes of the especially intelligent and gifted.[1] Hilda Bruch's classic account of anorexia nervosa is entitled '*The Golden Cage*' (Bruch, 1978). The title carries the implication that the typical sufferer is the affluent golden girl and indeed hints that it may be something about her material good fortune that leads her to become trapped. Specialist treatment centres see disproportionately more people from affluent and educated backgrounds. However, such observations of people *presenting* to services – especially prestigious specialist services, the kind that tend to produce papers – are unlikely to reflect accurately the social class distribution of all people with the disorder. Where access to such services depends upon the ability to pay, this is clearly likely to be the case. However, even in countries with socialised health services, the well-educated and more affluent are notoriously better at working the system and getting more than their share of the better services. The apparent skew in social class distribution of anorexia nervosa is to be viewed warily. Indeed, it seems to be absent or less apparent in some recent reports (Rastam, 1992; Gard & Freeman, 1996).

It may be that the apparent vulnerability of the affluent and 'westernised' classes in poorer and/or 'non-western' countries could also be attributed to similar forces of *selection* into services and reported series rather than vulnerability to disorder. Such an explanation is just about plausible for anorexia nervosa of pure restricting type where the evidence for an increase in prevalence over time in western countries is less compelling. By extension, the case for this type of anorexia nervosa emerging as a truly new disorder in other countries may be less convincing. Perhaps what is new is that the illness is being recognised as anorexia nervosa and recorded as such. Of course, both some increase in prevalence *and* an increase in recognition may be occurring together. This seems most likely.

The distribution of bulimia nervosa across countries, classes and cultures is more complex. As has been noted already, bulimia nervosa is a 'new' disorder. However, as soon as evidence from surveys became available, it showed that the disorder was widely spread within young women and that there was little or no skew in social class distribution at least in 'western' countries. There may, however, be rather more cases in towns and cities than in rural areas (Hoek *et al.*, 1995). Likewise, bulimia nervosa may be especially common in higher education students. By contrast, in 'non-western' countries, it seems likely that there is a social class bias in the prevalence of bulimia nervosa. The disorder seems to cluster in the more affluent classes, probably because they are more likely to embrace the particular 'western' culture described above (Nasser, 1997). Indeed, it may well be that that culture is noxious not so much in relation to eating disorders in general but more to bulimia nervosa in particular. A recent study in Curacao set out to identify cases of the two main eating disorders (Hoek, van Harten, van Hoeken & Susser, 1998). Cases of anorexia nervosa were found but none of bulimia nervosa. Curacao is relatively untouched by the 'western' culture described above and a possible conclusion is that this has meant that there is little or no bulimia nervosa. On the other hand, anorexia nervosa may well occur to some extent in all cultures although it remains likely that its prevalence is somewhat greater in 'western' countries and cultures.

The question of the differential vulnerability of ethnically or subculturally defined groups within 'western' societies is difficult to answer. In the United Kingdom, there is somewhat conflicting evidence about the rates of bulimia nervosa in young women with a personal or family background in the Indian subcontinent. In the main, surveys suggest that rates of the disorder are as high or higher in these groups as in the rest of the population (Mumford, Whitehouse & Platts, 1991). However, there is also evidence that their rate of referral to secondary services is lower (Ratan, Ghandi & Palmer, 1998). There is less evidence about community prevalence rates for people of Afro-Caribbean background, although they too seem to present to services less than would be expected (Lacey & Dolan, 1988). In the United States of America, the evidence of differential risk of disorder and presentation is likewise equivocal (Gray, Ford & Kelly, 1987; Abrams, Allen & Gray, 1993).

Certain subgroups defined by occupation and pre-occupation do seem to be especially vulnerable to eating disorders. Not surprisingly, people who are more likely to restrain their eating, or to do so with greater force or determination, seem to be at greater risk. Thus, for instance, ballet dancers both student and professional have been shown to have above-average rates of disorder (Hamilton, Brooks-Gunn & Warren, 1985; Szmukler, Eisler, Gillies & Hayward,1985a).

FILTERS ON THE PATHWAY TO CARE

Goldberg and Huxley (1980) introduced the idea of the filters on the pathway to care to describe the inevitable funnelling and selection which occurs between the act of self-recognition by the sufferer that something is wrong and that person's arrival before various kinds of helping agency. Hans Hoek, in his important review of the epidemiology of the eating disorders, used this framework to arrange his estimates of their prevalence and incidence (Hoek, 1993). This chapter will do likewise, although the estimates given are not those of Hoek, or at least not his alone.[2]

The idea of filters starts off with the rates of disorder in the community. Such rates have to be studied by specially arranged surveys and the results may be affected by problems in sampling, response rate and case detection. The most efficient surveys have two stages and involve the use of an initial screening to detect people thought to be worthy of going on for more intensive study in the second stage because they are thought to be more likely than the rest to be 'cases'. Often the first stage involves the use of self-report questionnaires sent through the post and the second involves diagnosis using standardised interviews. Community surveys of psychiatric disorders nearly always require sufferers to recognise and admit that they have the problem if they are to be detected. Those who lack insight may be missed, and those who wish to go undetected will usually do so. That could be described as the first filter.

The second and third filters involve the numbers of cases presenting to the first level of clinical service. In, for example, the United Kingdom and the Netherlands, primary care physicians (general practitioners or family doctors) and their teams occupy this position and it is to such health care systems that the Goldberg and Huxley model best applies. The second filter involves the sufferer, not only in recognising that she has a problem but also in seeking help. The third involves the doctor (or other clinician) appropriately diagnosing that problem and counting it as a case. Studies of eating disorders have mainly countered cases after the third filter. The numbers of individuals with eating disorders who come forward and present themselves in primary care is likely to reflect the prevailing perception of the disorders and judgements as to whether or not useful and congenial help is likely to be available. Most sufferers have mixed feelings about their state and, in the absence of evidently caring or competent services, many may decide that it is better to suffer in private than to risk the embarrassment, or worse, of revealing their problem with little prospect of a remedy. Likewise, the primary care doctors' judgements about the quality and availability of specialist care will importantly influence the numbers of people who are referred on through the next filters.

The forth and fifth filters involve the selection of those sufferers (they may now appropriately be called patients) who are referred on to secondary and more specialist care as outpatients or inpatients respectively. Once again, it is important to note that the flow and filters may be different in countries and systems where people have more direct access to specialists. Some such systems have very clear demarcations between 'office' and hospital practice. Such differences will be mentioned again in Chapter 11.

Each of the main disorders will now be discussed in turn with the numbers of people who are likely to be encountered at each stage of the filtering process. It is important to point out that all figures, such as those which follow, are *estimates* and certainly cannot give more than an approximate prediction when widely generalised. Rates may differ from place to place and from time to time. They are, however, better than nothing. They are likely to apply best to European and North American populations.

HOW MANY PEOPLE SUFFER FROM ANOREXIA NERVOSA?

Estimates of the community prevalence of anorexia nervosa are bedevilled by both the relative rarity of the disorder and the reluctance of many sufferers to declare their disorder in surveys. Furthermore, surveys usually concentrate on samples of young females. Typical results suggest prevalence rates in the range between 2 and 8 per 1,000 in this group with most estimates being nearer the lower end of this range (van Hoeken, Lucas & Hoek, 1998). Taken with other evidence, this might translate into an overall estimated point prevalence of between 10 and 30 per 100,000 total population. However, most studies are likely to underestimate prevalence in the community and this figure reflects what research surveys have detected. As people with anorexia nervosa are likely to hide away from such studies, the true prevalence may well be substantially higher.

By contrast, once patients present themselves in primary or secondary care then diagnosis may be fairly reliable and cases can be counted. Of course, if such an estimate is to relate to a total population, then all relevant care facilities will need to be included. The process will be helped if a register or similar system is in operation. The best estimates suggest that the annual incidence of anorexia nervosa detected in all services, including primary care, is likely to be between 4 and 10 per 100,000 total population per year (Szmukler, McCance, McCrone & Hunter, 1986; Lucas, Beard, O'Fallon & Kurland, 1991; Hoek *et al.*, 1995; Turnbull *et al.*, 1996; van Hoeken, Lucas & Hoek, 1998). Again it should be emphasised that this estimate is for *detected* disorder. The true incidence of new cases in the community is unknown.

HOW MANY PEOPLE SUFFER FROM BULIMIA NERVOSA?

There have been many surveys of the prevalence of bulimia nervosa in various communities and populations. Many have had snags and problems. There are often problems of sampling or of studying particular populations and then generalising the results too widely. For instance, a lot is known about the self-report characteristics of young female psychology students. They have been studied repeatedly because they are accessible and compliant. However, they are unlikely to be representative of wider womanhood. Another issue has been that of changing criteria for diagnosis. Thus, most studies conducted in the early 1980s used the DSM-III concept of 'Bulimia' (APA, 1980) which defined a rather wider group of people than Russell's original definition of 'Bulimia nervosa' (Russell, 1979) or the developments of it, which were incorporated into the later classifications DSM-IIIR (APA, 1987), ICD-10 (WHO, 1992) and DSM-IV (APA, 1994).

The literature up to the late 1980s was reviewed by Fairburn and Beglin (1990) who concluded that the best estimate of the community prevalence of bulimia nervosa was, in round figures, about 1% of young women. This figure is a reasonable summary of the findings of the better studies. However, it too is likely to be an underestimate and, furthermore, it is not easy to guess the proportion of all sufferers that fall into the category 'young woman'. Probably, men suffer from bulimia nervosa at a rate less than one-tenth that of women, but the number of older women who have the condition is unclear. There seem to be cohort effects, with women born before 1950 being at low risk (Kendler *et al.*, 1991). However, as the years pass, the number of 'older women', say aged 40 or above, who still have the disorder may well increase. Furthermore, it seems likely that, compared to anorexia nervosa, the incidence of bulimia nervosa is both more variable between populations and volatile over time and this will affect the prevalence. Based upon the available evidence and some guesswork, a reasonable estimate of the overall point prevalence would be of the order of 100 per 100,000 total population.

Figures for the incidence of presentation of bulimia nervosa vary widely between studies (van Hoeken, Lucas & Hoek, 1998). For those suffering with bulimia nervosa the filters on the pathway to care may be especially complex. The number of new cases counted depends crucially on where in the filtering process the counting is done and the nature of the particular filters which the sufferer encounters. Many filters are clogged. Thus, if the counting is of the incidence of presentation to secondary care the numbers will likely be much higher where there is a good service than where is a poor one. The best estimates of overall incidence of presentation to health care are likely to be those derived from special studies in primary care settings. Such estimates fall in the range 10–15 per 100,000 per year (Hoek, *et al.*, 1995; Turnbull *et al.*, 1996). Probably a majority of sufferers do not seek help and are not counted in such figures.

BINGE EATING DISORDER

Binge Eating Disorder (BED) is a 'new' disorder and estimates of its frequency vary widely. Furthermore, the difficulty in defining some of its features, their ambiguity in self-report instruments and doubts about the extent to which they cohere into a syndrome which is stable over time mean that good evidence for the incidence and prevalence of the condition is largely lacking. It is said to be most common in obese populations seeking help with weight reduction where up to a third may fulfil criteria. It is less common in the obese population in general where less than 10% have BED. In the community, perhaps a third of sufferers are male and, furthermore, only a minority are obese. A fair estimate for the point prevalence in the population as a whole might be of the order of 100 per 100,000 (Hay, 1998). However, in contrast to the case with the two main disorders, it is as likely that such a figure represents an overestimate of clinically significant disorder as it does an underestimate. It is not clear how stable the untreated syndrome is over time (Cachelin *et al.*, 1999) There is a need for the 'further study' envisaged in the designation in DSM-IV.

COMORBIDITY

Many sufferers from eating disorder also experience other psychological symptoms, and some may fulfil diagnostic criteria for other psychiatric syndromes. Furthermore, some pairings of coexistent disorders occur much more frequently than would be predicted by chance association. This has been mentioned before and will occur again later in the book. For the present, it is probably sufficient to point out that, from the clinical viewpoint, the degree of association between two disorders is likely to be exaggerated because an individual with, say, bulimia nervosa and alcohol dependence may, all other things being equal, be more likely to be known to services than someone who has just one of these problems. This is a problem for aetiological theorising, but it may just be those 'doubly troubled' individuals who most tax clinicians and services. The chief comorbid pairings are of either anorexia nervosa or bulimia nervosa with major depression and anxiety disorders – especially social phobia and obsessive compulsive disorder. Bulimia nervosa is also linked with substance abuse and borderline personality disorder (Cooper, 1995; Wilson, 1995).

THE COURSE AND OUTCOME OF THE EATING DISORDERS

It would be good to be able to make clear statements about the typical course and outcome of the two main eating disorders. If this were possible, incidence and point prevalence figures would fit together and the idea of a natural history for each of the disorders would be meaningful. Unfortunately, for a variety for reasons this is not the case. Most good longitudinal data are derived from the study of series of subjects who are even more highly selected than clinic samples in general. There is little uniformity of criteria for recovery, and patients from specialist clinics are over-represented. Where such patients have had a higher rate of expert treatment it might be thought that they would have better outcomes. On the other hand, they may have been more ill in the first place and so have a worse outcome. On balance, follow-up studies probably give an overly gloomy view of the typical course of disorder.

The outcome studies of anorexia nervosa give a rather varied picture (Hsu, 1988; Steinhausen, Rauss-Mason & Seidel, 1991; Herzog, Deter & Vanderycken, 1992). Crudely put, 'recovery' rates at ten years or more range from 18% with a 6% death rate (Eckert, Halmi, Marchi, Grove & Crosby, 1995) to 76% with no deaths (Strober, Freeman & Morrell, 1997). Most studies suggest that most sufferers eventually recover. Perhaps a quarter typically have a truly chronic course over many years. Development of bulimia nervosa or of a partial syndrome as a fairly stable state is not uncommon. However, anorexia nervosa has a significant mortality and estimates of the standardised mortality ratio (SMR) are almost always raised (Sullivan, 1995; Neilsen *et al.*, 1998). High crude death rates are often quoted from selected studies of severe cases followed up over many years (Theander, 1985; Ratnasutiya, Eisler, Szmukler & Russell, 1991). A more measured estimate from a number of studies would suggest a death rate of around 0.5% per year within the condition (Neilsen *et al.*, 1998). Of course, the crude mortality rate of any cohort eventually reaches 100% but anorexia nervosa afflicts young people who would not be expected to die, and the 0.5% figure reflects a notable mortality. Deaths by suicide are markedly elevated, as well as other causes – many of which are directly related to the disorder (Emborg, 1999).

The long-term prognosis of bulimia nervosa is even less clear than that of anorexia nervosa (Hsu, 1995; Keel & Mitchell, 1997). Most longer term follow-ups have studied patients who were the subjects of treatment trials or at least of treatment in specialist centres (Collings & King, 1994; Fairburn *et al.*, 1995; Fichter & Quadflieg, 1997; Keel, Mitchell, Miller, Davis & Crow, 1999). The overall picture seems to be one of a tendency towards recovery via an intermediate stage of a partial syndrome status which may itself be quite enduring. The movement from bulimia nervosa to anorexia nervosa is unusual. At about five years after treatment, a majority of subjects are recovered or nearly so, although perhaps a quarter are still highly symptomatic. Many sufferers – perhaps a quarter – have the condition for many years. It may be of significance that the bulimia nervosa subjects ascertained in the community in the Oxford Risk Factor Study had an average length of history of nearly four years (Fairburn *et al.*, 1997). Some studies paint a rather more gloomy picture than the trial follow-up studies, and furthermore emphasise that symptomatic recovery may be followed by relapse (Keller, Herzog, Lavori, Bradburn & Mahoney, 1992). The estimates available suggest that bulimia nervosa sufferers are at increased risk of premature death and thus have an elevated SMR (Patton, 1988).

BEYOND DIAGNOSTIC CATEGORIES

Until now the discussion in this chapter has tended to ignore the relationship between our diagnostic categories and the way things are in the world. Epidemiology depends upon defining entities and then counting them. However, these very activities tend also to make clear the limitations of these definitions and of the boundaries of the entities which they demarcate. As a stimulus for thought about the nature of diagnosis, there is nothing like doing a community survey and having to decide which kind of suffering or difficulty is to be counted as a case and which is not. Such things can turn upon exactly how much weight has been lost or whether there have been eight binges or only seven in the last month. The arbitrary nature of many of these defining boundaries becomes all too evident, and yet it is only by using such definitions that much epidemiological work can be done. However, that does not mean that our classifications are always optimal or, as the famous phrase goes, that they 'carve nature at her joints'. Even for research purposes our systems should be thought of as provisional. For clinical purposes they should be used with due caution and care. It is not ethical to treat or not to treat – or fund or not fund – people on the basis of whether or not they exactly fulfil diagnostic criteria. We should not punish people who have a clinical need just because they seem to have had the affrontery not to conform to the small print of our systems.

Epidemiology tends to rely on categories which define caseness. However, many relevant variables are essentially dimensional – weight and body mass index being examples – and others can be arrayed dimensionally. In a sense, the full syndrome eating disorders, bulimia nervosa and anorexia nervosa, are archetypes which may be placed at the end of a spectrum ranging from the healthy to the unequivocally morbid (see Box 2.1). In cases of the full syndromes all of the relevant defining features are present to the extent required by the diagnostic criteria. Other people show all of these features to a lesser extent or some symptoms fully and some not at all. Such people may be said to show partial syndromes. Community surveys of eating disorders, behaviours and attitudes usually show that partial syndromes outnumber full syndromes. Also, of course, partial syndromes differ in terms of their clinical significance and implications. Some are certainly of equal severity to full syndrome disorders whereas others are likely to be much less disruptive or problematic. However, there has been little systematic study of these issues.

Within the DSM-IV classification and its predecessors, any eating disorder which is of clinical significance but which does not fulfil criteria for one of the main disorders should be classified as 'Eating Disorder Not Otherwise Specified' (EDNOS). This category has no defining criteria but is there to collect the misfits and remainders in diagnostic terms. Some of these will be truly unusual states which are different in important respects from the full syndrome disorders. (These will be discussed further in Chapter 9.) Others will differ from one of the main disorders only in severity or detail. These latter are given categories of their own in ICD-10 as 'atypical anorexia nervosa' and 'atypical bulimia nervosa'. They are more or less the same as the states which are often referred to as 'partial syndromes' in epidemiological work, although the latter is perhaps a broader term which also includes milder states of less clinical significance.

Box 2.1 The Spectrum of Eating Disturbance and Disorder

The two main eating disorders may be thought of as archetypes which lie at the end of a descriptive spectrum of states characterised by eating restraint. Such restraint seems to play a part in the origin of most such eating disorders. This is less the case for BED and hence that diagnosis cannot be placed neatly on this spectrum. In many populations the number of people falling into each category would decrease from left to right. However, in some, the number of restrainers might outnumber those who do not restrain. In all community populations partial syndromes are likely to outnumber full syndromes. Some partial syndromes will be clinically significant – that is, cases of EDNOS.

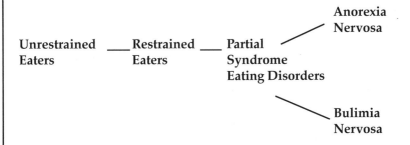

EPIDEMIOLOGY AND AETIOLOGY

This chapter has outlined the chief findings of epidemiology with respect to the crude distribution of the disorders within populations and the number of sufferers which are likely to be found in the community and presenting to services. More particular and focused studies may reveal possible associations and risk factors in more detail. For instance, the major case control studies of eating disorders conducted by Christopher Fairburn and colleagues are good examples of epidemiological research which sought to examine possible aetiological factors (Fairburn et al., 1997, 1998). Some of the findings of these studies will be discussed below. However, it may be important to emphasise at this stage that a number of factors may each be found to be associated with a markedly increased risk of having an eating disorder and yet each may be found in only a minority of sufferers and the combination of all of them in none. Having a low self-esteem, being a ballet dancer and having an eating-disordered sibling and older than average parents may all be associated with eating disorder, but a series of a hundred sufferers is unlikely to contain even one self-critical ballerina with elderly parents and a suffering sister. Likewise, a factor may be very importantly linked with a disorder and yet only a minority of those showing the risk factor may develop that disorder. Even most smokers do not develop lung cancer. Furthermore, arguing backwards from the existence of a disorder to the likely presence of some putative causal factor is justified only in the rare cases where the link has been established as a necessary one. Thus, the clinical picture of mumps *is* evidence for the presence of the mumps virus. However, a myocardial infarction is *not* evidence that the sufferer was under stress, had a type A personality, hypertension or a raised cholesterol and much less all four, even though each has been proposed as a risk factor for heart attack. In the field of psychiatric disorder there are almost no causal accounts as strong as the mumps story. Most are weaker even than that of the cardiac account. Certainly, it is illegitimate to argue that because an individual has an eating disorder she must have been sexually abused or have come from a particular kind of dysfunctional family, or whatever. Even strong associations – and I have no desire to suggest that these are especially strong – do not justify that kind of reverse inference. And yet sometimes it is all too easy to use the findings of research to bolster just such inferences which should really be thought of as the prejudices that they are.

A full account of aetiology should ideally involve a theory which is able to account for the origin of the disorder and which is compatible with what is observed about risk factors and the like. The theory should be robust in the sense that it has explanatory and predictive value. Furthermore, it should in principle be vulnerable to, but survive attempts at, refutation. Theories about the origins of the eating disorders are not that good or that robust, but there are plenty of ideas and even more observations. These will be described and discussed in the next chapter.

NOTES

1. Sometimes the families of patients and, less commonly, patients themselves emphasise this flattering image of the typical sufferer. It is clearly easier to swallow the idea of being the victim of an illness to which the bright and privileged are especially vulnerable than it would be if the disorder was seen as mainly the preserve of the dull and downtrodden. In clinical practice, if the person is confronting her disorder, it may be best not to take time challenging this view even though it is unlikely to be true. The sufferer and her family have enough on their plate both literally and metaphorically. However, what one might call the 'golden

girl' image is also perhaps part of the widespread ambivalence of many people about anorexia nervosa. Viewed from a distance, and not taken too far, the disorder seems to embody – an apt word – many socially valued attributes such as slenderness, self-control, youth, a kind of beauty and even health and fitness. Furthermore, these attributes are visible and evident whereas the misery and fear is hidden. Eating disorder buffs at parties are used to hiding their cringe when yet another person quips: 'Oh, yes. Anorexia nervosa, I could do with catching just a bit of that.' (As Kelly Vitousek has pointed out, people do not say that they could do with catching just a bit of schizophrenia, depression or agoraphobia.)

2. I have used the same idea of filters on the pathway to care although the precise definition of each of the filters may differ from those of some other accounts. For instance, it seems to me to be useful to define the first filter as located inside the subject and as involving her recognition of her state as a disorder for which she might appropriately seek clinical help. Actually doing so involves passing another filter.

FURTHER READING

Hoek, H W (1993) Review of the epidemiological studies of eating disorders *International Review of Psychiatry*, **5**, 61–74.

van Hoeken, D, Lucas, A R & Hoek, H W (1998) Epidemiology. In: Hoek, H W, Treasure, J L & Katzman, M A (Editors) *Neurobiology in the Treatment of Eating Disorders*. John Wiley & Sons, Chichester and New York.

Nasser, M (1997) *Culture and Weight Consciousness*. Routledge, London.

3

WHAT CAUSES EATING DISORDERS?

This chapter is entitled 'What causes eating disorders?'. It should start with a statement of the fact that we really do not know the answer to this question. However, the chapter will ramble on for many pages, so perhaps this negative response is not a simple one. Many answers have been proposed to the question and there are those who are convinced that their answer is *the* answer. Sometimes the arguments about the origins and nature of the eating disorders can become quite heated. Unfortunately, when there is so much heat there is often little light. Furthermore, the outsider or non-partisan may be left not knowing who or what to believe. However, when so many answers are put forward to a question it is best to be cautious about accepting any of them wholeheartedly.

It seems likely that eating disorders arise for complex reasons and we may need theories and explanations with many elements. However, we should not think that we have said much if we mutter pious words about multifactorial aetiology and leave it at that, resting on a comfortable bed of woolly thinking. This should not satisfy our intellectual curiosity and, more importantly, will not get us far in finding ways of helping our patients. We should try to tease out the factors that are the most important in bringing about the eating disorder in the first place and lead to its perpetuation. These need not be the same factors. However, both kinds may in some sense be said to cause the present eating disorder in the sufferer.[1] What follows is a brief discussion of many of the issues that have been invoked as playing some part in the causation of the eating disorders. It is quite a long list but even this catalogue is not complete. The order of presentation is not random but should not be thought of as an order of probable importance. Furthermore, the following discussion will not emphasise the way in which the different issues relate to each other. Some elements may not seem to go together in any obvious way. Not all have been proposed as part of a coherent causal scheme. Indeed, there is no one coherent causal scheme. This chapter will mainly review ideas and evidence. Some attempt at synthesis will be made in the next chapter. In the present chapter anorexia nervosa and bulimia nervosa will in general be discussed together.

EATING RESTRAINT AND ITS CONSEQUENCES

Restrained eating seems to be a crucial part of the background of the development of anorexia nervosa and of most cases of bulimia nervosa. Both disorders characteristically arise in people who are trying to eat less. The relationship of eating restraint to binge eating disorder is less clear.

The concept of restrained eating refers to a state in which the individual deliberately eats less than her hunger or drive to eat would otherwise lead her to do. People who have a truly reduced drive to eat and are eating little as a consequence are not showing eating restraint in the relevant sense. (They have *true* anorexia in the sense of lack of appetite.) The idea of restrained eating seems to contain two elements. Firstly, there is the idea that in the normal state the urge to eat is driven by deprivation and diminishes with feeding and is eventually capped by satiety. Secondly, the idea that the person who is exhibiting restraint is resolved to stop eating before she reaches that 'natural' stopping point. Indeed, she keeps herself in a position where hunger would usually push her towards further consumption. She may fail to achieve the 'zone of biological indifference' where eating usually stops and certainly will not come up against the aversive consequences of pushing the satiety barrier (Herman & Polivy, 1984). Both of these elements of the idea are necessary. What is not necessary is that the person should be fully successful in limiting her eating in the way that she intends. Someone may be said to be restraining if she aims to cut back her eating, does so for a few hours or days but then breaks out into binge eating. She may not have reduced her net intake over a day or a week but her intention would have been to do so and her position would therefore be one of restraint. Such a story is commonplace. At the margin it may be difficult to describe as restrained someone who always intends to eat less but never does. However, even in this case, some of the consequences of restraint may be evident (see Box 3.1).

Eating restraint involves a tendency to behave in a certain way, the behaviour itself and the consequences of that behaviour. The motivation for restraint varies and so do the consequences of the behaviour. Most cases of eating disorder arise in the context of eating restraint, which is motivated by a wish to lose weight – that is, by slimming or attempted slimming. For the present, that will serve as the exemplary case. Sometimes different motivation may lead to behaviour which is different in detail and this, in turn, may have consequences which are likewise

Box 3.1 Restraint diagram

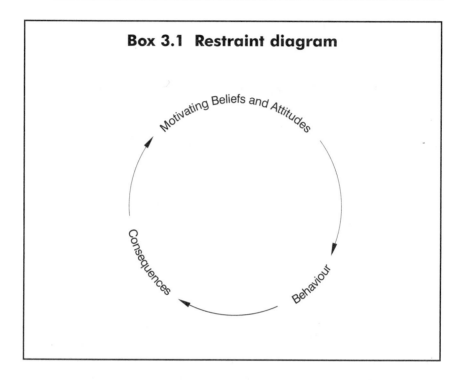

different in subtle ways. However, although the details may differ, there tend to be elements which are common to most or all instances.

The common elements of sustained eating restraint are still best illustrated by the results of a classic experiment, the Minnesota Starvation Study, which was conducted over 50 years ago in the USA by a research team led by Ancill Keys (Keys, Brozek, Henschel, Mickelson & Taylor, 1950).[2] The study examined the effects of limiting the dietary intake of a group of healthy young men over six months so that they lost around a quarter of their former body weight and then allowing them to re-feed back to their former size. The circumstances, the subjects of the experiment and their motivation could not have been much more different to those which apply to most people who develop eating disorders. For a start the subjects of the Keys experiment were male. Secondly, their motivation for restraint was complex. They volunteered to take part in the experiment to study the effects of starvation out of altruism and duty. They were conscientious objectors to military service at a time when many people were starving in a war-torn world. Furthermore, within the experiment the circumstances of their undereating were quite different from those of someone deciding to go on a slimming diet. Nevertheless, despite these differences – or perhaps in some ways because of them – their experiences when undergoing semi-starvation are useful in illuminating what may happen to people who restrain their eating in quite other circumstances and go on to develop eating disorders.

At the start of the Minnesota study there were 36 subjects who had been selected from a larger number of volunteers because of their physical and mental health and their motivation. Nevertheless, the men found the whole experience very testing and four were withdrawn from the study. The subjects became preoccupied with food largely to the exclusion of other topics. For some the preoccupation was extreme and some broke out into binge eating even when they were supposed to be starving. More had difficulty in eating normally when in the re-feeding stage. Some would eat oddly and in a ritualistic fashion. Furthermore, the volunteers experienced emotional changes. They tended to become subject to variable mood, were often depressed and occasionally elated, irritable and nervous. There was some shoplifting, violent outbursts and 'talk of suicide'. In general, the men were not their usual selves and the changes often took many weeks to reverse on re-feeding. For a while their whole world had come to be centred on food and eating.

The basic experience of the Minnesota volunteers is replicated in the experience of most people who attempt to restrain their eating so as to reduce their weight. The more they restrain the more they think about food and have an urge to eat. This has been called the dieter's dilemma. Such urges are often accompanied by a feeling of impulsivity with respect to food and of general emotionality. Of course, all of these are experienced too, often in heightened form, by people suffering from eating disorders. The Minnesota experiment suggests that such feelings may be importantly promoted by undereating even when this is not itself part of any morbid or internally motivated process.

The usual response of most slimmers to the dieter's dilemma is to escape by giving up. People who go onto to develop eating disorders also continue restrain and so experience the consequences of such restraint with full force.

COUNTERREGULATION

One consequence is the phenomenon known as counterregulation (Polivy & Herman, 1995). This is in some ways the reverse of the regulatory processes which occur when most people eat.[3] A person who is not restraining her eating will eat until she is satisfied ('full') and then stop. Within an episode of eating, the more she has already eaten the less she will be likely to eat. This makes simple sense. However, a person who is restraining her eating will be trying to eat less; but if, for one reason or another, she eats in a way that feels as if it has violated her rules, she is subsequently likely to eat more. In these circumstances, the more she has eaten previously the more she is likely to eat later – within limits, of course. This is known as counterregulation and is the reverse of the usual pattern. This phenomenon is probably best understood in cognitive terms. It seems to be the restrained person's beliefs about what she has eaten that predict later consumption (Herman & Polivy, 1984). It is the breaking of a rule that leads to the increased eating. Indeed, the whole thing has been called the 'what the hell' effect. However, there is just a bit of evidence which hints at a physiological component to the mechanism of counterregulation (Thompson, Palmer & Petersen, 1988). Furthermore, there is evidence that undereating leads to an alteration in the serotonin (5HT) mechanisms which play some part in satiety, although interestingly this change seems to occur only in women (Goodwin, Fairburn & Cowen, 1987).

It is tempting to think that the mechanisms which underlie counterregulation may play some part in the causation of bulimia nervosa and also perhaps, of anorexia nervosa. Pathogenesis might have a part for a regulatory system that has been pushed out of kilter and develops for a while the characteristic of positive feedback and the associated instability. However, the relevance of counterregulation to eating disorders is at present speculative. Even more speculative is the idea that the mechanism of counterregulation may have been selected for in evolution. However, if it were scarcity that was leading to undereating, it would probably be advantageous to suspend satiety mechanisms at first when food became available. The starving animal may do well to gorge when it comes across a plentiful supply of food. It does so without guilt or regret. Things are more complex when undereating is a decisive act in the midst of plenty.

MOTIVATION FOR RESTRAINT

The possible motivations for eating restraint are many, and may include religious fasting, secular ideas about the need to cleanse the body, worries about food allergies or quirky notions about 'nutritional balance' or fitness.[4] Such motivation may sometimes lead to the development of a clinically significant eating disorder although this would usually be strictly definable as an atypical disorder or EDNOS because the criteria for the main disorders specify that the sufferer must have ideas about weight as her central concern (Palmer, 1993). It is not clear whether all kinds of eating restraint carry similar risks of promoting eating disorders of some kind in those who pursue them. This seems unlikely. However, it is clear that most people who develop eating disorders seem to have done so in the context of restrained eating. Furthermore, by definition in the case of the strictly defined syndromes, most of those who end up suffering from an eating disorder have been motivated in their restraint by ideas about their body size, shape and weight.

The consequences of eating restraint tend to be broadly similar whatever the motivation. Thus the slimmer and the person who undertakes a sustained fast for religious reasons may both experience an increase in urge to eat and thoughts about food. However, they may differ in the way they think about these consequences. Perhaps the former is more likely to think of herself as a potentially greedy person with a propensity to be fat which she must try to control. The latter might think more in terms of sin and the need to control the urges of the flesh. Furthermore, it may be that different motivations lead to different restraint behaviour. Some people may deprive themselves of all foods equally whilst others may selectively cut back on their intake of certain kinds of food – for instance, many slimmers cut down on fats or carbohydrates or whatever they believe to be most 'fattening'. Such differential deprivation may affect the consequences of restraint but the matter has not received much study. However, it does seem that a low carbohydrate diet may be especially likely to promote a tendency to binge.

CONCERN ABOUT BODY WEIGHT AND SHAPE

Most people who develop eating disorders restrain their eating because they are concerned about their body size and often its shape also. They wish to be thinner, slimmer, smaller, lighter, less fat. The associations of each of these attributes may differ slightly but their overall meaning is much the same. To achieve these aims, they seek to lose weight. In doing so, they are, of course, acting in tune with a much more widespread concern and wish which is shared by a substantial proportion of their peers.

For young women, in particular, there seems to be a fairly general consensus that a slender body shape is considered desirable and desired. Slimming is endemic in so-called 'western' societies, as was touched upon above. It seems likely that this widespread pursuit of an ideal body shape is highly relevant to the aetiology of eating disorders.

This ideal has changed over the decades but has been markedly slim for at least the last 30 years. The change towards the slim ideal was illustrated by a study published in 1980 which looked at the 'vital statistics' of women who were entrants to the Miss America pageant over the 1960s and 1970s (Garner, Garfinkel, Schwartz & Thompson, 1980), and subsequent study showed that these trends had continued into the 1980s (Wiseman, Gray, Mosimann & Ahrems, 1992). Over the years there was a tendency for the cohorts of women to become taller, slimmer and have bigger waists and smaller busts and hips. Their weight for height (BMI) declined and, in general, the later women were longer and leaner than their predecessors. Furthermore, the authors showed similar trends in women chosen for *Playboy* centrefold pictures over the same time. The study is of note largely because it illustrates in real figures (in both senses) what is more usually the stuff of anecdote. Arguably, Miss America pageants and certainly *Playboy* centrefolds represent a notably male ideal of female pulchritude, but it does seem that such ideals influence real women and in turn are influenced by them. There is a debate about the extent to which the ideal of slimness is better thought of as imposed by men on women or as actively embraced and promoted by women themselves. There is no simple answer.

As was discussed in the previous chapter, the ideal of the slim woman is especially associated with 'western' societies. Likewise, within such societies, certain subgroups are more likely to restrain their eating in the pursuit of slimness. Women who have some additional reasons for being especially slim – for instance, dancers – may be at greater risk. Nevertheless, such particular social pressures are unlikely ever to be all important. Even in ballet schools not every dancer develops an eating disorder. It seems likely that for some any external pressure to restrain and be slim resonates with more personal characteristics to produce frank eating disorder. Furthermore, it could be that, for some, there are less specific aspects of their social situation that render them vulnerable.

THE SOCIAL CONTEXT

The above discussion leaves out the crucial question of why slimness is valued so highly in many contemporary societies. Not surprisingly, in view of the preponderance of women sufferers, feminist writers have made important contributions on this topic (Striegal-Moore, 1995). However, they provide no one clear answer but plenty of interesting speculation. For instance, it has been suggested that the valuing of slimness goes along with a valuing of youth, health and fitness. However, the degree of slimness involved in the iconic figures of the day is not really associated with reproductive health. A recent paper suggested that if the plaster mannequins used to display clothes in shop windows were real women they would not menstruate (Rintala & Mustajoki, 1992). Indeed, eating disorders are said to be common in the real life models of the fashion world although the supporting evidence for this is merely anecdotal (van Hanswijck de Jonge & van Furth, 1999). Perhaps the pursuit of thinness is part of a flight from a traditional femininity constructed around motherhood. It has been suggested that the thin ideal approximates to a move towards an androgenous or even a male figure. This has been linked to the changing social role of women in general. Others suggest that the thin ideal has to do with an infantilisation of women by men who are threatened by their emerging social power. Underlying the whole issue may be deep cultural beliefs about the opposition of the mind and the body, with the latter being often associated with the female. Eating restraint and slimming may represent impulses both to control and to perfect what, within much of western culture, has been thought of as out of control and imperfect. The fact that such restraint and control, unless taken to extremes, seems to also carry the promise of a body that is sexually desirable adds a complex twist to the matter (Abed, 1998). Denial and control may form an unlikely but workable alliance with sexual aspiration. However, each side of this alliance is arguably a response to social imperatives which have been predominantly controlled by males. Hitherto the shape – both metaphorical and literal – into which women have felt obliged to mould themselves has been determined largely by men.

The ideas about the social meaning of thinness are many and varied. Unfortunately, it is difficult to assess where the truth lies. Perhaps it is worth considering that the most powerful images are often ones which are overdetermined and manage to convey different and even contradictory meanings. This may well be the case for the modern idea of the slim woman.

Of course, not all sufferers are female. Most men with eating disorders seem to resemble their female counterparts quite closely in their thinking and beliefs by the time they are fully within the disorders. Yet in as much as the social context is relevant to the origin of their disorders they have presumably experienced different influences or reacted differently to similar influences when compared either to their suffering sisters or their male contemporaries. It is of interest that a disproportionate number of male sufferers are homosexual in orientation and that gay men in general seem to be more weight and shape concerned than heterosexual men (Andersen, 1995; Schneider & Agras, 1987). It has been argued that this increased risk may arise through a combination of internalised homo-negativity leading to problems of self-esteem and certain dominant images within some gay subcultures which emphasise slimness and attractiveness (Williamson, 1999). These influences may parallel those which surround many women. However, most male sufferers are not gay. The particular social worlds of the relatively few males who do succumb to eating disorders would repay careful study because they have in a sense developed the disorders against the general tide. Interesting subgroups of men who sometimes develop significant eating disturbance are jockeys and wrestlers who have to struggle to attain their fighting weight (King & Mezey, 1987; Opplinger, Landry, Foster & Lambercht, 1993).

Not everyone who develops an eating disorder has decisively restrained her eating in the pursuit of slimness or indeed for any other reason. Some bulimic disorders, perhaps especially binge eating disorder, may arise without apparent restraint. This may also be true of a disorder in which undereating rather than bingeing is central. Limiting eating or overeating may be part of an emotional response to circumstance. It has been suggested that undereating may be associated with certain kinds of social difficulty and distress in a way that is quite distinct from eating restraint in the cause of slimness. For instance, a position of social powerlessness could be relevant (Katzman, 1997; Katzman & Lee, 1997). However, within such a model the proximal cause and indeed meaning of undereating is less clear than when restraint is used in the service of slimming. Of course, in certain special situations, such as hunger strikes, the social meaning of refusing to eat is evident. Perhaps less strident versions of the use of undereating as a way of expression and influence may occur. Clinical observation and experience suggests that this is the case. However, it is difficult to generalise with any confidence.

One way in which the social context may well be relevant to the risk of developing eating disorders is in relation to the way in which it affects the sense of self-worth in the person concerned, whether this is through compliance with a social trend or fashion or by defiance of an unwelcome personal pressure.

SELF-ESTEEM

Most people who suffer from eating disorders seem to have low self-esteem. They have a poor opinion of themselves either in general or in certain important particulars. In principle it is possible that this self-esteem might be construed equally well as an aetiological issue, as a part of the disorder or as promoted by it. Finding herself in the midst of a miserable condition to which, to a degree, her own behaviour has contributed doubtless does little to boost an individual's sense of self-worth. Indeed, attempted slimming and its attendant failures may itself be undermining. However, it is likely that people who seek determinedly to lose weight are disproportionately drawn from those who do not like themselves much. By definition a slimmer is dissatisfied at the very least with her body otherwise she would not be seeking to change it. Low self-esteem is probably a risk factor both for slimming and for the development of eating disorder. Indeed, there is some evidence for this (Button, Sonuga-Barke, Davies & Thompson, 1996; Fairburn, Welch, Doll, Davies & O'Connor, 1997; Fairburn, Cooper, Doll & Welch, 1999). Most likely of all is a situation where low self-esteem, slimming and 'failure' to achieve the goals of slimming each come to form part of a circular mechanism in which both restraint and problems of self-esteem are increased in strength.

Low self-esteem does seem to be important as a risk factor for eating disorders. However, once again, it is important to remember that most people who have a low opinion of themselves are not – and do not become – eating disordered. Nevertheless, those who suffer from eating disorders do stand within the ranks of those with low self-esteem – at least by the time they are eating disordered. It seems very likely that this plays a part in causing these disorders although whether that part is predominantly in their origination or perpetuation or both is less clear. Furthermore, in a society where those who were especially self-critical did not tend to criticise themselves for being too fat, it is unlikely that those with low self-esteem would be at an increased risk of developing an eating disorder.

THE PERSONAL CONTEXT

The risk of developing an eating disorder varies greatly with easily definable personal characteristics such as sex and age. Presumably some of the increased risk involved in being a young woman relates to the way in which this status goes along with a greater tendency to restrain eating in the service of slimming. But undoubtedly not all of it.[5] It is likely that there are things about being a young woman in the modern world that increase the risk by other means. For instance, puberty, adolescence and growing into a young adult is, for a female, associated with profound and evident changes in her body as well as in her social role and sense of self. The onset of menstruation and breast development are events which are inevitably endowed with personal and social meaning which may tend to entangle body weight, shape and the eating which sustains them with wider issues. These may lead to eating restraint and its consequences, but such meanings can have direct influences too. Issues such as a sense of attractiveness or otherwise, of responsibility or otherwise, of expectations of independence or otherwise, may all seem to be signalled to the person herself and to others by changes in her body. Furthermore, they may change from time to time and differ between individuals. Some such experiences may be welcome to one person and terrifying to another. Some of the meanings attached to the body may be personal and idiosyncratic. Thus, although some of these influences go along with being young and female in general, others may relate to particular characteristics of the person and her circumstances. For instance, growing up to have a particular body shape may mean that the person feels that she is especially like her mother – which may be thought of as positive or negative. The probable importance of individual characteristics is entirely compatible with ideas of the importance of wider social influences. Indeed, without some such individual factors it is difficult to explain why pervasive social factors could produce disorder in some people and not in others. Furthermore, different influences may play different roles. Some factors may be mainly involved as precipitants of disorder, others as leading to its perpetuation. For instance, a young woman who decides to try to lose weight along with many of her friends may continue when they stop because for her it triggers feelings which they do not share.

Particular and personal meanings may be attached to the whole spectrum of relevant issues from body size and shape through over- and undereating to the details of the relationship with those with whom the person eats. The drive to eat is basic and looms large in any developmental narrative. Thus the range of psychodynamic accounts of personal and psychological development accord a central place to feeding. The evidence for the details of such accounts as theories of development may be lacking in most cases. However, there is no doubt that eating and body size and shape are soaked with meaning for many – perhaps most – people. Furthermore, psychodynamic ideas can be of great value in describing how such meanings relate to other aspects of an individual's internal world and how the whole is managed and experienced. The empathetic understanding of such issues may be as important in therapy of all kinds as it is in everyday life. The rather general factors discussed above have relevance to the individual sufferer only in conjunction with her own particular interpretation. Thus, to use starkly contrasting examples, the consequences of eating or of eating restraint may have quite different associations for each of the following.

- Someone who has always been obese and has felt that she was accused of being greedy throughout her childhood.
- Someone who has been the subject of childhood sexual abuse involving fellatio.
- Someone who was deprived of adequate food for crucial periods of her childhood.
- Someone who has been fed regularly but strictly and with much comment about eating up and not wasting food.
- Someone who has been able to eat anything and everything in an unconstrained manner without any comment.
- Someone who was comforted or bribed with food at times of emotional trauma.

And it would be not impossible for someone to have had a childhood in which each of these experiences had occurred at one time or another. Such personal experiences will at the very least colour the way in which an individual reacts to social and other expectations. Furthermore, the less notable influences of more average lives may still contribute to the variety of beliefs and attitudes which may affect the risk of a person developing an eating disorder and influence its detailed form and content if it does happen.

PERSONALITY AND TEMPERAMENT

Some individual difference in vulnerability could be accounted for by definable differences in personality or temperament. The two terms overlap but are different. Temperament suggests a relatively fixed and perhaps innate way of reacting. Personality includes temperament but is a somewhat wider concept. However, in practice, it is usually difficult to define or measure either term. It is, for instance, difficult to be sure that any relevant features observed in sufferers – particularly when they are patients – are indeed enduring characteristics of the person and hence might be causes rather than consequences of the eating disorder. In prin-ciple, it would be necessary to demonstrate that people with particular pre-morbid features were at greater or lesser risk of developing anorexia nervosa or bulimia nervosa. Measuring such features before the onset of disorder is impractical, inferring them from findings after the onset of disorder is prone to error. There are, however, some broadly defined and fairly consistent differences in personality between the typical restricting anorexia sufferer and the typical patient with bulimic features at low or normal weight.

People with the restricting type of anorexia nervosa tend to show obses-sional personality features and perfectionism. If they have a personality disorder it tends also to be of that kind, namely DSM-IV cluster C anxious–fearful (Wonderlich, 1995; Gillberg, Rastam & Gillberg, 1995). However, it must be acknowledged that whilst it is entirely plausible that obsessional features may in appropriate circumstances promote eating restraint, it also may be that semi-starvation might promote obsessional behaviour. Personality traits that have been described as 'autistic' (in a broad sense) and lacking in empathy seem to be over-represented in anorexia nervosa (Gillberg, Rastam & Gillberg, 1995).

People with bulimic disorders tend to be more emotionally reactive, and when they have definable comorbid personality disorder it tends to be of the cluster B dramatic–erratic type (Herzog, Keller, Lavori, Kenny & Sacks, 1992; Wonderlich, 1995). Borderline personality disorder is particularly notable because of the way in which it complicates management.

It is difficult to be sure that the 'personality' features evident in a sufferer are truly features characteristic of that person before she fell ill, and so could in principle be of aetiological significance. However, in many cases, sufferers do tend to report that the traits of low self-esteem and perfectionism were present before the onset of the disorder. This is true of many clinical accounts and has also been confirmed by systematic research (Fairburn *et al.*, 1997, 1999).

BODY IMAGE

Disturbance of body image is an important feature of anorexia nervosa and also occurs in bulimia nervosa (Cash & Deagle, 1997). It is at least plausible that such disturbance might play a part in the origination or perpetuation of the disorder. A simple proposition might be that the sufferer has sought to lose weight because she perceives herself to be fat and continues to do so because losing weight fails to change that perception. Certainly it is a characteristic of body image disturbance that the individual may feel as fat after losing, say, 20 kg as was the case before. This would promote a kind of vicious circle and it could trap the sufferer into the disorder. However, put in this way the proposition is almost certainly too simple. Body image disturbance is a complex phenomenon (Smeets, 1997). Such disturbance is essentially an experience in which a person feels subjectively that she is a different size or shape – usually bigger – than she really is objectively. Sometimes a sufferer will say that she *knows* that she is underweight but *feels* that she is not. Attempts to pin down the phenomenon by various methods have produced a variety of results which do not always simply confirm the impressions obtained at clinical interview. However, it is the subjective experience reported at such clinical interviews which arguably taps the 'real' body image disturbance. However, not all people who suffer from anorexia nervosa experience this disturbance in its classic form. Furthermore, it is certainly not confined to people who suffer from eating disorders. Many people who are preoccupied with their bodies have some disturbance of body image – for instance, many obese people, pregnant women and indeed many young women who do not have an eating disorder but are nevertheless preoccupied with their figures. On objective tests such people may show results as inaccurate as anorexia sufferers, although it seems unlikely that they report quite the same subjective experience as do those patients who show the 'classic' disturbance in its full form.

There is a sense in which the description of the clinical phenomenon of body image disturbance and the attempts to pin this down in objective terms in research have both seemed to have run their course, although these have diverged somewhat. It is time for new thinking (Smeets, 1997). However, for the present, the whole issue continues to seem tantalisingly relevant, but any particular role for body image disturbance in the precipitation or perpetuation of clinical disorder remains unclear.

EATING AND EMOTION

Those who suffer with eating disorders are troubled people – which is to be expected of people with troubling disorders. However, many seem to be troubled in wider ways and indeed substantial numbers warrant other psychiatric diagnoses. Thus, most sufferers from bulimia nervosa are unhappy and low spirited, and about half may be said to have current or previous comorbid major depression (Cooper & Fairburn, 1986; Laessle, 1990; Cooper, 1995). Likewise, anxiety symptoms are common in both anorexia and bulimia nervosa and a substantial number have comorbid social phobia (Halmi *et al.*, 1991; Bulik, Sullivan, Carter & Joyce, 1996). Obsessional symptoms are a common feature of anorexia nervosa and there is an increased risk of full obsessive-compulsive disorder (Matsunaga *et al.*, 1999). Indeed, there has been speculation that anorexia nervosa and obsessive–compulsive disorder are as closely related as bulimia nervosa and affective disorder (Holden, 1990; Hsu, Kaye & Weltzin, 1993; Swift, Andrew & Barlage, 1986). There is also evidence that eating disorders and other psychiatric morbidity, especially affective disorder, tend to run together in families (Halmi *et al.*, 1991; Strober, 1995; Lilenfeld & Kaye, 1998). Furthermore, there is evidence that eating disorders share risk factors with other emotional disorders (Fairburn et al., 1997, 1999). What aetiological inferences can be drawn from these observations? What part do disordered emotions play in the pathogenesis of the eating disorders?

There is some evidence that anorexia nervosa sufferers tend to have difficulties in handling and talking about emotion. They are said to tend towards the quality of alexithymia – a relative inability to put words to feelings (Cochrane, Brewerton,Wilson & Hodges, 1993; Schmidt, Jiwany & Treasure, 1993). In some this may be extreme and there may be so-called empathy disorder (Gillberg, Rastam & Gillberg, 1995; Rastam, Gillberg, Gillberg & Johansson, 1997). By contrast, high emotion is arguably more evident in the bulimic disorders. However, sufferers from either kind of eating disorder tend to cope with emotion by avoidance (Troop, Holbrey, Trowler & Treasure, 1994).

It has been suggested that the emphasis upon eating restraint has tended to belittle the role of emotional factors in the genesis of bulimic symptoms (Meyer, Waller & Waters, 1998) and there is considerable evidence that emotions may trigger binges. Furthermore, there are speculations about the psychological mechanisms that may promote or perpetuate bingeing behaviour. It is suggested that binges may divert attention from painful or difficult emotion and/or that binges may arise when attention is narrowed onto immediate cues and the higher order inhibitory functions are avoided. These ideas accord with clinical accounts and the introspections of sufferers. The psychopathological concept of dissociation may be relevant to the idea that binges involve a diversion or narrowing of attention and awareness. The general propensity to dissociate in association with a history of trauma does seem to be present in many of those who suffer from severe bulimia nervosa. Vanderlinden and Vanderycken (1997) have drawn parallels between such dissociation and the defensive systems of prey animals under threat. Such defensive reactions may involve food abstinence interrupted by short episodes of rapid food intake.

It seems most likely that sustained disturbance of eating behaviour will be promoted by emotion mainly when the scene has already been set by some disruption of 'normal' feeding. That disruption may be a decision to restrain eating but could also be a predominantly emotional event. Anecdotally, people do differ in the extent to which they are readily 'put off their food' by emotional upset and, indeed, in the extent to which they 'eat for comfort'. Such individual differences may well be relevant to the risk of developing eating disorder, although at present they are poorly understood. Satisfactory explanatory models of eating disorders are likely to involve both restraint and its consequences and emotional issues (McManus & Waller, 1995; Meyer, Waller & Waters, 1998); however, it should be remembered that a proportion of cases of bulimia nervosa seem to lack a history of notable eating restraint, and this proportion is substantial for cases of binge eating disorder. In such cases, it may be that emotional factors alone, or with some primary problem of eating regulation, lead to clinical eating disorder.

FAMILY INFLUENCES

Troubled people often come from troubled families. Families provide food for children and are the context for emotional development. It may well be that styles of eating and relating to food are set down in childhood as a result of family influences. It is plausible that families may be involved in triggering or perpetuating eating disorders. There has certainly been a lot of speculation along these lines. However, it is also true that troubled people upset families and the presence of an eating-disordered member in a family is likely to upset and trouble the other family members. The evidence from clinical observation and the theories that arise from it need to be considered with this in mind.

Many theorists have made bold statements about the way in which family life and parenting promote eating disorders. For instance, Bruch (1973) asserted the importance of the mother–child relationship and Selvini-Palazzoli (1974) that of the whole family system. However, such theories are largely unsupported by systematic research and seem insupportable as particular and specific aetiological theories. Furthermore, they have sometimes led to regrettable attributions of blame which tend to hinder rather than help any therapeutic endeavour. What evidence there is about the current family life of those suffering from eating disorders suggests that there is a wide variety rather than one or two consistent patterns (Rastam & Gillberg, 1991). On the whole, the stereotypes of the theorists have not been found (Eisler, 1995). However, there is some evidence that sufferers remember their childhood as characterised by a variety of negative features, most of which they share with people with other psychiatric disorders. Furthermore, some adverse family environmental factors, such as low contact and high expectations, have been found to be more common in the recollections of both bulimia and anorexia sufferers than in comparable subjects with other psychiatric disorders (Fairburn et al., 1997, 1999). Indeed, the general force of such family risk factors seems to be especially great for bulimia nervosa. A large twin study used multivariate analyses to try to tease out the likely influence of genetic and shared familial and non-shared environmental factors in bulimia nervosa and five other psychiatric disorders (Kendler et al., 1995). Alone amongst the six disorders studied, the model for bulimia nervosa suggested a significant aetiological role for familial environmental factors. Some studies suggest fewer overt problems in the childhood background of anorexia nervosa sufferers (Schmidt, Tiller & Treasure, 1993; Webster & Palmer, 2000).

CHILDHOOD ABUSE AND ADVERSITY

It is intuitively plausible that people who have had bad experiences in childhood are likely to become distressed at the time and that, furthermore, some may be damaged by them in the sense that the experiences may have lasting negative effects. Such is our everyday understanding. Over recent decades, research in sociology, psychology and psychiatry has tended to confirm such common wisdom (Browne & Finkelhor, 1986). In doing so it has tended to meet the criticism that it is merely discovering at great cost what is known already. However, formal confirmation of what may be considered obviously true is important. The past is littered with examples of assertions that seemed 'obviously true' or common-sensical but are now untenable. For instance, few would now hold that the sun goes round the earth, that people with white skins are innately superior or that incestuous sexual contact is extremely rare. Yet such beliefs have been held quite respectably in the past and it would be arrogant for us to think that we, too, cannot hold views which may be open to similar condemnation, ridicule or, more importantly, refutation by our successors. Although itself not perfect or immune from error, well-conducted research is our best defence against such mistakes. Furthermore, good research may sometimes lead to the refinement as well as the confirmation of some 'obvious' proposition and to a filling in of important details which common sense leaves out. And, of course, it goes without saying that what turns out to be true is often far from obvious.

Much of the above seems to apply to the issue of the relationship between childhood adversity and the later development of eating disorders. This is especially so with regard to the issue of childhood sexual experiences with adults – what is generally termed sexual abuse.[6] Only 20 or so years ago, such experiences were mentioned little in relation to the causation or provocation of eating disorder. Indeed, that was the case for all disorders until the 1980s saw increased attention to the issue. Later the pendulum swung markedly in the opposite direction until some explicitly took the presence of an eating disorder to be prima facie evidence of prior sexual abuse.[7] Fortunately there is some research which allows both extremes to be put into a more rational perspective.

There is now a substantial body of work which demonstrates that groups of women with clinical eating disorders report – if asked – substantially greater rates of childhood sexual experiences with adults than do groups of similar women unselected for disorder (Palmer, 1995; Wonderlich, Wilsnack, Wilsnack & Harris, 1996; Schmidt, Humfress & Treasure, 1997). There is, therefore, support for the view that such experiences could play a role in the causation of eating disorders (Wonderlich, Brewerton, Jocic, Dansky & Abbott, 1997). This is certainly the case for bulimia nervosa and for anorexia nervosa with bulimic features, although the evidence for such an association with restricting anorexia nervosa is somewhat less clear (Fullerton, Wonderlich & Gosnell, 1995). But is this plausibly causal association particular and specific to the eating disorders? The enthusiasm with which the idea has been taken up by some therapists would suggest that it might be. Furthermore, it seems intuitively likely that childhood sexual abuse might be especially associated with disorders which differentially afflict young women and are often considered to involve a process of personal and sexual development that has become derailed. Surely it makes sense that adverse sexual experiences might be behind the complex negative attitudes to the body which not uncommonly occur in these disorders? Indeed, it is common sense.

However, research has failed to confirm such a special association. Thus, although there is an association between childhood sexual experiences with adults and later eating disorders, the strength of this association is no greater and may even be weaker than that between such experiences and mental disorder in general. Such abuse is a risk factor for later psychiatric disorder in general, including eating disorder but not *especially* for eating disorder (Palmer & Oppenheimer, 1992; Welch & Fairburn, 1994; Fairburn *et al.*, 1999).

There has been somewhat less systematic research on physical or emotional abuse and on the wider aspects of childhood adversity in general reported by those who later develop eating disorders. The studies which have been done support the view that women who suffer from bulimia nervosa have experienced more than their fair share of such adversity. On average, they report more physical abuse than do comparable women in the population at large (Fairburn *et al.*, 1997; Schmidt, Humfress & Treasure, 1997). However, this excess of bad experiences resembles that reported by other groups of troubled women suffering from other psychiatric disorders, such as major depression. Bulimia nervosa sufferers seem to resemble these other sufferers in the way they report their childhood background. Interestingly, this seems to be less consistent for sufferers from restricting anorexia nervosa, who tend to report less troubled childhoods than their bulimic equivalents (Schmidt, Tiller & Treasure, 1993). They may describe only average amounts of adversity in childhood and, in this respect, resemble women who have no psychiatric disorder (Webster & Palmer, 2000).

PRECIPITATING LIFE EVENTS AND ADVERSITY

As with childhood troubles, it makes sense that later troubling events might precipitate eating disorder. In listening to the history of individual sufferers, it is often the case that difficult and testing occurrences seem to have closely preceded the onset of the disorder. Part of the clinician's task is to try to understand the problem by making links of this kind. Once again it is common sense to do so. However, it is a very well-developed human capacity to make such links and to search for meaning in this way, although our very facility in this respect can sometimes lead us astray.[8] There is not a lot of research on the topic of precipitation of eating disorders by life events and difficulties. However, the little systematic research available tends to support the idea that the onset of bulimia nervosa coincides with an excess of life events in the preceding year (Welch, Doll & Fairburn, 1997). In this respect, once again, bulimia nervosa seems similar to many other psychiatric disorders which have been studied in this way, whereas for anorexia nervosa this is less clearly the case. However, life events may play a part here too (Rastam & Gillberg, 1992; Gowers, North, Byram & Weaver, 1996). There is some work that suggest that events of a sexual nature may be especially relevant for anorexia nervosa (Schmidt, Tiller, Blanchard, Andrews & Treasure, 1997).

BIOLOGICAL ISSUES

To call an issue 'biological' in the context of psychiatry and clinical psychology is often simply to signal that the discussion which follows will be concerned with physical measurements. Thus the term 'biological psychiatry' is characteristically concerned with studies of neurotransmitters, neuroimaging and the like. Many observations have been made. Of course, anorexia nervosa is the psychiatric disorder which most evidently affects the body and, not surprisingly, starving people have bodily dysfunction. The facility with which it is possible to go on fishing trips, find abnormal results and wrap them up in papers has led to the accumulation of a substantial literature. There have, of course, been some interesting findings, but the term 'biological' ought also perhaps to refer to discussion of such findings within a wider framework in which physiology and psychology are brought together and, perhaps, even included within the framework of wider biological thinking, such as that of evolutionary theory. Such a synthesis is too rarely attempted. Many observations and speculations float around but are not often made to interact in a way which is really interesting or put together into a hypothesis that risks refutation. Perhaps that has yet to come.

An example of a speculation that did attempt some such synthesis was that which is implicit in the thinking of Arthur Crisp of St George's Hospital, London, who has made a big contribution to the understanding of anorexia nervosa over the last 40 years.[9] He saw anorexia nervosa as a derailment of adolescence construed as a psychological and biological process going on within an individual who, in turn, had to be considered within a family (Crisp, 1980, 1997). Crucially for the present discussion, he emphasised the way in which adolescence is driven by physical puberty and, furthermore, that puberty is a body-weight-related and triggered developmental event. By reducing weight, the anorexia nervosa sufferer not only changes the external appearance of her body but also its internal environment. Her sex hormones levels come to resemble those of a pre-pubertal girl. Crisp suggested that these changes have their experiential components which may be rewarding or relieving to a young person struggling with the process of growing up – and perhaps to her family also. A psychobiological regression takes place which is seen as importantly unpinning the disorder. Psychosocial difficulty leads to undernutrition which leads to a change in internal environment which leads to psychological relief – albeit relief which is bound up with a new kind of disorder and potential for suffering. Crisp subtitles his book on anorexia nervosa – *Taking the heat out of the system*, and this phrase captures the essence of the idea.

The above account is a simplification and does little justice to Crisp's complex view of anorexia nervosa. However, it notes the attempt to put into some kind of meaningful theoretical context the hormonal changes that occur with fully developed anorexia nervosa. These affect principally the hypothalamic-pituitary-gonadal axis. In anorexia nervosa at low weight, levels of the pituitary hormones, luteinising hormone (LH) and follicular stimulating hormone (FSH), which are both produced by the anterior pituitary gland, are low – as are the gonadal hormones, such as oestrogen. This whole system seems to be have been 'switched off' by weight loss below a threshold just as it was 'switched on' in normal development by the body weight passing a threshold on the way up.[10] Anecdotally this can indeed seem to have notable effects upon the emotional state of the person and, occasionally, there are observable changes such as the remission and re-emergence of acne as the weight threshold is passed on the way down and on the way up. It seems quite likely that mechanisms involving these changes may have some part to play in the perpetuation of low weight anorexia nervosa. However, the existence of states with very similar psychopathology at essentially normal body weights and with normal hormonal environments which sustain menstruation suggest that such psychobiological regression is unlikely to be the crucial or originating factor.

Other endocrine systems are also affected in anorexia nervosa, although none so predictably or dramatically as the pituitary–gonadal axis. Thus thyroid hormones and thyroid responsiveness are only subtly changed and growth hormone is often raised at low weight but reverts to normal with weight gain. Both of these issues are likely to be directly related to nutritional status (Fairburn, 1995a). The endocrine findings in bulimia nervosa are less consistent and probably reflect the highly variable general state of sufferers (Pirke, 1995).

Cortisol levels are usually normal or high in anorexia nervosa. Connan and Treasure (1998) have postulated that severe and chronic stress operating at a crucial developmental time may lead to a situation in which the hypothalamic–pituitary–adrenal (HPA) axis becomes set at a level which is relatively insensitive to cortisol feedback and pushes the system that controls body composition and weight out of kilter. This is a bold and interesting synthesis which attempts to combine a variety of observations into a hypothesis with testable predictions. However, if this model predicts that anorexia nervosa sufferers are, as it were, set at a low weight – in a way that is broadly analogous to how a healthy individual is set at a normal weight – it would seem to suggest that they should not have a big or unusual urge to eat. The experience of hunger in sufferers varies but many feel themselves to be battling against a major urge to eat. It is difficult to reconcile this with theories that seem to predict the opposite.

There have been numerous observations with regard to neurotransmitter levels in eating disorders, and especially in anorexia nervosa (Kaye, 1995). However, at present they fail to provide the basis for an impressive aetiological theory. Research into neurotransmitter systems in the eating disorders is bedevilled by the twin problems of the indirect methods which are necessary when studying human sufferers and the questionable relevance of animal experiments to disorders which seem to involve an essential place for human psychology. The latter have, and doubtless will continue to provide, much useful information about basic mechanisms of feeding, hunger, satiety and the control of body composition which are probably largely conserved in evolution. For instance, the dopamine reward system, the various serotonergic systems involved in feeding and satiety and the roles of leptin, cortisol and insulin in body weight control may well be similar in human beings and laboratory animals. However, the ways in which these systems could go awry and be distorted in patients may be distinctly human. An idea like 'naughty but nice' is unlikely to be replicated in a rat. It is therefore perhaps surprising that there are any plausible animal models of disorder. However, attention has been drawn recently to a number of animal syndromes which could be relevant and are certainly fascinating (Owen, 1998). Notable amongst these is the 'wasting pig' or 'thin sow syndrome' which seems to have many striking similarities with anorexia nervosa.

In general, at the time of writing, the field of biological research into anorexia nervosa and bulimia nervosa would seem to be full of many promising green shoots but the full harvest is still some way off. There is a need to combine the results of biology – narrowly defined – with those of psychology and clinical observation. When the ideas of one side can be reconciled with the other in a way that makes better sense than each alone, then a truly biological account, in the wider sense, will be available. In the meantime we are left with a variety of poorly connected observations from neuroimaging (Ellison & Foong, 1998), neurotransmitters and physiology (Treasure & Campbell, 1994; Kaye,, 1995; Pirke 1995), and little sense of much added explanatory value. However, this could all change quite rapidly.

GENETIC ISSUES AND OBSERVATIONS

In principle, almost every feature of human life may at some level of analysis be usefully thought of as involving the interaction of genes and environment. Few can be described entirely adequately in terms of only one of these although, of course, either genes or environment may sometimes provide a good enough explanation. The relevant question is whether there is evidence of a detectable and potentially *definable* genetic component in the aetiology of the eating disorders.

There are already studies that suggest that genetic variation does indeed predict risk. Family studies have shown a fairly consistent excess of cases of anorexia nervosa in the first-degree relatives of people with the disorder (Strober, 1995; Lilenfeld & Kaye, 1998). Indeed, there seems to be a tendency for the two main eating disorders to be found to excess in the families of sufferers of either kind (Lilenfeld & Kaye, 1998). At least part of the increased risk seems to be for both disorders.

That the increased risk in families is genetically transmitted is suggested by the results of twin studies. Such studies compare the rate of concordance for disorder in monozygotic (identical) twins with dizygotic (non-identical) twins. If the first significantly exceeds the second then this strongly suggests that the wholly shared genetic make-up of the monozygotic twins is playing a detectable role. Several such twin studies have been carried out in both anorexia nervosa and bulimia nervosa (Lilenfeld & Kaye, 1998). The evidence is fairly consistent in favour of genetically inherited risk for anorexia nervosa (Holland, Sicotte & Treasure, 1988). There is also some evidence with regard to bulimia nervosa and indeed for some shared risk between the two disorders (Kendler *et al.*, 1991; Lilenfeld & Kaye, 1998). Furthermore, a twin study has been shown that eating attitudes also tend to run in families and do so in a way that suggests a genetic basis for the familial tendency (Rutherford, McGuffin, Katz & Murray, 1993).

If there is a common genetic predisposition to the two eating disorders it is unclear what its phenotype might be. However, it may be complex and relevant only in conjunction with other genetic predispositions or in the presence of particular environmental factors. Furthermore, the type of eating disorder which occurs may be influenced by other factors: for instance, obsessional traits may tip the balance in favour of restricting anorexia nervosa, or predisposition towards affective disorder or emotional instability may make bulimia nervosa a more likely outcome.

A number of studies have investigated the relationship between the eating disorders and other psychiatric conditions (Lilenfeld & Kaye, 1998). Rates of mood disorders tend to be elevated in the families of both bulimia and anorexia sufferers. Furthermore, some studies have found that the risk is greater if the eating-disordered person is depressed, although the findings are inconsistent. The evidence for a genetic link between eating disorders and alcohol or substance abuse is less clear (Kendler, 1995; Lilenfeld & Kaye, 1998). There does seem to be a familial association between anorexia nervosa and obsessive compulsive disorder (Halmi, 1991; Lilenfeld & Kaye, 1998).

The new genetic methods which detect in various ways the variation of either genes which have actual relevance or marker genes which are closely related in their position on the chromosome are beginning to be used to study the eating disorders. A number of candidate genes have been examined in relation to anorexia nervosa. However, at the time of writing, it would seem that no results of real potential significance have been replicated (Pieri & Campbell, 1999; Collier, Sham, Arranz, Hu & Treasure, 1999), which is not surprising as the entire enterprise is at a very early stage. The promise remains that genes may be identified which play a definite role in these disorders. This promise includes the probability that deciphering genetic variation will also throw important light on the necessary environmental contribution to the genesis of eating disorders.

CONCLUSIONS

This chapter has considered aetiological ideas. It started with the bold statement that the causes of the eating disorders are not known and proceeded to discuss possible aetiological issues at some length. If this seems to reflect contradiction and uncertainty, that is probably a fairly accurate picture of the current state of our attempts to understand and explain these disorders. We cannot say that we know *the* causes but we do have many ideas which have some use and value. From the point of view of the researcher and the academic, we should cherish our scepticism and our capacity to be critical. And in this sense we should all be 'academic' at some stage if we are not to be carried away into needless error. However, most of us are also clinicians and need to be active, practical and resolved in what we offer to our patients. Wearing our everyday clinical hat, we need less scepticism and more enthusiasm, less dithering doubt and more action confidently offered. This is *not* contradictory. To the extent that we are critically knowledgeable of the findings of any relevant research, we can enthusiastically offer our patients what we genuinely – and defensibly – think is the best advice. Such advice will be informed both by the general findings of our predecessors and peers and by our particular assessment of the person before us. We may know that our advice is in no sense the last word but we should aim to make it the best we can offer. It should be, in the jargon of the consumer magazine, the current 'best buy'. Using the same terminology, the next chapter will offer a personal view of what might be the current 'best buy' with regard to how to think and talk about the eating disorders in the clinical context. It will include a somewhat idiosyncratic attempt at a provisional synthesis of some of the aetiological ideas reviewed in this chapter. It will lead towards the following chapter's discussion of what is involved in recovery and to the more practical orientation of the rest of the book.

NOTES

1. Causation is a surprisingly slippery concept. Philosophers can get into wonderful contortions trying to clarify what is meant by one thing causing another. This can be fascinating stuff. However, if one is not in the right frame of mind it can seem silly or self-indulgent. Surely everyone knows what causation means, don't they? Well, no actually – it does seem that there is real room for uncertainty. Should this affect our enterprise as clinicians or even as researchers? Probably not, at least not most of the time, except to give us yet another reason for being appropriately sceptical of both received opinion and the latest products of empirical research on our topic.

   We should keep a double dose of doubt in the back of our minds. Not only do we not quite know what causes eating disorders but also we cannot be entirely sure what kind of thing a cause would be if we were to stumble across one.

   Furthermore when discussing human beings there are additional complications. People and their brains are mechanisms and can sometimes be explained in mechanistic terms. However, people are also conscious persons with thoughts, feelings, desires and intentions. In everyday terms, the best account of human behaviour and experience is almost always couched in this latter kind of way; that is, by accounts that are amenable to empathetic understanding. We get by – and more than get by – through using such understanding. To seek to avoid using such accounts is to seem to think about our fellows in less than fully human terms. And yet at times empathetic understanding lets us down and it is then useful to seek explanations of other kinds. However, the relationship between mechanistic explanation and empathetic understanding is a philosophical quagmire that is deeper even than the nature of causation. Psychology and psychiatry are disciplines which are built upon this quagmire. Yet, like the citizens of Los Angeles who live out their lives above the San Andreas fault, on the whole we manage to get on with our business with modest success whilst not even thinking about what lies below. Perhaps, in this spirit, having flagged up the issue, it is time to get on.

2. The original two-volume report of this study is well worth reading. However, it is difficult to get hold of and an alternative is the substantial summary of the work, which is given by Garner (1997).

3. The regulation of 'normal' eating is doubtless a complicated business. I do not know enough about it to do more than paint a very simple picture of eating and satiety with which to contrast the phenomenon of counterregulation. In real life and in experiments, satiety depends upon far more than the total amount that has been eaten.

4. A few years ago I had come across only three male sufferers from bulimia nervosa or something like it in Leicester where I work. Two of them knew each other, although not well. They had not influenced each other but had moved in broadly the same circles. They were both interested in a kind of poorly defined 'eastern' religion which probably had more links with California than with the Indian subcontinent. However, both felt that they should engage in fasting, both found it difficult to sustain, both broke out into bingeing behaviour, both resorted to self-induced vomiting and both ended up caught within an apparently self-sustaining pattern which was essentially that of bulimia nervosa. Strictly, neither could be diagnosed as having that disorder because both denied weight concern. One would regularly make a tour of fish and chip shops, gorge what were to him, except in the midst of a binge, forbidden products and then vomit before proceeding to repeat the whole cycle. It must be pointed out that most young men vomiting fish and chips on the pavements of Leicester on a Saturday night are not suffering from bulimia nervosa but from some quite other malaise.

5. I sometimes ponder a thought experiment which conjures up a society where there is no pressure on young women to be slim but where that pressure is experienced only when women reach an age of, say, 40. Would the incidence of eating disorders be the same although shifted by a couple of decades or so? Would there be much less – or more – disorder? My guess is that there is something about the developmental position of the young that makes them more vulnerable. This vulnerability is likely to have to do with the still continuing development of a secure sense of self. It might involve biological issues also. So my best guess would be that in my imaginary society many 40 year olds would diet – they do now – but a smaller proportion would develop eating disorders. What do you think?

6. I prefer the rather longer term 'childhood sexual experiences with adults' (CSEA) for use in discussing research about the noxious nature of such experiences. It is more neutral and descriptive and avoids the

clearly condemnatory and arguably sometimes question begging use of the term abuse. However, I have no doubt that the term abuse is almost always appropriate. The sexual exploitation of children is to be condemned unreservedly. Nevertheless, in defining terms for research, the definitions often have to draw somewhat arbitrary boundaries. For instance, a common distinction is for sexual contact between someone of, say, 14 and an adult at least five years older to be included within the definition of CSEA. However, the age gap of the definition may exclude potentially damaging experiences where the older person is just 59 months older and include some potentially less negative experiences where the older person is 61 months the senior. Issues of betrayal of trust, coercion and whatever do not map absolutely onto age differences. However, most childhood sexual experiences with adults involve an adult who is a generation or more older than the child. In such cases – as in many of the others – the word abuse is clearly appropriate.

7.   There is an interesting history to be written about the emergence during the second half of the twentieth century of attention, first, to the physical abuse of children and then to their sexual abuse. The rediscovery of childhood sexual abuse had been complicated by the influence of Freudian theory, which tended to consider accounts of childhood sexual experiences with a sophisticated scepticism (Masson, 1984). Although, as is well known, Freud himself had at first thought that neurosis was based upon real sexual abuse, he later revised his ideas. Subsequently, accounts of sexual contact in childhood were usually thought of as fantasies, albeit significant and universal fantasies, with indirect relevance to adult disorder. This tradition clouded the question of the role of actual abuse. I recall that as late as the early 1980s when at a meeting I presented data on systematically collected recollections by adult patients of such experiences, the eminent chairman of the session pointed out that 'of course' he assumed that I was not suggesting that the events recalled by the subjects of the research had necessarily really happened. He added that the observations were of interest anyway even if many were fantasies. I responded by saying that I tended to believe these accounts just as much as other things which patients told me – no more but no less. I still think that that is the appropriate stance. It is important to hear such accounts and to believe them except when there is a clear reason not to do so. However, the giving of exceptional credence to such accounts, or the interpretation of tiny hints or suggestive symptoms as if they were solid evidence of abuse, seems to me to be just as likely to cause harm as the previous studied scepticism or neglect of the matter. The whole issue of so-called 'false memories'

apparently induced by pushy therapy lies in a murky area. For what it is worth, my own view is that major abusive experiences in childhood probably can be truly forgotten in some sense and re-emerge at some significant later time. However, my guess is that this phenomenon is rare and certainly rarer than the situation where such events are never forgotten although they may be pushed to the back of the mind. Such memories may, of course, be vague – as are many childhood memories. Furthermore, the act of recall is itself a complex and active process. In most cases there will be much that inevitably remains uncertain. Conviction and certainty are not the same thing. A workable truth can only be found by a combination of careful clinical technique in the particular case and good research in relation to the general issues. However, it is important to recognise the change in the *zeitgeist* – at least that of the chattering and therapeutic classes. The earlier sophisticated scepticism mentioned above has now largely given way to a nose-tapping attitude of 'no smoke without fire', which prides itself on being able to see the previously unseeable. This extends into the arts. I am getting fed up with the number of books and plays that have as their 'surprise' element the revelation of childhood sexual abuse in the background of a principal character. How quickly yesterday's taboo has become today's cliché. In my view, both taboo and cliché may interfere with the clarity of our thinking about an issue of great importance.

8. A range of research techniques have been developed to try to get around the difficulties presented by such an understandable 'search after meaning' by people who are suffering from an illness, difficulty or catastrophe. Professor George Brown and his colleagues at Bedford College, London, have been important pioneers in this development. Their work on the social background of women suffering from depression set new standards. Their techniques have only recently been applied to the study of the eating disorders.

9. I am happy to acknowledge that it was working under Arthur Crisp in the early 1970s that got me going in the field of eating disorders. The richness of his way of thinking about and working with people suffering from anorexia nervosa has inspired and provoked many individuals in more than one generation into careers of practice and research with eating disorders. I am proud to be one of them.

10. The threshold is probably one of body fat rather than of weight. It may be that this weight or fat threshold represents a mechanism which has been selected for through evolutionary time (Frisch & McArthur, 1974). An animal that does not become pregnant unless it has a fatty insurance policy against scarcity of food would have an advantage over one that played its reproductive card whatever the circumstance.

It has been calculated that the typical amount of body fat which allows menstruation is about enough to sustain a woman through a nine-month pregnancy.

FURTHER READING

Gillberg, C & Rastam, M (1998) The etiology of anorexia nervosa. In: Hoek, H W, Treasure, J L & Katzman, M A (Editors) *Neurobiology in the Treatment of Eating Disorders.* John Wiley & Sons, Chichester and New York.

Palmer, R L (1998) Aetiology of bulimia nervosa. In: Hoek, H W, Treasure, J L & Katzman, M A (editors) *Neurobiology in the Treatment of Eating Disorders.* John Wiley & Sons, Chichester and New York.

Fairburn, C G, Cooper, Z, Doll, H A & Welch, S L (1999) Risk factors for anorexia nervosa: three integrated case comparisons. *Archives of General Psychiatry,* **56,** 468–476.

Fairburn, C G, Doll, H A, Welch, S L, Hay, P J, Davies, B A & O'Connor, M E (1998) Risk factors for binge eating disorder: a community based case-control study. *Archives of General Psychiatry,* **55,** 425–432.

Fairburn, C G, Welch, S L, Doll, H A, Davies, B A & O'Connor, M E (1997) Risk factors for bulimia nervosa: a community based case-control study. *Archives of General Psychiatry* **54,** 509–517.

4

WHAT ARE THE EATING DISORDERS ABOUT?

The previous chapters have described the eating disorders and discussed a variety of ideas about how and why they may arise. But they may still feel puzzling. There may well be some features of the experience of the sufferer that seem to make some sense on occasions but often many details and explanatory ideas do not. There remains an imprecise but forceful question which stays nagging in the back of the mind. 'What are eating disorders about?' Unfortunately, there is no neat and satisfactory answer. This chapter will attempt *an* answer of sorts, but please note, it is not to be taken as *the* answer.

In seeking to respond to such a broad question as 'What are eating disorders about?', it may be useful to look at the metaphors that are commonly used in framing an answer.

HORIZONTAL AND VERTICAL METAPHORS

In some sense, anorexia nervosa and bulimia nervosa are clearly about weight and eating and their control. However, it is often stated that this is a superficial view. It is said that they are not *really* about weight and eating at all. They are really about low self-esteem, a sense of powerlessness, difficulties with emotional control, or a variety of other such issues which are said to *underlie* the more apparent symptoms. These, in turn, are sometimes seen as underpinned by particular problems of development, circumstance or relationship. According to such views, the weight and eating symptoms are signs and signals of other problems. Or perhaps ways of coping with them. The symptoms are mere epiphenomena. The real problems lie deeper.[1]

This *vertical* metaphor of depth is, of course, a commonplace of discourse based within the broad tradition of psychodynamic thought. Indeed, according to that tradition psychological symptoms may be viewed as symbolic representations of 'underlying' conflicts which have been repressed. Furthermore, physical symptoms may sometimes be thought of in these terms also. However, this way of speaking and thinking has some unfortunate consequences. Most importantly, any vertical metaphor – because of the pervasive experience of gravity in real life – will always accord greater importance to that which is spoken of as below or deep and upon which other features rest and depend. But is this *always* the best way of speaking about the symptoms of the eating disorders? When speaking of the relationship between the weight and eating symptoms and the other issues it is at least arguable that is preferable to use a less usual *horizontal* metaphor in which the former is said to be tangled up with the latter. Using such a way of speaking, the matter of weight and eating can be given, at least broadly, equal importance to that accorded to deficits of self-esteem and the rest. That seems to be right since such weight and eating symptoms and their consequences often appear to have a role in the development and perpetuation of the disorder that is crucial and more than just symbolic. It is the tangle that matters. Furthermore, put bluntly, it is the low weight or the consequences of bingeing and vomiting that at worst kills some sufferers and makes far more ill and incapacitated. So the following discussion will be draped around the horizontal metaphor of 'entanglement' rather than the more usual way of speaking, using the vertical metaphor of depth. The story which will form the provisional answer to the question of what eating disorders are about will be organised in this way (see Box 4.1).

ENTANGLEMENT AND MOTIVATED EATING RESTRAINT

The entanglement mentioned above is to be thought of as being between two sets of issues. On the one side are ideas about weight and eating control, on the other side are the range of wider personal issues such as self-esteem, self-evaluation, self-confidence, emotional control and the like (see Box 4.2). The tangle is a cognitive one; a mix of ideas and beliefs. Each side of the tangle is itself not uncommonly experienced by many people as problematic. Some concern about weight and eating is very frequent indeed, especially in women. Likewise, to be concerned about the second set of issues – self-evaluation and the rest – is entirely to be expected, and to have no such concern is to be an unusual person and probably not an especially effective or pleasant one. Furthermore, for many people, especially young women, how they feel about themselves in general is influenced somewhat by the way in which they think about and experience their weight, shape and eating. Some degree of entanglement between these two sets of issues is, in this sense, normal. What is abnormal in the eating disorders is the *degree* of entanglement.

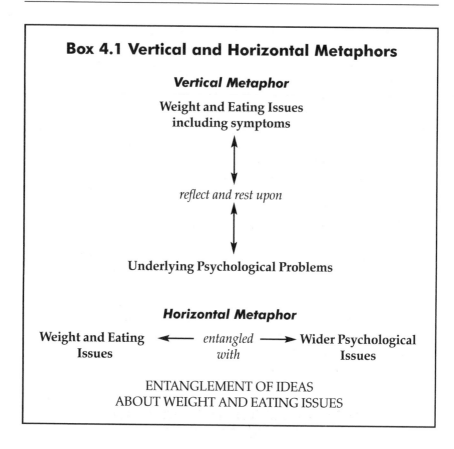

Box 4.1 Vertical and Horizontal Metaphors

Vertical Metaphor

Weight and Eating Issues
including symptoms

reflect and rest upon

Underlying Psychological Problems

Horizontal Metaphor

Weight and Eating   ←—— *entangled* ——→ Wider Psychological
Issues   *with*   Issues

ENTANGLEMENT OF IDEAS
ABOUT WEIGHT AND EATING ISSUES

The ideas which are said to constitute the specific psychopathology of the eating disorders are such as to reflect and confirm this tangle in that they emphasise the great and wide-ranging personal importance and implications of particular weights or shapes for better or worse. (If it would not spoil the metaphor, these ideas could be described as the glue that holds the tangle together, but tangles should not need glue.) Such ideas also provide the motivation for eating restraint. Sometimes it seems that such restraint may be motivated by ideas other than those specified in the diagnostic criteria. For instance, ideas about fitness, complex nutritional balance, food allergies, greed, spiritual purity or 'mortifying the flesh' may be what links eating – and sometimes weight – with issues of wider well-being (Palmer, 1993).

Discussion of entanglement of ideas about weight and eating control and wider personal issues is a useful starting point when considering what eating disorders are about – but it is only a start. It is necessary to look further at how weight and eating control might work.

Box 4.2 Varieties of Entanglement

Weight and Eating ◄——► *entanglement* ◄——► Wider Psychological
Issues   Issues

Ideas about

WEIGHT AND SHAPE

GREED AND SIN

FOOD ALLERGIES, ETC.

'YIN AND YANG'

'MORTIFYING THE FLESH'

WEIGHT AND EATING CONTROL:
THE SLIMMING PHILOSOPHY

The actual mechanisms involved in weight and eating control are likely to be complex and they are certainly not well understood.[2] However, that does not stop many people from giving a remarkably simple account of how weight and eating control work. They do so with every appearance of confidence that they believe the account to be true or even self-evident. This account goes something like this: 'If you eat too much, your weight goes up. If you eat too little, your weight goes down. And if you eat just the right amount, your weight stays just where you want it to be.' This account could be called the 'slimming philosophy' and very many people – perhaps most people – seem to believe it and indeed many act upon it. A smaller group of people make a living out of peddling its consequences in the form of slimming products, diet books and the like.

Is the 'slimming philosophy' true? It clearly contains some truth. Weight is more mutable than height. It can be changed. Undereating does lead to weight loss. Likewise, although less predictably perhaps, overeating may lead to weight gain.[3] However, the apparent implication, that changing weight is straightforward and easy, is false. Furthermore, the 'slimming philosophy' has a couple of significant problems. Firstly, it has the following sting in its tail: it promotes the view that if a person is not the weight – or even perhaps the shape – that she would wish to be or thinks others would have her be, then it is not only her misfortune, it is also importantly her responsibility – even her fault. These ideas promote self-blame, because if they are taken to be true then people who are not as they would wish to be – usually in our society this would mean that they thought themselves 'too fat' – tend to conclude that they have not tried hard enough to be slim. Such a person may begin to feel not only too fat but also lazy and lacking in resolve – in short, a fat slob. Furthermore, she may feel that other people also judge her in this way. Indeed, if she is heavier than average she may often be correct in feeling that that is what other people think of her. There is a large literature that documents the way that overweight people are negatively perceived (Stunkard & Sobal, 1995). The consequence of all of this is that any entanglement between ideas about weight and eating and wider issues of self-evaluation becomes confirmed, and strengthened. If slimming is attempted but fails, then such negative views are strengthened even more.

The second problem with the 'slimming philosophy' is less noxious but may be important none the less. This is that it seems to suggest that if eating varies then weight should change readily along with it. However, for most people most of the time – although not all people all of the time – there seems to be a surprising stability about their body weight over weeks, months or even years. This stability seems often to be more than might be expected from any parallel stability of dietary intake.[4] And it is this relative stability of body weight that suggests an alternative way of thinking about weight and eating control which may be more illuminating. This alternative account might even be nearer the truth, although that cannot be guaranteed.

WEIGHT AND EATING CONTROL: THE SPRING STORY

This alternative way of thinking about the control of weight and eating is that it behaves like a regulated system. A regulated system will tend to resist change and return to a predetermined set point. A spring is such a system. Whether a spring is stretched or compressed it will tend to return to its original resting state. It will settle at a predictable point or at least somewhere within a fairly narrow range. In general, body weight does indeed have something of this characteristic, at least for most people over short to medium lengths of time – say months or a few years.[5] The proposition is that the mechanisms which regulate body weight can be reasonably represented by the image of a spring. This is the 'spring story'.

What are the implications of this regulation model or spring story and how do they differ from those of the 'slimming philosophy"? The differences between the two models remain largely hidden until a person seeks to change her weight. The latter will then predict that the attempt to change should be easy and straightforward, but the spring story will

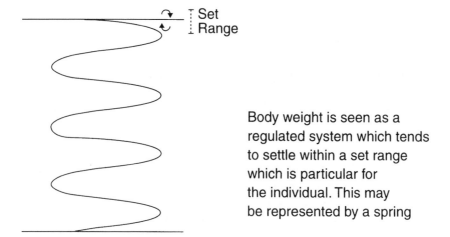

Body weight is seen as a
regulated system which tends
to settle within a set range
which is particular for
the individual. This may
be represented by a spring

Figure 4.1: Spring Diagram I

predict that the system will resist any change away from its set range
(Figure 4.1). The body will have a vote as it were and it will vote against
moving far. This will be true whether the person is seeking to raise or lower
her body weight. For instance, it is said that sumo wrestlers often
encounter difficulties when trying to substantially increase their body
weight. However, the more commonplace example of dieting for the
purpose of slimming will serve better and is certainly more relevant to the
eating disorders. Not all people who develop eating disorders have set out
to slim, but nearly all have restrained their eating for one reason or
another. For this purpose, the example of slimming will serve as repre-
senting these others too.

THE NATURAL HISTORY OF SLIMMING

The usual outcome of attempts to slim is failure. Sustained weight loss is
not usually achieved (Garner & Wooley, 1991). The typical story goes
something like this. Someone is dissatisfied with herself. At the very least
she is dissatisfied with her body otherwise she would not want to change
it. However, attempts at slimming often occur when the person is more
pervasively unsettled and displeased with herself or her life. So she sets
out to restrain her eating and restrict her intake. If this is at first successful,
the venture will often be immediately rewarding to the slimmer. She will
experience the positive consequences of slimming. She will feel better: she
is achieving something, and is in control. But soon she will typically

encounter negative consequences. She may feel hungry and find herself preoccupied with thoughts of food and eating. (This tendency for eating restraint to increase the urge to eat has been called 'the dieter's dilemma'.) She may feel impulsive in her urge to eat and may even feel an impulse to binge. Interestingly, she may feel more than usually tense, emotional and in particular irritable. The most frequent response to these accruing negative consequences of eating restraint is to give it up – sooner or later. The person in some sense makes a judgement that the whole enterprise is just not worth the effort. The emotions associated with 'giving in' may vary from an enjoyable sense of relief and 'letting go' to more negative feelings of failure. Not uncommonly the abandonment of slimming may lead to self-recrimination and further attempts at a later time. Indeed it seems likely that the experience of failure may commonly increase the very feelings of dissatisfaction and, perhaps, low self-esteem which may have triggered the behaviour in the first place. It may also increase the entanglement between ideas about weight and ideas about self-worth.

The natural history or usual course of slimming outlined above may be difficult to understand in the light of the 'slimming philosophy'. But they make good sense in the light of the regulatory model. The regulatory mechanisms represented by the spring in the 'spring story' – whatever their actual nature may be – will predictably resist the change threatened by the eating restraint of slimming. This resistance will be represented by the increased drive to eat, the food preoccupation and so on. It will build up as restraint continues and weight is lost until the forces involved may be properly represented by the image of a compressed spring. And that may well be how the would-be slimmer experiences it – as sitting on top of a potential jack-in-the-box. The 'spring' which had previously been an image of inherent stability is now pushed out of kilter and is a source of instability. It had previously been two way and a friendly force. It is now pushing only one way and, inasmuch as it is pushing against the intentions of the slimmer, it is experienced as unfriendly.

It is important to keep in mind that this image of the spring is just a way of talking and thinking about these matters. However, it is arguably a better way of thinking and talking than the more usual methods. Its advantages become more obvious when it is applied to the eating disorders themselves.

THE VICIOUS CIRCLE OF RESTRAINT

Most people give up slimming. They abandon eating restraint when the negative consequences build up. However, this is clearly not the case when someone develops anorexia nervosa. Then, typically, eating restraint is continued well beyond the point that was the original aim of the slimming attempt. For instance, someone who originally weighed 65 kg and wanted to weigh 55 kg, may still be restraining hard when she weighs 45 kg and end up severely ill with anorexia nervosa when she weighs 35 kg. How has this happened? Why does the slimmer continue to restrain after having reached her original target? Why does she continue and appear to become stuck in a pattern of behaviour which seems so disadvantageous to the outside observer.

The spring story may provide one possible answer. The regulatory model predicts that change – in this case weight loss – will be resisted. This resistance will be experienced as some mix of hunger, food preoccupation, impulsivity and emotionality. This is a force against which the slimmer may feel that she must fight. The more that she feels frightened of these forces, or rewarded by the sense of being in control of them, the more she is likely to persist with this fight. However, the more she persists and the more she succeeds in her fight, the more the force builds up (see Figure 4.2). The spring becomes increasingly compressed. The individual finds herself in the midst of a vicious circle because fighting the source of her fear leads it to increase. It feels as though it would take more and more courage to give in to the force. She hesitates to give up restraint because she worries that the pent-up force – represented by the compressed spring – might prove overwhelming if she did. If she does persist and indeed restrains harder, she may begin to feel that to do otherwise is to risk getting out of control in terms of her weight, her eating, her emotions or some mix of all three. She begins to feel that holding on to her exaggerated but precarious sense of control is the key to some minimal sense of well-being and the only way to avoid nameless disaster. Almost everything seems to be involved in this struggle to avoid weight gain even though she is now at a lower weight than her original target. She is trapped. She has anorexia nervosa. Or so this story goes.

THE VICIOUS CIRCLE OF FAILED RESTRAINT

Another vicious circle awaits the slimmer who restrains with force but who gives in and overeats in the face of the build up of forces represented by the compressed spring. She will feel that she has failed and that she has given up in the face of powerful forces. She may well interpret this 'failure' either as a reflection of her weakness of will or of the strength of the appetite within her, or both. The act of giving in and eating may begin to have a highly charged but varied emotional tone. It may include elements of guilt combined with a pleasurable excitement. However, provided her investment in restrain is too great for her to simply abandon the whole

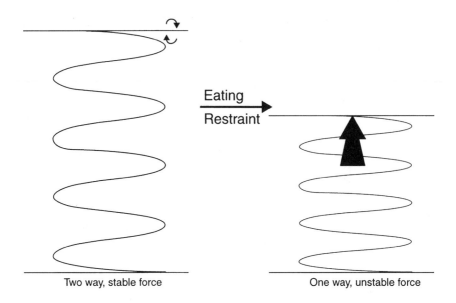

Figure 4.2: Spring Diagram II

venture, the would-be slimmer's response is to redouble her efforts to restrain her eating. Then, however, she too may find that the forces increase (see Figure 4.3). When they overwhelm her resolve again, she too finds herself caught up in a vicious circle. Each attempt to stop bingeing promotes the next binge. If she attempts to thwart the forces by vomiting or whatever, she will become even more trapped. She will come to be in the state of bulimia nervosa. Or so *this* story goes.

THE VICIOUS CIRCLE OF ENTANGLEMENT

An individual who finds herself trapped by either of the vicious circles described above is likely to feel that she is in a miserable and powerless position. It is an unsought after position but none the less she somehow feels that her own ideas and behaviour have led her into it. To a degree she is right. She blames herself, but in doing so may lower further the low self-esteem that has contributed to her entrapment in the first place. She is trapped by her difficulty in saying 'it's not worth while' and decisively giving up eating restraint. She feels that she cannot win but must nevertheless avoid the threat of losing everything. Paradoxically, her determination to persist is bolstered by failure. 'Failure' may further undermine her self-esteem, and, as she persists, the very ideas upon which the whole

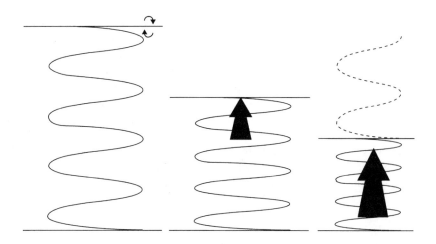

Greater restraint will lead to greater response and the risk of "escape"

Figure 4.3: Spring Diagram III

enterprise is based may be strengthened and become more extreme. Weight and eating become even more entangled with wider personal issues. This is a further vicious circle.[6]

A NESTING SET OF VICIOUS CIRCLES

This way of thinking and speaking about the clinical eating disorders portrays them as involving a nesting set of vicious circles, which is understandable in the light of the way in which eating restraint opposes the body's inherent regulatory mechanisms. Taken together they form a more useful story or way of talking than the more commonplace 'slimming philosophy'. It is their main claim to validity that they seem to make sense to many sufferers and may sometimes make their suffering and dilemmas more understandable.

DIFFERENTIAL VULNERABILITY

This account sees such vicious circles as being at the heart of the problem, but an advantage of this 'story' is that many other features commonly observed in the eating disorders can also be plausibly included, as can some other hypothetical mechanisms. Psychological variation may be incorporated. For instance, it seems likely that a person who lacks in self-esteem may well find it more difficult to adopt the healthily blithe 'what the hell?' response to the dieter's dilemma and is more likely to persist in or repeat attempts at motivated eating restraint. Low self-esteem may contribute to the risk of getting caught up in either the vicious circle of restraint or of failed restraint. Such low self-esteem and anything that increases the strength of the individual's determination to restrain may increase her vulnerability to either disorder. Moreover, someone who is obsessional and overcontrolled by nature may well find it difficult not to persevere with restraint when to give it up feels as if it risks loss of control and 'messiness'. Such a person might be especially vulnerable to the vicious circle of restraint and hence to anorexia nervosa. Conversely, it seems likely that someone who is more extroverted or impulsive in personality would be more likely to get caught up in the vicious circle that leads to bulimic behaviour.

More speculatively, it could be that a person may be more vulnerable to any of these vicious circles, perhaps especially that of restraint, if she is grappling with issues of emotional control which somehow parallel the control of appetite and eating which she attempts. Such issues may arise from the interpersonal context in which the individual finds herself. Thus, if she is in a circumstance where there is a premium upon sitting on top of her emotions and not expressing or acting upon them, she may be especially vulnerable to becoming entrapped. For instance, a young person who is struggling through the dilemmas of late adolescence may feel constrained from getting too angry or upsetting her parents if they seem to her to have an impaired capacity to cope with such emotion. (Examples of this might include situations where the mother is recently separated and floundering in the face her own troubles or the father has had a heart attack and suffers from unstable angina. See the illustrative stories in Chapter 1.) Sometimes it may be more distant events or emotional issues within the family that have set a style or tradition which makes overt distress or disruptive behaviour especially difficult to tolerate. To influence the outcome of slimming or other eating restraint in the young person it would be necessary only for the expectation or vulnerability of the parents to *seem* to demand that she stays in control and avoids rocking the boat.

Anything that changes the outcome of eating restraint may change the vulnerability of an individual to eating disorder. Within the framework of the 'spring story', it would be possible to postulate that the probably biological regulatory mechanisms which are represented by the spring might themselves be subject to variation in their strength or character between individuals in a way that altered the risk of disorder. It was noted in the preceding chapter that even what little is known of such mechanisms suggests that they may differ between men and women. Biological issues can also thus be incorporated into this framework.

Social issues may give the best account not only for the risk of an individual starting to restrain her eating but also for the outcome of such restraint in some cases. Thus, for some people, the social context in which they live may place such a strong premium upon sustaining restraint as to make them vulnerable to entrapment within the vicious circles outlined above. For instance, a young woman who is an athlete or a fashion model may experience a great pressure to conform to an ultra-slim ideal common to the subculture in which she performs. To some degree, perhaps most young women find themselves in the midst of such pressures, but they may be much stronger for some than they are for others.

Once the vicious circles have entrapped the sufferer, other forces may contribute to her staying trapped. She may find herself perversely rewarded by the consequences of her position. For instance, some potential sufferers may be hooked by the sometimes pleasurable sense of emotional release associated with bingeing and the distracting complexities of the secret life that goes with it. Others may find that the endocrine consequences of weight loss relieve them of some of their struggle with their sexual impulses. Still others may find that those near to them begin to deal with them differently, and this may be rewarding or at least simplifying. Sometimes, a whole family may reconfigure itself around the sufferer in a way which comes to have a stability that was absent before the illness occurred.[7] For instance, in some cases it may be more manageable for all concerned to have a sick child in their midst than a challenging teenager, even though the unity of purpose and family coherence is quite genuinely directed towards the care and hoped-for recovery of that 'child'. In all sorts of ways the situations which arise around the eating-disordered person may contribute to the perpetuation of the disorder. The whole thing may become a kind of meaning machine which sucks in and incorporates – an apt word in this context – the worries, concerns and vulnerabilities of everyone concerned. The eating disorder seems to take on a life of its own. The person feels more and more trapped.

SPRING STORY: RECAPITULATION AND WARNING

What has been called the 'spring story' is a way of thinking and talking about eating disorders. It portrays anorexia nervosa and bulimia nervosa as states in which the sufferer becomes entrapped by sets of vicious circles. These vicious circles may involve psychological and biological components but – the possibility of individual variability notwithstanding – they are construed as arising from a distortion of normal regulatory mechanisms rather than mechanisms that are essentially morbid. It puts determined eating restraint in the presence of an intact drive to eat at the heart of the matter.

The 'spring story' is an attempt to answer the imprecise question 'What are eating disorders about?'. However, it is an imprecise answer and, furthermore, a provisional one. Aspects of it do not bear much close scrutiny. It is offered not as a theory of the eating disorders but rather as a framework within which they may be considered. It may find a place especially in the everyday business of clinical practice where the need is for something to hold together diverse observations from several domains. It should not be taken too seriously. In its own terms it seems to work quite well for anorexia nervosa and for many cases of bulimia nervosa. However, it fails when confronted with some cases. For instance, it is difficult to encompass those rare cases of anorexia nervosa in which there seems to be true loss of appetite. Likewise, the minority of cases of bulimia nervosa in which bingeing appears to have preceded eating restraint, or in which bingeing continues in the absence of attempts at such restraint, are not easily construed within its framework. Most cases of binge eating disorder fit the model hardly at all.

A use for the 'spring story' is to give a picture of the nature of the trap in which the sufferer finds herself. As a consequence, it may help in thinking about what might be necessary for her to escape. It represents the trap as a set of vicious circles arising from essentially normal regulatory mechanisms which have been pushed out of kilter. The good news is that there is no inexorably morbid process at work. Escape is possible. The bad news is that vicious circles are vicious because escaping from them always involves effort and cost. The easiest thing in the short term is to keep going around them. The sufferer is presented with dilemmas about whether or not the effort and cost involved in escape feel worth while and are things she can face. The nature of these dilemmas and the necessary tasks of recovery are the subject of the next chapter.

NOTES

1. I once heard it proposed that the eating disorders should no longer be described as such but should be dubbed the 'disorders of self-esteem' or something of the sort. This seemed to me to be daft and I came to the conclusion that the proposer – for whom I have the greatest respect – was either making a wonderfully disguised joke or was having a real off-day. Even if low self-esteem were to be thought of as a necessary feature of 'eating disorders' – and that could perhaps be argued – it is certainly the case that many people have profoundly low self-esteem but are entirely normal in their eating. It also seems self-evident that if

their eating or weight is not affected they just do not have an 'eating disorder'. Furthermore, such a person would have a problem that was in an important sense different from someone who did have a classic eating disorder. The weight and eating symptoms are the defining and necessary features of eating disorders however important any other features may be.

2. This sentence should perhaps read 'the mechanisms involved in weight and eating control are not well understood by me'. However, I am not convinced that anyone has an entirely adequate account.

3. There is something of a tautology here if 'undereating' and 'overeating' are defined as patterns of eating which lead to weight change down or up respectively. Furthermore, any person who is obese has clearly 'overeaten' in the sense that her intake has led to a higher than healthy weight. However, she may well not have overeaten in the sense of eating in a socially excessive or gluttonous way.

4. It is perhaps difficult to be certain of what would be expected in the way of stability or otherwise of weight. Perhaps people's intake of food is, on average, steady enough. And then there is the issue of energy expenditure. The whole matter is complex. However, for the purposes of the present exercise – the attempt to answer the question 'What are eating disorders about?' – I would ask you to accept, for the sake of the next step in the argument, that the 'slimming philosophy' is not an adequate model of weight and eating control and that body weight is more stable in reality than it would predict.

5. Of course, people's weights do change. Middle-age spread is a real phenomenon as I can attest from personal experience. However, my own weight is, in general, stable now within a kilogram or two, just as it was a couple of decades ago. It is just that such stability now finds me weighing perhaps 10 kilograms or so more than I did then. I tell myself that I shall do something about this one of these days. As an eating disorders pundit and cynical sceptic about the value of slimming, I am not entirely immune to the prevailing idea that I would be better off if I were to lose just a bit of weight. However, I have not found it that difficult to resist actually doing anything about it.

6. I have come to be very familiar with a conversation which, at different times, has something like the following questions and answers within it. What weight are you now? *About 6 stones* (38 kg). What would you feel about weighing an average weight for your height, say 9 stones (57 kg)? *I think that I'd rather die than weigh 9 stones. I would be enormous.* How do you feel in general at present? *Not good.* When did you last feel that you were reasonably happy and things were going well? *About three years ago.* What did you weigh three years ago? *About 9 stones.* This is clearly a gross simplification of elements in a clinical conversation. However, it

illustrates how something about being in the state of anorexia nervosa coincides with a tendency for such ideas to become not only more entrenched but also more extreme.

7. Professor Arthur Crisp has especially emphasised the way in which anorexia nervosa may involve the whole family's response to the sufferer's adolescence, including the reawakening of issues from the parents' own earlier lives. The treatment approach which he developed over many years at St George's Hospital, London, was importantly based upon this emphasis. His writings contain many rich accounts of such matters. His book, *Anorexia nervosa: Let Me Be*, is a good place to start reading about these (Crisp, 1980).

FURTHER READING

Palmer, RL (1989) The Spring Story: a way of talking about clinical eating disorder. *British Review of Anorexia Nervosa and Bulima*, **4**, 33–41.

5

WHAT IS INVOLVED IN RECOVERY FROM EATING DISORDERS?

The preceding chapter portrayed the eating disorders as entrapping the sufferer in a series of vicious circles. Escaping from such entrapment involves breaking out of these vicious circles. In these terms that much is clear, but how may the task of recovery be best thought about? This chapter is about what is involved in getting better. What must the sufferer do? It will also touch upon what, in general terms, others can do for her. However, it is not about the details of treatment. It is rather an attempt to define what an individual needs to achieve – whether in relation to treatment or not – if she is truly to get better and stand a good chance of staying that way. Inasmuch as the discussion is framed within the speculative and provisional way of thinking outlined in the previous chapter, it is subject to the same caveats and warnings that were appropriate then. However, there is perhaps less here that is controversial. There is likely to be broad agreement about what is involved in recovery although, of course, much less about how this may best be promoted.

Recovery may be thought of as involving three tasks. They will be presented separately, but for the sufferer struggling to escape from an eating disorder they have to be confronted together. They are all of apiece.

TASK ONE: RESTORING WEIGHT AND EATING

The first task is that of restoring a healthy body weight and sustainable pattern of eating. This is at least fairly easy to describe although it may be very difficult for the sufferer to face and achieve.

In this context a healthy body weight means one which can be maintained in the long term without undue eating restraint and which sustains wider health and notably menstruation in the adult woman. In the terms of the 'spring story', it is a weight at which the individual is not in a state of continuous battle with the regulatory mechanisms represented by the spring. For most people, this weight is likely to be close to the average weight for their age and height. This is so almost by definition. However, for smaller numbers of people it will be significantly lower or higher than this average. Some people are 'naturally' skinny or plump, or so it seems. In principle, the weight at which a person is likely to find stability is better estimated by recourse to scrutiny of her own personal history rather than by examining standard tables of average weights. If an individual has had a period of a year or more in her adult life in which she has sustained a stable body weight without disordered eating or restraint, it is likely that she may be able to find stability again at or near that body weight. However, many people presenting for help have never had such a time of weight stability in their adult lives because their eating disorder or any preceding eating restraint started in their adolescence before they had had a chance to establish such a position.[1] In practice, an average weight or something like it may be the best guess that can be made in the case of sufferers who are currently markedly underweight. For those who are currently of average or above average weight, seeking a stable pattern of regular and unrestrained eating may be the better primary goal. If this is achieved they may 'discover' their inherently stable weight.

A sustainable pattern of eating may be taken as meaning a diet which sustains health – including a healthy body weight which is socially acceptable and does not involve marked eating restraint. All of these features are likely to be debatable in any one individual. An eating disorder sufferer, almost by definition, will have a tendency to engage in such debate from an unusual and exaggerated position. All sorts of evidence may be invoked to question what seems to be a commonsensical view of what is 'normal or 'healthy' eating. Not uncommonly, exaggerated versions of sensible advice, such as the health educators' admonition that people in general should eat less fat, are rehashed and used as justification for extreme dietary avoidance of one kind or another. Nevertheless, recovery involves the resumption of a diet with a content and a pattern with the characteristics outlined above. Such a diet, not surprisingly, usually resembles what most people eat.

TASK TWO: DISENTANGLING

The first task was easy to talk about even if it is often difficult to achieve. The second and third tasks may be just as difficult in practice, but are not easy even to describe adequately. Both are mental tasks involving thinking and, usually, talking.

The second task makes sense within the way of speaking that construes the eating disorders as involving a maladaptive entanglement of ideas about weight and eating control with wider personal issues. The task in these terms is to undo this tangle. It involves, as it were, putting ideas about weight and the like on one side and ideas about self-worth or whatever on the other. Of course, this notion of disentangling is all very well as a metaphor but the process is perhaps less clear in real life. However, to the person who is accomplishing it, the importance of weight and eating control for her sense of self-worth will decline. Ideas which constitute the specific psychopathology of the disorders will be challenged and found wanting. Their importance will diminish. The process of challenge may at times be direct, as in some kinds of therapy. At other times, life events and circumstances may have much the same effect as when, for instance, a young woman finds that her new boyfriend or her peers seem to love or value her regardless of her body shape and size.[2]

In practice, the process of disentangling which constitutes this second task of recovery would usually mean that the individual starts to view her world in a more varied and flexible way. What is involved is a loosening of the conceptual links between weight and eating and wider issues. In the terms of personal construct theory, this would be referred to as a lessening of the rigidity of construing which has been shown to be characteristic of the thinking of anorexia nervosa sufferers (Button, 1993). Presumably, in principle, this could mean that she simply adopts another equally rigid way of thinking and explaining her experience, and if this did not involve ideas about weight and eating she would no longer be eating disordered although she might be heading for another kind of trap. However, she would nevertheless have to face up to the issues that were previously caught up with her disorder, but now have to be dealt with in other ways. That leads on to the third task of recovery.

TASK THREE: GETTING LIFE ON THE MOVE AGAIN

This third task is perhaps best thought of as 'what would in principle remain if the sufferer were to use a magic wand to accomplish the other two tasks?' Thus, if an individual were to restore her weight and eating to a normal and stable pattern and, furthermore, overcome the conceptual tangles involved in the specific psychopathology of her eating disorder, she would still have to deal with whatever antecedent issues had contributed to her disorder and whatever unfortunate consequences the illness may have had for her. For instance, someone who was sexually abused as a child, troubled and uncertain as an adolescent, and eating disordered for five years as a young adult, would not automatically feel at ease with her sexuality, be full of confidence, have a secure sense of self and be able to build a new life even were she to have the services of the proposed magic wand. To recover fully, she would need to begin to deal with these issues. She would need to get 'on the move again' in respect of those aspects of her life which had been stuck.

In the inevitable absence of the magic wand invoked above, the third task is a variable and unpredictable business. The sufferer who is emerging from an eating disorder may feel exposed to all sorts of thoughts and feelings which are, at best, unnerving and, at worst, terrifying. The false certainties and familiarities of the world of her disorder may continue to be perversely attractive. Equally attractive may be the idea that the issues involved in the third task need to be sorted out before any progress can occur in the matter of the first and second tasks. This is almost always a misleading view and indeed it may be dangerous if it impedes any progress. All three tasks are bound up together. It is likely to be as true that the issues of weight and eating complicate and impede progress with regard to the wider issues as it is that these wider issues drive the actual disorder of eating. Furthermore, the whole idea of getting the wider issues definitively 'sorted out' once and for all can itself be misleading. Most people's lives consist of an somewhat erratic progression from one set of problems to the next. Arguably the difference between the psychologically healthy and the not so healthy resides not in the presence or absence of problems, but rather in the degree to which the latter become stuck, going round and round in circles in relation to one set of problems that feel intractable and not progressing to the next. Therefore, the person who is escaping from an eating disorder needs to begin to resolve those related problems before she can make any progress. She needs to turn the whirlpool of her life back into a flowing stream, even if she would be well advised to anticipate that there may be all sorts of rocks and rapids ahead.

THE ROLE OF OTHERS IN RECOVERY

The whole of this book seeks to address the issue of helping people with eating disorders. This brief section will discuss only in outline some of the broader issues which arise in relation to the role of others in the tasks of recovery as they have been set out above.

What is needed most by the sufferer is a sense that others appreciate not only the difficulty but also the complexity of the tasks of recovery. This applies whether these others are family, friends, colleagues or professionals. Of course, it is true that the anorexia nervosa sufferer needs to eat more and to put on weight. There is an irrefutable simplicity in this. However, the parent or professional who underestimates the enormity of the task when viewed through the eyes of the sufferer is unlikely to be experienced as helpful. Furthermore, when things do begin to change it is likewise unhelpful to fail to recognise that weight gain of itself is not enough and may bring with it more difficulty and suffering rather than less. The hopeful difference is that the difficulty and suffering associated with weight gain may be productive in the sense that the sufferer is beginning to react to her problem. The would-be helper needs to hold on to that aspect and assist the recovering sufferer to do so too. Many sufferers dread being thought of as 'better' or 'recovered' just because they have put on weight. The others in their lives need to validate their view that there is more to recovery than that. This can be difficult if these other people have been beside themselves with worry and are relieved merely to see their loved one retreating from what had seemed to be death's door. It can be difficult to appreciate that the sufferer may feel *less* safe now having gained some weight than she did when she was physically on the edge. Similar issues may arise in relation to the eating behaviour of the bulimia nervosa sufferer, although the more covert nature of the symptoms may mean that the different concerns of the sufferer and the other may influence each other less directly.

Overall, those around the person who is trying to escape from an eating disorder need to take seriously all three of the tasks of recovery. Furthermore, they need to keep in mind that only the sufferer can accomplish these tasks; they cannot be taken over by anyone else. Others can, however, provide the means and circumstance in which these tasks can be undertaken with an improved chance of success. Most of all they can try to help the sufferer to feel just about safe enough to tackle them. Such help may or may not involve the provision of complex circumstances – as, for instance, in the case of professionals offering admission to a hospital with a special treatment regime. However, it should almost always include a sense that the individual's suffering and struggle is understood or, if not understood, at least validated. The implication of this and what it may mean for professionals in various circumstances will be discussed in later chapters.

CAN ANYONE RECOVER?

The short answer to this question should be 'yes'. However, both the question and this answer need qualification. If the question is taken to be asking whether there is ever a time in the career of an eating disorder sufferer when recovery should be thought of as impossible, then the response should be that no case is hopeless. Improvement is always possible and full recovery can occur even after decades of disorder.

However, the psychological and physical effects of disorder may remain and continue to affect the individual. For instance, anorexia nervosa may lead to osteoporosis, with pathological fractures or collapsed vertebrae, which would remain even if the individual were to regain a normal weight, diet and attitudes. Likewise, spending 25 years from the age of 15 restricted by a severe eating disorder will have produced continuing emotional effects even if life does begin again at 40. We are all shaped by our experiences, and this is true of individuals whose psychological development has been distorted by chronic illness, but, some individuals seem to manage to put even these negative experiences to good use. So any sufferer should be thought of as potentially able to recover, and a wish to do so is probably the best sign that this potential may be realised. However, this is different to saying that all sufferers should be expected to recover in either sense of the word 'expected'. Certainly, if groups of people suffering from anorexia nervosa are followed up over many years, a significant minority do not recover (Herzog, Keller & Lavori 1988; Herzog, Deter & Vanderycken 1992). Data on the long-term outcome of bulimia nervosa are few but what there are suggest that that disorder too may run a truly chronic course in some cases (Herzog, Keller & Lavori, 1988; Herzog, Deter & Vanderycken, 1992; Collings & King, 1994; Fichter & Quadflieg, 1997). It would therefore be foolish, in the absence of some major advance in treatment, to expect everyone to recover in the sense of predicting that that would be the case. And that being so, it may be inappropriate to expect every patient to recover in the sense of feeling that everyone always should be pushed hard in that direction. For a few truly chronic sufferers it may be that they will want to make the best life they can within their disorder rather than strive for full recovery. That should be – and at the end of the day inevitably is – their prerogative and their decision. The role of others is to give information, support, encouragement and the means to help whatever efforts towards recovery the sufferer feels able to make. It is appropriate to try to instil hope but not to bully the sufferer who is feeling that she cannot face the rigours of trying to change too much. Such bullying – even when well intended – usually makes the situation worse.

Many people who recover from eating disorders remain more than usually sensitive or preoccupied by matters of weight and eating. Perhaps they should be thought of as only partially recovered. It is a question of degree. Some may continue to show partial versions of the full syndromes, but when these are mild and do not interfere with life, they come to resemble many people in the general population who have never had an eating disorder. Some certainly seem to lose all symptoms and unusual attitudes. However, those who have at one time succumbed to the full syndromes probably do face a greater risk of doing so again. They have a vulnerability. It is their Achilles heel. Indeed, there is evidence that when people with a past history of eating disorder become psychologically disordered again, it is usually into an eating disorder that they relapse. 'Symptom substitution' or falling ill in other ways is less likely, at least in the first decade or so. However, it would be wrong to say that 'once eating disordered, always eating disordered'. Most people eventually recover, and the remainder of the book will discuss ways of helping them to do so.

NOTES

1. In practice, some sufferers may seek to convince others – and themselves – that they did in fact have a stable weight in the past when they did not. They will choose a weight from the past which was low and which fits their current preoccupations. For instance, a woman of 23 who has had bulimia nervosa associated with variable weight for eight years might think of a time when, at 20, she tightly controlled her weight at 8 stones (51 kg.) as her 'normal' weight, even though this was achieved only for a few months and at the cost of restraint. Although she has almost always been markedly heavier, this is the weight that she would wish to be. However, it is unlikely to be the weight at which she can most readily achieve stability. Alternatively, such a woman might suggest that her proper weight is that which was the case before she developed an eating disorder, even though this was her weight as an early teenager and not an adult weight at all.
2. I tend to think that life and psychotherapy lead to change by similar mechanisms. Perhaps therapy is required when life has not provided the experiences which would allow the individual to escape from her particular traps and vicious circles. When someone is very stuck then the focused and especially contrived circumstances of psychotherapy may be vital. However, I would tend to the view that there is little that therapy can accomplish that 'life' cannot, given good luck. But, of course, good luck cannot be sought out or prescribed, whereas therapy can.

Part II

6

HOW TO ASSESS PEOPLE WITH EATING DISORDERS

This chapter is concerned with the issues involved when a professional meets someone suffering from an eating disorder and tries to assess her problems and the help she might need to escape from them. It sets out to inform and advise the professional. This is straightforward; however, when such an encounter occurs in real life it is likely that a double process of assessment will be taking place. Not only will the professional be assessing the sufferer and her disorder, but the sufferer will be assessing the professional. She will be trying to decide whether the professional is knowledgeable about eating disorders, understands something of her experience, is willing to listen and seems competent and trustworthy. Clearly for both parties the process of assessment is likely to continue well beyond the first meeting – especially in relation to the key area of trust – but first impressions are important. The professional needs to keep this in mind. Things can go wrong. However, it is not difficult to avoid the more obvious pitfalls. What follows is a discussion of some of the issues involved in making an assessment arranged around an account of one way of doing it.[1]

THE FIRST FEW MINUTES

The first few minutes of an interview are important. They are crucial in setting the tone. It is important to avoid getting off on the wrong foot. In order to do so the assessor has to begin quickly to try to develop some idea of what hopes, fears and expectations the sufferer brings to the encounter. Some of them may stay well hidden but she needs to be given an early opportunity to express such feelings. If she does not there is a risk that there may be problematic differences between what her expectations really are and what the assessor guesses them to be. However, the issue can be simply introduced by asking a direct question along the lines of 'What did you feel about the idea of coming along to see me today?' and then facilitating discussion of what may well be quite complex and mixed feelings. This is a useful preliminary to more focused questioning or a discussion of the eating disorder itself. A few minutes setting the stage in this way may save much time and avoid unnecessary difficulty and complication. It may also be useful to state clearly what the assessment is going to involve and to ask if what is proposed is acceptable to the sufferer. After all, what is familiar, expected and routine to the assessor may be frighteningly unfamiliar to the patient.

Another useful, if obvious, question is to ask simply what the patient is worried or concerned about. What might she want help for? The answer may not be what is expected. The sufferer may emphasise problems or issues which are quite different from what the assessor has anticipated. There may be surprises. It may be useful to suggest to the patient how important it is to state the obvious and assume nothing about what the assessor might already know. Otherwise, she may give the impression that she is worried about all sorts of things but not about her weight or eating because she is, as it were, taking that as read. On the other hand, a sufferer may not mention what may seem obviously a problem to the assessor because she sees things differently or has such mixed feelings about the prospect of change.

MIXED FEELINGS

The range of feelings and expectations which sufferers bring along to a first assessment interview vary widely. Some may be idiosyncratic and personal. However, it may be useful to outline what is a reasonable initial guess as to what the expectations may be of sufferers presenting with the two main disorders. The accounts which follow are stereotypes, but stereotypes, can be useful. They may be better than nothing provided that they are not treated as assumptions. The stereotypes will be illustrated by using again the stories of the two fictional sufferers who were introduced in the first chapter.

People presenting with anorexia nervosa typically have mixed feelings about seeking help. The sufferer tends to feel both dissatisfied with the unhappy state in which she finds herself and at the same time somehow in control – albeit tenuously so – and fearful of what would happen were she to lose that control. She may come to the assessment reluctantly – or with a show of reluctance – persuaded or propelled by others. She may feel that those who would help her are aiming to take her over and somehow remove her anorexia nervosa. She feels that she has something to lose as well as something to gain. Losing control is frightening. She may feel cornered.

The major problems that can ensue from the mismanagement of mixed feelings will be discussed later. These tangles may begin from the outset if the clinician inherits the role of the family or friends and takes over the part of the sufferer's mixed feelings that the family have previously carried. The sufferer may be enabled then simply to resist change if she can tacitly rely on others to push her.

Faith Goes to the Doctor

Faith was persuaded to go along to the doctor by her mother after a family Christmas that was dominated by her difficulty around food and eating. Initially she protested that there was nothing wrong with her and that going to the doctor was a waste of time. Her mother pointed out that her periods had stopped and that she had fainted twice. She also used mild moral blackmail by saying that she was worried about the extent that her husband, Faith's father, was worried and about the effect that this might have on his health. Reluctantly, Faith agreed to go along with her mother. At the appointment with the family doctor, her mother did a lot of the talking. Faith said little and felt rather like a child and somewhat taken over by her mother and the doctor. After weighing Faith and giving her a brief physical examination, the doctor stated that, in her opinion, Faith was suffering from anorexia nervosa and that she should be referred to the local psychiatric service without delay. Although her mother seemed relieved, Faith herself was alarmed at the proposal but went along with it rather than make a fuss. She told herself that she was going only to keep everyone happy and that really there was nothing wrong. She feared that the whole business might upset her work routine and spoil her preparation for her A level examinations. She wanted to do very well even though she had not been accepted at Oxford University. She wanted to prove to herself and to her father that if she tried hard enough she could do anything. She 'knew' that once her examinations were over she could sort out her eating if only everyone would not keep going on and on about it. She hated it when her family nagged her to eat but at the same time found herself thinking about food all of the time. She felt fat but also felt bony and uncomfortable when she sat on a hard chair at school. Just sometimes she allowed herself to wonder how she had allowed herself to get into such a mess and whether anyone could help her to get out of it. But she was alarmed by a half-remembered account she had once read of a girl being locked up and force fed for anorexia nervosa. When the appointment arrived, she resolved to go and see the psychiatrist but only to explain that everyone was making a fuss about nothing and that she was all right.

The stereotypic bulimia nervosa sufferer also has mixed feelings although they are somewhat different. She is likely to experience a muted version of the dilemma of anorexia nervosa. She may be concerned to hold on to her aim of controlling her weight and may feel uncertain what trying to stop bingeing would do to that. She may hope that this would reduce her weight but also may fear the effect of giving up the use of vomiting or laxatives. Most importantly she is likely to have mixed feelings about the bingeing itself. Mostly she will feel ashamed of herself for giving in to the impulse to binge. She may wish to hide the extent of her bingeing or the details of what she actually does when she binges. Furthermore, she may be full of negative thoughts and may doubt that anything can stop her bingeing. (After all, she has probably tried to do so often enough.) However, there may be a part of her that guiltily values the buzz that the bingeing sometimes gives her. She feels bad about this too. Many sufferers from bulimia nervosa do not seek help because they feel ashamed. Those who come along may show a mixture of desperation and wariness.

Rachel Goes to the Doctor

Rachel was 23 and her son, Rory, was aged 5 by the time she first sought help for her bulimia nervosa. By then she had had the disorder for over four years. As soon as the pattern of bingeing and vomiting was established she had known what was happening. She had read about the disorder many times in women's magazines and had seen a programme about it on television. Nevertheless, at first she told herself that she would soon get out of it. In the early days, each time she binged, she resolved never to do it again. After a few months she found this less easy to believe but still felt that she would be able to stop 'when things settled down'. And, indeed, life did move on; her studies went well and she decided not to go to University but got a job which she enjoyed as a doctor's receptionist. She was getting on fairly well with her mother who looked after Rory when he was not at the nursery. She went out regularly with her friends and had a couple of brief relationships with men. However, her bulimia continued, as did her deep sense of unhappiness. She found herself feeling upset and angry for no immediate reason. She thought of 'doing something about it' but was not sure what to do. She was wary of telling her family doctor who worked in the same Health Centre as she did. He seemed a nice enough man but she had heard him going on about some of his patients who had emotional problems. She feared that he would not take her seriously. On the other hand, she did not want to tell her mother because she feared that she might over-react. Also she liked giving everyone the impression that all was well. She felt ashamed of her problem. Her decision to seek help was finally triggered when one day Rory came upon her vomiting and asked her what she was doing. She felt mixed up and even more ashamed. The same day, she telephoned the Eating Disorders Association who gave her the number of a local self-help group, and she also arranged an appointment to see her doctor. In the event he was much more understanding than she had anticipated and readily agreed to refer her to a local specialist. She went along to that appointment still feeling somewhat wary but nevertheless also relieved at taking what she felt was the first step towards recovery.

If an individual says that she has come along only because others have cajoled or coerced her to do so, it may be useful to discuss this at length and ask her if she wishes to go ahead with the assessment. Giving someone the choice of opting out almost always leads them to opt in.[2] Furthermore, having thus actively chosen to continue with the assessment, the patient or client – as she now is – will usually be much more cooperative and collaborative in the whole process than she would have been if her resentment and mixed feelings had not be aired. This is, of course, a very adult interaction which emphasises the person's freedom to seek help or not, as she so chooses. It is a difficult position to sustain when the sufferer is *very* ill, although even here there may be a lot to be said for seeking in this way to avoid promoting potentially harmful opposition. It may be impossible or inappropriate when the sufferer is a child. Then the parents do have an entirely legitimate say in the whole matter and the mixed feelings of the sufferer may need to be handled differently, perhaps by adopting a whole family approach from the outset. It is possible to involve the whole family from the beginning even when the patient is an adult, and some notable authorities advocate this especially for those presenting with anorexia nervosa (Crisp, 1997). However, if this is not to undermine the sufferer's sense of autonomy and complicate further her mixed feelings, the whole business has to be conducted with clear – even ostentatious – regard for these issues.

ENGAGEMENT

Implicit in what has gone before is the fact that in clinical practice the process of assessment is carried out in parallel with the process of engaging the sufferer. Engagement involves building a relationship between the sufferer and the clinician or, more generally, with the whole enterprise of change and recovery. The clinician needs not only to make an assessment of the sufferer's clinical condition but also of her feelings about it and her motivation for change. Mixed feelings are usual and those feelings in the patient which are positive with regard to the possibility of recovery need to be cherished and promoted. However, if the clinician is too pushy it may provoke negative feelings and resistance. The art is to help the sufferer to hold in her mind the dilemmas facing her rather than avoiding them, whilst at the same time working towards providing the means to help her to do something about her state.

The degree to which an individual is willing to change varies widely even amongst people who come along apparently asking for help. One way of talking about this issue is in the terms of the so-called transtheoretical model of change put forward by Prochaska and DiClementi (1986, 1992) and advocated in the field of eating disorders by Janet Treasure and others (Treasure & Ward, 1997). This is outlined in Box 6.1, and is a useful way of thinking in clinical practice. At present there are limitations to the methods available for empirical research using this conceptual framework. Real people remain messy in their thinking and sometimes defy the ability of questionnaires to capture their complexity. However, the model does provide a way of thinking about the otherwise slippery concept of 'motivation'. Furthermore, it can help the clinician to make appropriate responses tuned to the perceived stage of the patient. Thus, a sufferer who is in the precontemplation stage may benefit from lengthy discussion to help her clarify the pros and cons of change, whereas discussion of the means of change and too much advice on how to achieve it may be useless or even harmful. On the other hand, for someone who is in the preparation or action such advice may be welcome and useful. Motivational Interviewing (Miller & Rollnick, 1991) is a style of clinical interaction based around these ideas. It was developed in the field of substance abuse but has been adapted for use with eating disordered people (Killick & Allen, 1997; Treasure & Ward, 1997).

INTERVIEWING STYLE

The interviewing styles adopted by different clinicians vary. There is clearly a balance to be struck between styles that emphasise different functions of the assessment interview. For instance, it is desirable to encourage a sense of autonomy and choice in the patient so that a truly collaborative relationship can develop. This may require a good deal of listening and the facilitation of discussion about the sufferer's feelings – not least her feelings about the consultation itself. However, it is also important that the assessor obtains a detailed picture of the sufferer's current problem and the story of its development. There is information to be gathered. This may require direct questioning in addition to facilitation. Typically obtaining a good history involves some questions, a good deal of facilitation and a certain amount of gentle controlling by the assessor in order to maintain focus and direction. A skilful clinical interviewer is able to combine elements of widely different styles within an encounter which nevertheless seems to have something of the flow of a natural conversation.

At the end of one or two such assessment interviews the clinician should feel that he has a fairly well rounded view of the sufferer and her disorder

BOX 6.1 Motivation and the Stages of Change

The Transtheoretical Model suggests that people may be thought of as occupying a number of positions with regard to the prospect of psychological or behavioural change. These positions are relevant whatever the problem and whatever the proposed way of managing it. 'Motivation' is thought of as a characteristic of the interaction between clinician and patient rather than as something inherent in the latter. The person is described as being in one of five **stages.**

Precontemplation is the stage where the person does not see a problem and does not consider attempting any change. She is not really thinking about the problem as a problem.

Contemplation is a stage which is often characterised by mixed feelings. The person is able to see that an issue is problematic but may also be aware of the advantages of staying as she is and the difficulties or dangers of change. However, she is thinking about the possibility of change.

Preparation is, as its name suggests, a stage where the person is – perhaps only on balance – convinced by the need for change and is planning to do something. She is getting ready. She may be 'psyching herself up'.

Action is the stage of doing something and actively changing.

Maintenance is the time when the change is accomplished and the need is for the person to consolidate the change and make it a part of her normal life. Ambivalence may still be present and there is a danger of lapsing back into the problem.

Even in principle a person is unlikely to progress simply through these stages one by one. Indeed, people may go round and round, adding more elements of change, or may retreat from changes which they had achieved. People attempting to help need to tune their offers to the relevant stage of change if they are to be maximally effective and not provoke opposition or otherwise do more harm than good. The full model includes the concepts of 'process' and 'level' which refer to the means and nature of the changes respectively.

upon which to base any offer of help. She should feel that she has been listened to and understood and that the clinician has come to know enough about her for that offer to be well informed. Ideally, the sufferer should also have the impression that the clinician is competent and – in as much as any wariness will allow – trustworthy.

The following sections will focus on the appropriate content of assessment interviews – that is, on what may need to be asked. Nevertheless, how the asking is done is of great importance. However, the manner of questioning is a matter of skill and books are not a good method for teaching and learning skills. Furthermore, the skills required for talking with people about their eating disorders are general clinical skills. There is little that is special or peculiar to the field about the form of interviewing that is required. Indeed, there is likely to be much that is general – that is, shared with other kinds of assessment – about even the content of the assessment interview of an eating-disordered patient. What follows will concentrate mainly upon what needs to be especially considered or emphasised.

THE IMMEDIATE AIMS OF ASSESSMENT

A complete assessment will enable the clinician to make a **diagnosis of the eating disorder** from which the patient is suffering, together with a description of any **comorbidity, complications** or **additional problems** associated with it. The assessor should also know enough about the sufferer and her life to be able to set this diagnosis in a particular and personal context. Such a **wider description of the person** and her problem is sometimes called a case formulation.[3]

Since human beings are three-dimensional creatures, it is to be expected that a good assessment will have included consideration of issues best thought of in psychological, social and biological or physical terms. It may be useful to check at the end of an assessment that each of these dimensions has received attention to some degree. Furthermore, a good assessment will include more than diagnosis and description. It will give consideration to the question 'Why did this person develop this problem?'.

In general, the answers to this kind of question will be couched in the language of empathetic understanding That is, they will talk of hopes, fears, beliefs, intentions, dilemmas and the like.[4] The aim is to develop a **story about why the person has got into difficulty or fallen ill** when and how she has. Thinking about such a story is an important part of any assessment. It enables the assessor to have some feel for what it is like to be the sufferer. Moreover, a good story may allow the clinician to pitch offers of help in a way that makes sense to the patient. The assessor should try to be, in the various senses of the word, understanding.

It is often helpful for the assessor to share his version of her story with the sufferer; and, of course, discovering the story that the sufferer tells about herself is a key part of assessment. This may or may not be the same story as that held by the assessor. The stories of sufferers tend to include an unduly large measure of self-blame. For instance, she may feel that a statement such as 'I've got into this mess because I am a weak person' is all there is to be said. Developing a shared 'story' may well come to be a central component of therapy, but such sharing can be started as part of the process of assessment and engagement. However, it is important that at every stage the clinician should be aware that his favoured story is just that – a story – and that as such it may well not be correct or even close to the truth. A story should be valued and used when it seems to be the best account available at the time. However, it should always be thought of as provisional even when – perhaps especially when – it seems to be a good account of the events and issues. Much harm may be done in attempting to foist a story upon a sufferer.

In order to arrive at a diagnosis, a description and a story, it is necessary to seek information. The parts of the history and examination which are special to the assessment of people with eating disorders not surprisingly relate to the issues that are special to those disorders – namely the issues of weight and eating. Of course, a much more wide-ranging history is required to put them into an appropriate context. However, such a wide-ranging history is not special to the field of eating disorders and presents no new problems to the generally experienced clinician.

THE HISTORY OF WEIGHT AND EATING

A good initial question is to ask when it was first the case that weight or eating were experienced as a problem *of any kind*. The patient may answer by describing the time when these issues first became a major problem or perhaps when she first sought help or was considered 'ill'. It is important to emphasise the phrase 'of any kind' and to push the account back until it is possible for the sufferer to say that before the time in question she was really not at all concerned or troubled about weight or eating. Thus, someone who is now presenting with bulimia nervosa at average weight at 22, may have had the disorder for four years, have had a brief episode of undiagnosed anorexia nervosa at 17 and a career of on-and-off dieting for the previous three years, following a plump early adolescence and a history of having been a faddy eater as a 7 year old. All of these could have some relevance to her present state and to how she thinks about it. Unprompted, she may feel that much of this is not worth reporting. The assessor may need to be gently persistent to elicit anything like the full story (see Box 6.2).

Box 6.2 Assessment of Weight Issues

Some topics to be included

- What is the patient's own complaint about her weight?

- When did she first become concerned about such issues in any way?

- Ask about food fads, dieting, physical illness – anything that has changed her weight or eating over the years.

- Has she restrained her eating – and if so when, to what extent and why?

- What is her highest ever weight? When was that and what were the circumstances?

- What is her lowest ever adult weight?

- Has she had a stable weight as an adult? Was she restraining at that time?

- What weight would she like to be if she had a free choice and a 'magic wand'?

- Take a detailed history of weight change since the onset of frank eating disorder.

At the end of the assessment, the clinician should be in a position to draw – in reality or at least in his mind – an approximate lifetime graph of the sufferer's weight. An important issue in such a graph is the timing of puberty, physical development and the menarche. Of course, such an account brings in issues wider than that of weight and physical development. It leads into a history of menstruation in females but also into discussion of the reactions of the patient and others to all of the changes of adolescence. It is useful to relate the physical changes of growing up to the person's feelings even as the history is being told. Such links are of the essence.

It is useful to try to make some guess as to what the person's body weight would have been were she not restraining, bingeing or otherwise distorting her pattern of eating. Although the concept may be questionable in detail, it is useful to think of a person as having a 'natural' adult weight. This corresponds to the weight at which their body might regulate itself given a regular and substantial diet. (Within the useful myth of the Spring

Story, it is the weight at which the spring is neither stretched nor squashed.) For most people this approximates to an average weight for height, age and sex, but for some individuals it may not. Some individuals are naturally slim. Some are plump. In this regard it is useful to ask about the person's highest ever weight and lowest adult weight. If she has been at any time an adult and not eating disordered, then the weight that she was then may be a useful guide, even if this is markedly different from the average. However, many sufferers will be keen to give the impression that their natural weight is lower than it might seem to be. Some individuals may have a 'natural' weight which is markedly high. This should not be taken as meaning that they were necessarily eating disordered in a relevant sense at that time. It is also useful to ask about the weights of all of the first-degree relatives and perhaps even of the wider family.

It is important to establish the patient's current pattern of eating and how this has developed. Again gentle persistence may be required to obtain a clear picture. A good history will enable the assessor to add to the lifetime graph of body weight the times when slimming or other restraint occurred, the presence of any abnormal behaviours such as vomiting or laxative use and so on. The account of current eating needs to be more detailed. It is usually a good idea to go over a typical day, asking the sufferer about what she intends to eat then finding out what she actually eats. Sometimes, if assessment occurs over more than one session it may be useful to ask the patient to start keeping an eating diary. However, the assessor should not consider this to be a trivial request. Often it is experienced as a burden or as an intrusion, and if that seems to be the case then it may be better to postpone such diary keeping until it may form a part of therapy within an established treatment alliance. Of course, the eating pattern that is discovered by whatever means, may be highly variable or have a definite pattern of variation. For instance, it may be different at weekends. Details which may be of interest may include the degree to which eating is ritualised and the reaction of those around the sufferer to her eating. Does she hide away and eat in secret? Do others nag her or, on the other hand, appear not to notice that anything is amiss? Does she try to keep up appearances or is her disordered eating evident? In trying to gauge amounts of food eaten, it may be useful to ask whether the person would feel all right about swapping her meal with you or someone else without an eating disorder. Sufferers tend to describe portions as 'normal' which, by most standards, are meagre. On the other hand, a few anorexia nervosa sufferers may say that they eat 'nothing', when clearly they are gaining some nutrition from somewhere. They may be discounting nibbling or unplanned eating or sometimes they may indeed be eating nothing but sustaining themselves on calorific drinks. Of course, the amount of fluid that a sufferer takes is important. The majority even of those suffering from severe anorexia nervosa drink sufficient fluids to avoid dehydration. However, a minority restrict fluids also, and this can be dangerous.

An especially complex issue may be that of the individual's experience of hunger or urges to eat. Surprisingly, there is even now a lack of clarity about what is typical for either anorexia nervosa or bulimia nervosa. Some sufferers complicate discussion of the topic by using words in rather idiosyncratic ways when discussing such matters. They may feel it is wrong to describe themselves as ever being hungry even though they may admit to an urge to eat. However, it does seem that most sufferers from either eating disorder experience their drive to eat as present and often as problematically increased. They are engaged in a struggle with this drive and the individual in assessment needs to be encouraged to describe how she experiences this (see Box 6.3).

Lastly, of course, the assessor needs to establish the presence or absence – and frequency – of binge eating and of abnormal methods of attempted weight control such as vomiting. Binges may be objective or subjective. The former involves the eating of a substantial amount of food which is unequivocally excessive in the circumstances whereas for the latter the subject feels that she has eaten excessively when she has not in the judgement of a detached observer. Both should be accompanied by a subjective sense of loss of control. Some sufferers may be embarrassed to give a detailed account of what they eat in a binge. However, it is always of interest and sometimes important to get the details if at all possible. Indeed, the telling of the story to an interested clinician who seems neither surprised nor disconcerted by the account may be importantly comforting to the patient. It may be of interest to know about whether binges are, in general, impulsive or planned.[5]

- What does the person feel as she goes through the cycle of bingeing and then purging?
- What foods does she binge on?
- Exactly how does she induce vomiting, if she does?
- Is some part of the behaviour experienced as positively rewarding?
- Does she get a buzz out of it?
- How does the episode of bingeing end?
- What does she feel afterwards?
- How does she manage any negative feelings?

Other issues which may be important are the drinking of large quantities of fluids as a wash out after a binge, or the vomiting of blood. The former can occasionally lead to the risk of water intoxication. The latter, if substantial, may be a sign of oesophageal tears and need investigation. However, minor bleeding is more likely to be caused by abrasion of the throat with the fingers or whatever and is not of itself alarming.

BOX 6.3 Assessment of Eating Issues

Some topics to be included

- What is a typical days eating? To what degree is the patient attempting restraint?

- Is there a pattern? Does it vary? Is eating ritualised?

- Does she avoid particular foods? And if so why?

- Does she restrict fluids?

- What is the patient's experience of hunger or of any urge to eat?

- Does she binge? Are these objectively large binges? Does she feel out of control?

- Are the binges planned? How do they begin? How do they end? How often?

- Does she make herself vomit? If so how? Does she vomit blood? Does she wash out with copious fluids afterwards?

- Does she take laxatives, diuretics, emetics, appetite suppressants? With what effects?

- Does she chew and spit? Does she fast for a day or more?

- Can she eat in front of others?

- Does she exercise? Is this to 'burn off calories'?

Some sufferers do unusual things and one or two open questions about eating behaviour may elicit surprises. Chewing food and then spitting it out before swallowing is not uncommon as an occasional behaviour but may sometimes be a frequent or even central feature of an eating disorder. Enemas and the like are occasionally used.

IDEAS AND ATTITUDES

In hearing the sufferer's account of her weight and eating, the assessor will have had the opportunity to detect clues as her attitudes and beliefs about these matters. Perhaps more importantly still he will be able to assess how these are related to beliefs and attitudes about herself in general. In other words, the extent and nature of the entanglement between weight and eating and wider issues can be examined. This involves the detection of what might be called the specific psychopathology of the eating disorders. However, the rather simple sets of words which are to be found in the various diagnostic criteria are merely summaries of what is thought to be typical. It is useful to explore the particular ideas which are important to the individual sufferer. For instance, some people with eating disorders are especially concerned about overall weight, others about the overall shape of their bodies and still others about particular body parts. As was noted elsewhere, some others deny – often convincingly – that they have any unusual concern about the size or shape of their bodies but describe being concerned about control of their eating for other reasons. Their 'entanglement' is different and yet they may have disorders which in other respects are closely similar to the eating disorders which are specified in the diagnostic criteria.

It is therefore useful to try to explore and describe the sufferer's beliefs about herself and her body. It is also useful to discuss her attitude towards these beliefs. For instance, a sufferer may say that she feels that she is fat. Sometimes this may be simply true. In other cases the sufferer may find herself *feeling* that she is fat, *knowing* that she is thin and worrying about the fact that she finds herself thus torn. She may worry that weight is so important to her and that she knows that the issue has become for her quite distorted and out of proportion. To worry about her worry may auger well for therapy, but unfortunately it does not of itself allow the individual to escape. Worry about worry can be debilitating. Nevertheless, talking about the complexities of belief in the context of assessment may be the start of undoing some of these tangles (see Box 6.4). However, maladaptive beliefs can be strengthened by the opposition of the clinician who mishandles the situation and either assumes the presence of textbook ideas or jumps in with premature confrontations along the lines of 'but you're not fat, are you?'.

Body image disturbance is especially subject to complexities and variations which are not encompassed by the over simple phrases of diagnostic criteria and common belief. Thus the sufferer who simply misperceives herself as fat when she is thin must exist but, in general, the experience of the body in anorexia nervosa, and indeed in bulimia, is much more variable and complex. Furthermore, the relevant complexity is probably better revealed by skilful interviewing than by recourse to any of the many methods which have been devised to 'measure' body image disturbance. These have their place in research but are unlikely to add much in clinical practice.

An overarching issue seems often to be that of control and the fear of loss of control. This is especially the case in anorexia nervosa. Most sufferers readily speak about their dilemmas in terms of control. Again, however, it may well be worth while beginning to explore, even in the context of first assessment, what the individual sufferer means by control and what would be the consequences of its loss. Of course, the ready answer may be in terms of weight gain and perhaps obesity. But what are the special implications of this for the person? What would it mean for her? In what way are weight and eating mixed up with wider personal issues?

WIDER ASSESSMENT

It is, of course, necessary to find out about more than just weight and eating. It is important to hear an account of the sufferer's childhood, her parents and other caregivers, her schooldays, subsequent career and relationships. This amounts to a brief story of the sufferer's life so far,

---

Box 6.4 Assessment of Psychological Issues

Some topics to be included

- What does the patient feel about her body and her weight?

- If she is restraining her eating, what is her motivation?

- Does she feel fat? Does she dislike her body? If so, in what way?

- Does she have a distorted body image? If so, in what way?

- What does she feel would happen if she did not control her weight or eating?

- Does she fear loss of control? Is she able to say what she means by this?

- Does she feel guilt or self disgust? If so, what leads her to feel this?

- Does anything about her disorder lead her to feel good?

- If she binges, what are her feelings before, during and after bingeing?

- What has she told others about her eating disorder – if anything?

- How does she think about her disorder? What does she make of it?

including her personal, social and sexual development. This enables the assessor to gain some insight into the issues which may have become tangled up with weight and eating. It enables him to make a formulation and think about a possible story of how things have reached their present stage.

In asking about the wider aspects of a person's life there are pros and cons of direct questions. There is the old psychotherapist's dictum that if you ask questions, all you get are answers. There is some truth in this and the patient must be given an opportunity to tell her own story in her own way. On the other hand, some systematic enquiry is also required if important issues are not to be missed. Getting the right balance is a matter of skill and judgement.

Some issues are thought of as being especially sensitive and personal. These include sexual matters, childhood abuse and drug use. However, sensitivity should not lead to squeamishness or undue reticence. A direct question asked with confidence and without equivocation gives the patient implicit permission to talk about things which she might otherwise find very difficult to broach. It indicates that the clinician can consider such topics without embarrassment.[6] If the sufferer wants to talk, she can then do so. If she does not, she should not, of course, be coerced. The clinician should not give the impression of having a mission to dig up certain kinds of revelation. Even when the patient is not forthcoming, at least in the assessor's mind – and perhaps in the conversation – any difficult issue is flagged as being of possible importance. A genuinely open mind is required about what seems to be important for and in relation to the particular patient. Furthermore, it is enough in the context of an assessment to establish an issue as possibly relevant rather than seek to explore all the details. Such exploration may – or may not – eventually be relevant in the context of ongoing therapy.

As the person's account of her life unfolds, it may sometimes be useful to ask quite pointed questions or make comments, albeit in a tentative way. For instance, the clinician might venture a remark about how the patient might have felt in a particular situation. If well done, this can facilitate the sufferer in considering what she did indeed feel and talking about it even if her feelings were different from those suggested by the clinician. The patient's response may also indicate something of the person's ability or willingness to talk about the kind of issue being raised and the kind of way in which she thinks about it. This may give useful clues to what kind of help she may want or be willing or able to use. It may also signal to the patient that issues of feelings and emotion are considered relevant and of interest to the clinician. The box contains examples of such comments or questions using, once again, one of the fictional cases introduced earlier in the book.

Faith Sees the Psychiatrist

Faith had been reluctant to attend the appointment with the psychiatrist suggested by her general practitioner. However, in the event, when she did she felt that the first interview did not go too badly. Most of the time was spent talking about her weight and eating problems and how they had developed. Faith was still worried that the doctor might try to pressurise her into doing things that she did not want to do. However, she found herself quite relieved to be able to tell her story to someone who listened but who was not involved in the sense of being upset by what she said. Furthermore, some of the psychiatrist's questions and comments made her think. When she was talking about her studies, he asked her whether she sometimes felt angry with her father for expecting so much of her. Faith had rarely allowed herself to acknowledge this feeling but nevertheless agreed that she had felt this at times, although adding that she had mainly wanted to do well for herself. The doctor then suggested that working so hard, aiming to do well and to go to university allowed her both to please her father now and to plan her future escape from him and the difficult situation at home. He then added, 'It seems to me that something about your efforts to get everything right and please everybody has led you to find yourself doing things you never intended – like seeing me, for instance. That must be pretty upsetting.' This remark made Faith feel tearful. Although she still tried to hide it, she knew that the psychiatrist had noticed. She was relieved when he moved on to ask her questions about more neutral topics. However, she had a feeling that she might like to talk more about the mess she felt that she was in.

It is, of course, necessary to bring the whole assessment of wider issues up to date. The taking of a history is completed with an attempt to gain a picture of the person's current life, her relationships, her daily life, what supports her and what threatens her. Who are the important people in her life? How does her problem influence her life? What are her hopes and aspirations for the future and does continuing disorder threaten these?

Once again there is nothing very specific to the eating disorders about the skills and methods which the professional needs to employ to assess these matters. However, some people suffering from an eating disorder do have a notable capacity to deny the likely implications of the disorder for their future plans. The fear and mixed feelings which have been mentioned so often before sometimes blind them to the ways in which failure to escape from their illness may shrink their options for the future.

MENTAL EXAMINATION

Many people who suffer from a clinical eating disorder also suffer from concurrent syndromes of mental disorder of other kinds. Many more still have symptoms and distress which are not directly related to weight or eating. It is important that such comorbidity should be detected. Professionals from within a medical or mental health background will have the skills to look for such problems. However, they will need to avoid the danger of being distracted by the salient eating disorder to the extent that they miss the major depression, the alcohol abuse, the social phobia or the obsessive-compulsive disorder that also undermines the life of the patient. Likewise, it is important to ask about suicidal feelings and related behaviours. Both of the main eating disorders are associated with an elevated risk of both completed suicide and of a whole range of self-harming behaviours.

PERSONALITY ASSESSMENT

The whole concept of personality is open to question as is the idea of personality disorder. In particular, it is doubtful if the variety of relatively enduring but maladaptive characteristics of people can be adequately summed up in the kind of categories to be found in diagnostic systems such as DSM-IV. Nevertheless, people differ in their usual ways of relating to themselves and to others and, for some, patterns of difficulty are discernible. An assessment of an individual with an eating disorder should include an attempt to describe such patterns and whether or not definable disorder is thought to be present.

- What does the sufferer feel about herself?
- Does she trust other people?
- Is she an affectionate person?
- Is she usually quiet or noisy?
- Is she organised or disorganised?
- Is she a perfectionist?
- Are there things that she likes about herself?
- What does she dislike?

The issue of self-esteem may be especially relevant to eating disorders. However, just as with personality in general, self-esteem may be a complex issue. Someone may be critical of herself to the point of self-loathing in many respects, but not in all. People experience themselves differently in different circumstances. For instance, it is not uncommon for someone with a significant eating disorder to be successful at work and, indeed, to know that this is the case. However, it would be most unusual – almost unbelievable – for such a sufferer to feel satisfied with all aspects of her life. Indeed, the eating disorder itself will often seem to corrode the sufferer's remaining self-confidence and esteem. This is so even when 'success' at exaggerated self-control has for a while given some fragile bolstering to the sufferer's sense of security. The assessor may explore the patient's view of herself both by direct questioning and by noting the tone of the account she gives of herself and her life.

Being caught up in the vicious circles of disorder tends to distort not only the person's view of herself but also her relationships with others. However, it is likely that individuals with notable difficulties in these respects may be especially vulnerable to becoming eating disordered. Again it is by listening carefully to the history and the way that it is told that the assessor is best able to define the patient's style of relating to others. Indeed, the way in which the patient relates to the clinician may itself give clues to the patient's usual patterns of relating, although it is important to keep in mind the strangely demanding nature of the clinical encounter. It is through these techniques of using the history and the interview itself that most information relevant to the assessment of personality arises. In general, direct questioning is less useful. Likewise, pencil and paper questionnaires and tests tend to be disappointing and misleading in the assessment of individuals in the clinic, although they are useful in comparing groups of people in the context of research. However, even then the results of such tests of personality should not be taken too seriously.

PHYSICAL ASSESSMENT

Anorexia nervosa and bulimia nervosa are disorders with major physical components. These components need to be assessed. Such assessment may present different problems in different settings. However, failure to attend appropriately to the physical aspects of the disorders may increase the risk to the sufferer and place the practitioner at risk of accusations of negligence. The important thing is that physical issues should not be ignored and that somehow they should be addressed, even though there may be difficulties in doing so.

Firstly, there is no universal consensus about what is appropriate in the way of physical assessment. Even full syndrome cases of anorexia nervosa or bulimia nervosa differ markedly in the degree to which the sufferer is physically compromised or at risk. Some clinical judgement is required and 'rules of thumb' are no substitute. Box 6.5 gives some advice about what may be appropriate.

Secondly, the professional involved in assessing someone coming along for help for an eating disorder may not have the knowledge or skills to assess fully the physical state. Their professional training may have been in other areas. The appropriate response to this problem will depend upon the context. One plan would be to seek to involve another professional – for instance, the sufferer's general practitioner or family physician – in assessing and monitoring the sufferer's physical state. This may work well although there may be problems of coordination or patient reluctance. However, in the context of a service which is multidisciplinary and which sees substantial numbers of people with eating disorders, it should be possible for physical issues to be addressed 'in house' even where the main person in touch with the patient is not medically trained. Indeed, there is little that is very special or technical about the whole matter in most cases. Common sense, general clinical confidence and a bit of ad hoc knowledge, together with a willingness to call in others in a worrying or puzzling situation, are adequate safeguards most of the time. For instance, someone suffering from bulimia nervosa at normal weight may require ongoing monitoring of her blood electrolytes until such time as she is clinically improving. A flexible system would allow such blood tests to be ordered by the clinician chiefly involved with the patient whatever his profession might be. Inflexibility could arise through inappropriate rigidity in the system or through professional chauvinism on the part of the medics involved. It can also occur where other professionals assert that the assessment of physical issues is not part of their job. Either way the patient may end up receiving a response to her problems which is less than adequate or unduly complex.

Thirdly, the patient herself may be reluctant to allow an adequate assessment of her physical state. She may have particular fears – for instance, in relation to physical examination or venepuncture – or her reluctance may be a part of more pervasive mixed feelings. Then discussion of these feelings needs to become a central part of assessment.

A mundane but important part of the process of assessment is the issue of weighing. Clearly, body weight can be measured more easily and more reliably than other important aspects of the sufferer's condition. However, she may be reluctant to be weighed for a variety of reasons. Sometimes the handling of this issue can become pivotal for the patient and clinician alike. Both face dilemmas. The assessor can make the mistake of pressing the matter too hard and promoting a battle. Or he may avoid the issue and seem to collude with the sufferer in a denial of the importance of weight. Of course, it is likely that she is reluctant because the issue of weight feels so important and is mixed up with so many other issues. Again, for the assessor it is a matter of getting the balance right. It will usually be best for him to explain that measuring weight is important and that omitting it will make the assessment less than adequate. But at the same time he should avoid any kind of coercion. Thus the final decision rests with the patient, but so does the responsibility for what may be an assessment which is less than optimal. However, the situation may be used as an opportunity to explore the patient's feelings about her body weight, about the consultation and the prospect of change. Once again, these issues may well become central in any subsequent therapy but they can be very usefully broached as part of assessment. Indeed, the simple act of weighing can, in a sense, form part of the therapeutic process. Alternatively, such discussion can be damaging to the process of engagement if it is mishandled.

Although special investigations have a part to play in the assessment of the physical state of the patient, it is the history and general appraisal of the apparent health of the patient that are most vital. If the patient is losing weight rapidly, say at more than a kilogram per week, and is already at a low weight, say a BMI of less than 15, it does not take a medical degree to tell that there is cause for concern. Likewise, if a sufferer has been stable – or stuck – even at a very low weight for months or years, there may be less cause for immediate alarm and more time for reflection. A commonsensical appraisal of the stability or otherwise over time of the physical state of the patient is a valuable guide to the risks she is facing in the short-term future.

INVOLVING OTHERS

There are pros and cons of involving others from the adult patient's life in the initial assessment of her problem. There can therefore be no hard and fast rules about the matter. Of course, if the sufferer is a child then the parents or other caregivers would – and should – usually be involved from the outset.[7] However, adults need to be able to choose whether or not their parents, siblings, spouses, partners, friends or others are invited to contribute to the assessment. Of course, the clinician can make suggestions but the final say rests with the patient. And with the final say goes a measure of responsibility. For instance, it may be the case that an adult sufferer attends her first appointment with a friend or relative and asks that that individual be present during the whole interview. The presence of such a third party will inevitably alter the content of the assessment, and if the patient insists upon having someone else at the meeting then she has to accept that the assessment will thereby be changed. The interaction about this matter should enact the principle that the sufferer is ultimately in charge of herself and that her meeting with the clinician is a grown-up encounter in which both parties have their responsibilities.[8] In general, a primary interview which includes only the assessor and the adult sufferer is likely to be more revealing about the sufferer and her views, and that is the most important perspective.

Box 6.5 Assessment of the Physical State

For All Patients

- Measurement of body weight. It is usually useful to calculate the Body Mass Index.

- General enquiry about any complaints or physical symptoms. These should be followed up by specific questioning and investigation as necessary.

- History of any notable physical illnesses.

For Patients who Vomit or Abuse Laxatives or Diuretics

- Enquiry about extent and nature of these behaviours including the vomiting of blood or the use of 'washing out'.

- Take blood for estimation of urea and electrolytes.

For Patients who are at Low Weight*

- Take blood for full blood count, estimation of urea and electrolytes and liver function tests. A mild neutropenia is common in anorexia nervosa. Thyroid function tests may be relevant especially if there is any doubt about the diagnosis.

- Perform physical examination especially if there are physical symptoms. Note especially resting heart rate and blood pressure.

- Perform ECG. Look especially for abnormalities of rhythm and prolonged QT interval. Estimate serum calcium and magnesium if suspicion of cardiac problem.

- Ask patient to squat and then rise to test for myopathy.

*What counts as low weight is to some degree a matter of judgement. A stable low weight is less worrying than a rapidly declining weight. However, a weight of below BMI 15 in an adult patient would normally suggest that these investigations should be done.

The simplest asset that involvement of a third party may bring is additional information about the history or present state of the sufferer. However, this information is inevitably derived from a particular perspective – that of a particular mother, lover or whatever. It may be valuable but it will not be wholly objective and should not be treated as such. Indeed, the most relevant information may arise from observation and exploration of the reaction of the sufferer to the other's view of her problems. That is one reason why it is usually best to talk with such others in the presence of the patient unless she explicitly opts not to be there. Another reason for hearing the views of others in the presence of the patient is that she is thus a party to what goes on and knows what has been said about her by both the other and the clinician. Ordinary rules of clinical confidentiality need to be emphasised, as do the adult responsibilities of all concerned.[9] Furthermore, information gained in the presence of the sufferer is information that can be used; information gained behind her back is complicated by its provenance and is usually much less useful. Indeed, information of itself is perhaps rarely as useful or as powerful as expected in such situations. Relatives and other informants often seem to think that if only the doctor or whoever *knows* a particular thing, then that will mean that he can *do* something about it. This is perhaps not an unreasonable expectation but it is derived from clinical situations where diagnosis is more powerful and treatment is more instrumental. Thus, if a doctor is told by a relative that a patient has been passing blood in her urine, this may raise particular diagnostic issues and lead to particular treatments. Provided the patient gives informed consent to the procedures, the treatment is done to them rather than by or with them. The situation is very different when the information relates to suspected and undeclared self-induced vomiting by a person with an eating disorder, and treatment is a collaborative business.

The receipt of unsolicited communications about a patient from others, along with the request that the fact of the communication or its content should remain secret, creates dilemmas for the clinician. It effectively puts him in a position of conflict between his relationship with the patient and his relationship with her relative or important other. Almost always the relationship with the patient should take precedence and the would-be informant should be told that the condition of secrecy is not acceptable. If the communication has already taken place, as with a letter, it is usually best to tell the patient that it has been received and tell the sender that the patient has been informed. Rare exceptions to this kind of principle might be where the information concerned is not about the patient or her immediate circumstance, but has nevertheless been offered by the informant because it says something indirectly about the patient. Such confidences might perhaps be kept from the patient but they should be flagged up with the informant as special in this respect, with the usual rule emphasised.[10]

There may be advantages beyond simple information gathering in the involvement of a family member or other important person in the sufferer's life at some stage in the process of assessment. As was hinted above, the encounter may allow the assessor to observe directly the inter-action between the patient and the other, and this may be illuminating. Furthermore, the relative or whoever may be experienced by the sufferer as a crucial support or, as importantly, having an undermining influence or something more complex. In any case it may be useful for the other person to have an opportunity to have her say. The other's view of the situation may sometimes be influenced for the good by the meeting. Indeed, the consultation may be as important an event for that person as for the patient. The meeting may serve to reassure the other person when appro-priate or to inform or educate her view of the situation. To be denied such an opportunity might sometimes influence the situation for the worse. Once again, the balance of advantage is usually in favour of the assessor meeting with the other in the presence of the sufferer. There may then be some opportunity for the sharing of views.

STANDARD INTERVIEWS AND QUESTIONNAIRES

A number of standard interviews have been developed over recent years for the documentation and measurement of the features of the clinical eating disorders. In addition, numerous self-report questionnaires are relevant to the field. (For a review see Nathan & Allison, 1998.) The use of such standard interviews and questionnaires has been invaluable in research, but their role in everyday clinical practice is less clear. The inter-views may be unnecessarily cumbersome and undue reliance on self-report questionnaires can be misleading.

The most widely established of the standard interviews is the Eating Disorders Examination (EDE) (Fairburn & Cooper, 1993). This is a semi-structured interview and set of rating scales that have been developed by Christopher Fairburn and colleagues at Oxford. The EDE can be used to rate the behaviours as well as the beliefs and attitudes found in the eating disorders. It is perhaps especially focused on the features of bulimia nervosa. Reliable use of the instrument requires special training. Its main use is in research where it has become the most commonly used instrument. There is no doubt that clinicians may benefit from familiarity with the concepts used in the EDE and similar instruments such as the Clinical Eating Disorders Rating Instrument (CEDRI) (Palmer, Christie, Cordle, Davies & Kenrick, 1987; Palmer, Robertson, Cain & Black, 1996) and the Structured Interview for Anorexia and Bulimia (SIAB) (Fichter, et al., 1991; Fichter, Herpertz, Quadflieg & Herperttz-Dahlmann, 1998). However, few practitioners who are not also researchers are likely to use these interviews in everyday clinical work.

The interviews are seldom used outside of research because they take time and effort to master and use. By contrast, the use of self-rating questionnaires is easy and therefore tempting. There are many such instruments, of which the Eating Attitude Test (EAT) (Garner & Garfinkel, 1979; Garner, Olmsted, Bohr & Garfinkel, 1982) and the Eating Disorders Inventory (EDI) (Garner, Olmsted & Polivy, 1983) are the most commonly used. There are several others, including a self-report version of the Eating Disorders Examination called the EDE-Q (Fairburn & Beglin, 1994) and the Bulimia Investigatory Test Edinburgh (Henderson & Freeman, 1987), which undoubtedly acquired its inelegant full name to enable it to be abbreviated to the catchy BITE.

The EAT is the oldest and has been widely used as a screening questionnaire for the risk of being a case of eating disorder, for instance, in two-stage epidemiological surveys. In that role it performs fairly well. It does *not* diagnose eating disorders, nor have its authors claimed that it does. It should not be used to make or even bolster a diagnosis. It may have some use in clinical practice to monitor change in attitudes over time in an individual case or in the evaluation of an intervention. The EDI, which has similar uses, has a number of scales only some of which relate to issues specific to the eating disorders. The other scales purport to measure issues – such as 'maturity fears' and 'personal ineffectiveness' which may be thought relevant to the eating disorders but are not at all specific to them (Hurley, Palmer & Stretch, 1990). A newer version, the EDI-2, has two additional scales of this kind (Garner, 1991). The EDE-Q and the BITE are more focused upon symptoms and have some claim to be diagnostic. However, they are no substitute for clinical diagnosis in practice.

PUTTING IT ALL TOGETHER

The purpose of assessment in practice is to gain a view of the sufferer and her problems so that an offer of help can be made which is relevant and appropriate.[11] A part of this is the making of a diagnosis. In practice, this is a real problem in only a minority of cases. If the problem is whether or not the patient fits the diagnostic criteria in their finest detail, the matter is rarely relevant to treatment. Thus, if a patient has not quite binged often enough to fulfil the criteria for bulimia nervosa, or has not lost quite enough weight for anorexia nervosa, the implication may be little different than for those who have. However, occasionally, people do present with problems that are either genuinely unusual or really taxing in diagnostic terms. One kind of problem may arise when a patient at low weight and/or poor physical health is suspected of having some other physical disorder. Then the diagnosis of anorexia nervosa should be made positively on the basis of the mental features. There is, of course, a separate question of whether the person also has some other disorder, and this should be investigated. It is possible for both anorexia nervosa and another disorder to be present together. Likewise, psychiatric comorbid conditions are frequently present and they, along with the eating disorder, should be diagnosed positively. In general, anorexia nervosa should not be a diagnosis of exclusion.

Typically the process of assessment will end with such an offer or an explanation of why an offer is unnecessary, inappropriate or impractical. An adequate assessment may often take more than one interview. If it is anticipated that this will be the case then it may be useful to warn the patient that there may be no clear outcome of the first meeting. In these circumstances the first interview is typically taken up with asking questions and hearing the story. The sufferer gives a lot and may feel let down when the clinician says rather little in return if she has not been warned that this may happen and that there will be little feedback before the second session. Thus warned, most patients agree with the proposition that it is sensible to defer making offers of help or even giving advice until she has had an opportunity to describe fully her predicament.

Towards the end of assessment and before the assessor gives his view, it is useful to give the sufferer a clear opportunity to say what she thinks about her problem. Of course, something of her view will have emerged during earlier parts of the conversation, but an opportunity to expand or summarise is likely to be illuminating. A direct but open question is usually sufficient to introduce the topic. If this fails then a multiple-choice question may be tried such as: 'Do you think of your difficulties as an illness visited upon you, or a meaningless bad habit, or as a weakness, or as something mixed up with other things in your life, or what? How do you think about the situation?' It is not, of course, the function of such questions to suggest any particular answer to the patient even if – as is likely to be the case – the assessor himself has a preferred view. Rather the immediate purpose is to gauge the difference between the sufferer's view and the assessor's view as a preliminary to the practical business of discussing what might happen next. The ultimate aim is to create a way of viewing the patient's situation which allows her to work with someone to improve it. A good deal of talking about such issues may form an important part of any subsequent therapy, but even at the assessment stage some discussion is useful. Remember that assessment and engagement go hand in hand.

The final part of assessment typically involves the assessor in sharing his view of the situation with the patient and explaining what – if anything – he or his colleagues are able to offer to the patient. The assessor needs to explain what he thinks about the problems the patient brings and what she might do about them. He needs to be straightforward and truthful about matters such as diagnosis, complications and risks but should present these in a way that is digestible by the patient. This should include treatment options which are presented as ways forward. It is to be hoped that, by this time, the clinician and the patient may have built up sufficient rapport for there to be a discussion within a framework with at least some shared elements. The assessor needs to put forward his ideas but he must also take account of what he has learned about the sufferer's perspective of her problem. In the discussion about options it may sometimes be useful for the assessor to play the devil's advocate and to suggest that one option is for the sufferer not to change. This usually leads the sufferer to emphasise the more positive options. Likewise, in presenting aspects of the problem that have the characteristics of a vicious circle, it may be thought provoking to point out that vicious circles are vicious because the easiest thing to do is to keep going around them. Getting better should be presented as being hard work.

There are many ways of discussing what is involved in recovery. The framework outlined in Chapters 4 and 5 can be used explicitly.[12] However, what is important is that the patient should feel that something of the nature of her difficulty has been understood and that, as a result of the consultation, she has the option of working towards recovery with help. It becomes her dilemma whether or not she can bring herself to take up any offer of help and do so wholeheartedly and successfully. In offering treatment it may sometimes be useful to ask the patient to take time making her decision rather than take an initial 'yes' for an answer. A day or two waiting for a real decision may be time well spent.

The next two chapters will discuss what kinds of help are likely to be appropriate to offer those who suffer from each of the two main eating disorders. The dilemma of the clinician is how to maximise both the autonomy of the patient and her chances of recovery. Some of the things that may go wrong are discussed in Chapter 10.

NOTES

1. There are, of course, many ways of carrying out an assessment. The account given here is inevitably based upon my own practice. Obviously, I think that this way of doing things has merit otherwise I would not work in the way that I am about to describe. But equally obviously others commonly do things differently and would advocate and defend their practice. Details of style do not matter as long as the job gets done. Furthermore, different settings are associated with different styles. My style merges from a specialist psychiatric setting where people are referred – usually by their general medical

practitioner in the context of the British National Health Service – and come along by appointment, often after having waited some time for that appointment. Some things may be different in an emergency situation or in a setting where self-referral is the norm. However, many things will be the same whatever the setting. Of course, the expectations of all concerned may differ somewhat with the setting, as may the language that is used. One – to my mind minor – issue of language concerns the use of the terms 'patient' or 'client' to refer to the person seeking professional help in a health setting. Some people get quite concerned about the supposed difference of implication between these terms. I am not one of them. I tend to favour the word patient. My understanding is that it derives from the Latin for 'one who suffers' rather than having anything to do with passivity – or even the qualities involved in coping with waiting lists.

2. In what must be hundreds of assessment interviews over the years, I can remember only one patient who chose to opt out when given the opportunity to do so. A few weeks later she opted to be seen and subsequently stayed in touch for years.

3. Terms like formulation and even diagnosis come from the vocabulary of psychiatry and may feel unduly 'medical' to some readers. However, if this troubles you, I leave it to you to translate what is my preferred and familiar language into terms with which you feel more comfortable. Nevertheless, I hope that in doing so you may find that the substance of what I say makes sense. A full assessment – and the vocabulary in which it is couched – needs to be able to cope with the variety of issues which may be relevant from defence mechanisms and self-construing through alcohol abuse and suicidal feelings to low potassium levels and cardiac arrhythmias.

4. Some philosophers describe such language as 'folk psychology'. This term has a somewhat pejorative tone. This kind of understanding is what allows human beings to interact with each other, predict the behaviour of others and describe their own mental states. It rarely lets us down and is thus our preferred way of answering 'why' questions about ourselves and others. Indeed, it is only when our own thoughts or the behaviour of others prove especially puzzling or problematic that we even consider recourse to other kinds of explanations and invoke other mechanisms.

5. There is some tension between the idea that binges must involve 'loss of control' and that they are often planned. However, this is neither truly incoherent nor unique to bingeing. For instance, a heavy smoker may be trying to stop but nevertheless may buy cigarettes because he or she has an urge to do so. Loss of control would seem to apply to sustained urges or problematic drives as well as to brief impulses.

Indeed, the urge to binge seems usually to be based in the heightened attention to food and drive to eat promoted by undereating. This is likely to be continuing rather than episodic and impulsive. Apparently impulsive behaviour is likely to arise when the individual either suddenly fails in her efforts to distract her attention onto other matters or when opportunity to act presents itself, or both.

6. There is sometimes discussion about what kinds of issue can easily be raised and discussed between what kind of people. In particular, the childhood sexual abuse of a female is sometimes thought of as a subject which should be raised only by a professional who is also female. I tend to disagree. I am a middle-aged male but almost always ask patients of either sex whether or not they have had any unwelcome or inappropriate sexual experiences in childhood or since. The majority answer simply one way or the other and very few seem to find such a question out of place or upsetting. If the patient answers positively, then she should be given the opportunity to give some account of the experience but should not be pressed to do so. Undue interrogation about details could itself be abusive and is neither necessary nor useful.

7. Even here there may be questions about where to draw the line between childhood and adulthood. I am going to cop out of suggesting a particular age below which an individual should be considered a child and above which she should be considered an adult. For this purpose I would assert the rather circular argument that if the patient is construed as a child then the parents should be routinely involved. If the patient is construed as an adult, then she should certainly call the shots about this matter. In my view, any person of normal mental competence who is aged 18 or above has a right to elect to be treated as an adult in this respect. Many who are younger may wish to do so also.

8. My way of dealing with such a situation is to have a brief discussion – preferably with the sufferer alone – in which I encourage the patient to accept an interview by herself with the possibility of a threesome at a later stage. In doing so I point out that the interview would be different in the two cases and probably more relevant if the patient is able to talk freely and not constrained by the presence of someone else whose feelings she may want to spare. (Of course, the interview may also be constrained in the other case by increased feelings of nervousness or whatever, although that kind of constraint may say something about the sufferer which is relevant to future therapy.) Most sufferers agree to an initial solo interview. Not a few say that they had not wanted the other person in on the interview anyway and that it was the other person who had wanted it.

9. When first interviewing a family with an adult member with an eating disorder – especially when that member is a 'child' of the family – I usually set out by talking pointedly to the sufferer. I bring in others to give their view only after having asked the sufferer in each case whether that is all right with her. This may seem a bit over the top but it does dramatise the special position of the sufferer and the fact that she is ultimately in charge of herself and of the encounter. It may be especially useful to do this when the habitual interactions of the family around the topic of the illness have come to be like those of parents and a 'child-child'; a pattern of interaction which may include a lot of unproductive battling or overprotection. The sufferer's expectations – and indeed those of the family – may be that the clinical situation is going to replicate this regressed position. Such ostentatious playing out of the adult rules of the clinical game may help to change such expectations.

10. Real life can test out simple principles to the limit. The following story is based upon a real situation, although I have changed it in detail. A patient's mother told me 'in confidence' that two of her children had been conceived as a result of a secret extra-marital affair. The patient's father was the husband and 'father of the family' who was said to be ignorant of the paternity of two of 'his' children although it was said that 'he may have his suspicions'. The patient was said to know nothing of all this. Nevertheless, the mother wanted me to know because she thought it might enable me to understand things better. Perhaps it did, but it gave me little in the way of any increased ability to help. The mother seemed to be giving the information in good faith, but also perhaps to relieve herself. I talked about it with her in these terms. I did not divulge anything to the patient – partly on the basis that she was not directly involved. It was not my secret to pass on. However, this family secret may well have been indirectly relevant. I felt burdened rather than empowered by being made a party to it. What would you have done?

11. Perhaps I should have made this obvious statement at the beginning of the chapter. It is my usual practice to make such a statement at the beginning of most first assessment interviews. It is a useful prelude to asking the sufferer what she wants and expects and, furthermore, demonstrates the importance of stating the obvious and not taking it as understood. Of course, occasionally the function of an assessment interview is not so simple, for instance, when the consultation is entirely for the purposes of giving a second opinion or for medico-legal reasons. Then it is even more important that the sufferer knows what is what.

12 I quite often – but not always – use the spring story as a framework for presenting both a view of nature of the disorder and the tasks of recovery. In doing so I commonly go as far as to use a flip chart to draw out the spring story and decorate it with the particular features of the patient. This use of the spring story is described in more detail in Palmer (1989).

FURTHER READING

Crowther, J H & Sherwood, N E (1997) Assessment. In: Garner, D M & Garfinkel, PE (Editors) *Handbook of the Treatment of Eating Disorders* (second edition). Guilford Press, New York and London.

Fairburn, C G & Cooper, Z (1993) The Eating Disorders Examination (12th Edition). In: Fairburn, C G & Wilson, G T (Editors*) Binge Eating; Nature, Assessment and Treatment.* Guilford Press, New York and London.

Nathan, J S & Allison, D B (1998) Psychological and physical assessment of persons with eating disorders. In: Hoek, H K, Treasure, J L & Katzman, M A (Editors) *Neurobiology in the Treatment of Eating Disorders*. John Wiley & Sons, Chichester and New York.

Wilson, G T (1993) Assessment of binge eating. In: Fairburn, C G & Wilson, G T (Editors) *Binge Eating; Nature, Assessment and Treatment*. Guilford Press, New York and London.

7

WHAT HELPS PEOPLE WITH ANOREXIA NERVOSA?

There is a sense in which recovery from anorexia nervosa is so simple. The sufferer has to eat enough to restore her weight to normal, maintain that position and then cope with the consequences of doing so. If she can manage that she may be unhappy or even disordered in other ways but she will no longer have anorexia nervosa. That seems straightforward enough but of course, in practice, making such a change is a fearful business for the sufferer and often a frustrating one for those who would help her.[1] The sufferer's fear and helper's frustration may each promote the other. A situation that has a basic simplicity may come to be very complicated indeed.

The sufferer who comes to the clinic may have decided for herself that she wishes to try to escape from her condition. However, she may well have been cajoled along by others who are worried and concerned about her. Commonly, she will come along with all sorts of uncertainties and reservations, perhaps telling herself that it is worth exploring the possibility of help if only to be seen to be doing something about what others see as her problem. She may not see herself as 'sick'. The classic sick role involves the individual feeling able for the duration of the illness to give up some of the usual obligations of life and to have the right to expect the help of others. In return, the sick person has a duty to strive for recovery, including seeking help or treatment as appropriate. However, matters are rarely that straightforward in the case of anorexia nervosa. Typically the sufferer embraces the sick role only partially and sometimes not at all. She approaches the prospect of treatment with notably mixed feelings. The response of the clinician to these mixed feelings has been discussed above and some of the major difficulties that may arise will be discussed again in Chapter 10. For the moment, the management of mixed feelings will not be emphasised. But such feelings are nearly always present when someone seeks help for anorexia nervosa. Furthermore, anorexia nervosa cannot be treated instrumentally. For better or worse, there is no magic pill or procedure that can be applied to a passive or protesting patient.

Treatment has to involve the development of a partnership with the sufferer within which she can do what is necessary to recover. She needs to feel safe and secure enough to try to change and such a relationship has to be fostered from the beginning, as was discussed in Chapter 6. However, it is never static, and even when things are moving it should not be taken for granted. It needs to be built up and sustained over time. The relationship may get damaged and need repair. It will have to support different functions at different times. And eventually, like scaffolding, it needs to be dismantled in such a way that the sufferer can prosper without it.[2] How, then, may a clinician help the sufferer to do what is necessary? What treatments are good and effective?

EVIDENCE-BASED PRACTICE

For the present, the treatment and management of anorexia nervosa cannot be based upon good research evidence in a way that would be desirable. There is one definite reason for this, and one which is more debatable. The clear reason is that there is at present a dearth of good evidence upon which to base clinical practice. The debatable reason is the nature of the present and any probable future regimes of management for anorexia nervosa. It could be argued that even were there to be mountains of evidence available there might still be major problems involved in generalising to the particular case because of the way in which such treatments make demands upon an ambivalent sufferer. The variability of disorder and circumstance means that no one prescription is likely to fit all cases. This kind of argument is not wholly convincing. However, there are likely to be real issues of generalisation when a clinician attempts to use thoughtfully the results of research in the management of disorders like anorexia nervosa, where the active participation of the patient in treatment is so vital. It is perhaps, in some ways, like expecting there to be evidence about how best to rescue someone from drowning in a swollen river. There may be tips and techniques which have been found to be useful in most cases; furthermore, it will be best for the rescuer to have confidence and training. A life guard will do better than most, but the particular characteristics of the drowning person, the river and the rescuer may mean that no two rescue attempts are exactly alike. However, at present we are so far from having good enough evidence in the case of anorexia nervosa that this kind of argument does not carry much force, and certainly it should not be advocated against the use of such techniques as randomised controlled trials to produce potentially generalisable knowledge.

The lack of good evidence may be explained, at least in part, by the real difficulties of research into the treatment of anorexia nervosa. Firstly, it is a disorder which is not common. It is not easy to gather large enough samples of similar sufferers to give adequate statistical power. Secondly, it occurs with a wide variety of severity. Formal treatment trials require clinicians to specify interventions and the variety of severity suggests that a varied rather than a uniform response may be indicated. Thirdly, successful trials require that a sufficient number of patients agree to accept the prescribed treatment. However, potential subjects may be reluctant to join in treatment studies because of the mixed feelings mentioned above. If they do agree they may not stick to the rules of the game, as it were. Lastly, those rules may attempt to constrain the clinician to such a degree that the management of the patient within the trial is so different from usual clinical practice that generalisation of results from the former to the latter becomes questionable. Either that or too many subjects are not included or fall out of the trial. Treatment regimes for anorexia nervosa are neither simple nor instrumental. Clinicians weave their complex interventions from elements in which they have faith.[3] The cloth thus produced may vary widely between clinicians and, furthermore, may be made up into treatments which are individually tailored to the perceived needs or characteristics of the patient. By contrast, treatment trials usually demand an 'off the peg' approach which both clinicians and patients may be reluctant to adopt.

It is important that there should be more evidence about what is good and effective treatment for anorexia nervosa. More research is urgently needed. There is a place for purely observational studies and for small studies of innovative treatment (Treasure & Kordy, 1998). However, the gold standard of treatment efficacy research remains the randomised controlled trial. Fortunately, there have been a few determined researchers who have tackled the problems outlined above and conducted such trials in anorexia nervosa. Their results are valuable and these will be mentioned in the following discussion of treatment. However, because of their scarcity, the few trials that have been completed have sometimes been asked to carry a greater weight of inference than they can comfortably bear. Unfortunately, at present, the treatment of anorexia nervosa is still supported in the main by opinion and clinical experience.

THE TASKS OF RECOVERY – AND THE AIMS OF TREATMENT

It is perhaps useful to review what getting better from anorexia nervosa involves however it may be achieved. Most evidently, of course, it involves the individual in regaining a healthy weight and a pattern of eating to sustain it. There needs also to be psychological change. In the terms used in an earlier chapter, the sufferer must disentangle ideas about weight and eating control from the wider issues about self-worth and so on with which she has become closely mixed up. In practice this means the lessening and ending of the specific psychopathology of the disorder. These two aims are all that is necessary for the individual to remedy her eating disorder, but some progress in getting life on the move in general is clearly desirable and perhaps even essential if there is not to be a high risk of the disorder returning.

Broadly speaking, the kinds of help which may be offered to the anorexia nervosa sufferer may be divided into two groups. The interventions which are aimed directly at helping the patient to restore her weight and eating might be called *clinical management*. The kinds of help which are aimed at promoting psychological change might be described as *therapy*. Of course, to a degree the distinction between what helps a patient to change her eating and what helps her to change her mind is artificial. Indeed, making it risks missing the point. The fact that these things are mixed up is the very essence of eating disorders. However, provided this is borne in mind, using these terms in the way outlined may be helpful. Sometimes the distinction between therapy and management is relatively clear, as when the patient is in hospital. It may be less so in the case of outpatient treatment when the interaction between the patient and her therapist may be focused upon both weight restoration and psychological change. Indeed, in this case any influence of treatment upon weight and eating will be achieved indirectly via helping the patient to change her own behaviour in this respect. The utility of the distinction between therapy and management may be most useful in discussing the third relevant element – that is, the *service organisation* within which they both occur.

These three terms have limitations but, nevertheless, it may be useful to employ them in discussing the complicated business of treating anorexia nervosa.

CLINICAL MANAGEMENT

There is ample evidence from clinical experience that most sufferers from anorexia nervosa can gain weight, and indeed restore weight to healthy levels, if they are managed within an experienced inpatient regime in hospital. At times such management seems to be life saving. Furthermore, it may be a stage in a progression towards a full recovery. But, of course, weight restoration in hospital is not such a recovery. At most it is a means to that end. What is also clear is that many sufferers make progress or recover without hospital admission. Outpatient management seems to be importantly helpful. Intermediate between these two forms of management, there is increasing exploration of the utility of day programmes and so-called partial hospitalisation of various kinds. These seem to have grown up in response to a perceived need for something that offers more than outpatient contact but which avoids some of the disadvantages of inpatient care – not least its high cost.

Each of these forms of management will be discussed in turn. However, it is important to emphasise that each is a means which can be offered to the sufferer in order to help her with her struggle. Each needs to be considered alongside issues and interventions which will be discussed under the heading of therapy.[4]

Inpatient Treatment

In order for a sufferer to receive inpatient treatment, she must go into hospital. In most cases this involves her agreeing to accept an offer of such treatment. Sometimes, a sufferer will feel, or perhaps be made to feel, that she has no choice other than to go along with such an offer. In a few instances, the sufferer will be pushed or coerced into hospital and, indeed, some sort of compulsory order may be involved. However, it is best if the decision to go into hospital for treatment is a real one made in a truly informed manner. The patient should know what she wants to achieve and what is being offered to help her to achieve it. Compulsion and issues around mixed feelings and reluctance will be discussed elsewhere. Likewise, there will be some discussion below of the issues which arise when a sufferer is severely ill physically and feels for that reason that she has little choice. For the present, the discussion will focus upon the situation where the patient is undertaking inpatient treatment on a voluntary basis and is no more reluctant to do so than is typical.

The best reason for accepting an offer of inpatient treatment is for the sufferer to feel that she wants to change, is trying to do so but cannot manage it without such extra help. The usual obstacle is that the sufferer cannot bring herself to eat in a way that leads her to reverse her morbid weight loss. Thus, the main aim of admission is usually to help the patient address her problems of eating and to gain weight although the whole experience may be designed to have wider positive effects of a psychological kind. However, psychological interventions such as individual or group therapies designed to have wider effects can usually be delivered as effectively on an outpatient basis as in hospital. They are rarely the essential justification for admission although they may be part of the overall inpatient treatment regime. Thus, inpatient treatment is mainly a method of clinical management rather than therapy in the senses of these terms set out above.

There may be exceptions to the rule that the reason for admission to hospital is mainly about achieving weight restoration. For instance, there are inpatient programmes that accept anorexia sufferers for treatment which do not set out to promote weight gain directly. For instance, they may offer a special milieu and other psychological treatments on a residential basis with the aim of exploring and changing 'underlying' issues in the same way as would be offered to people suffering from other kinds of disorder. Indeed, such treatment regimes often have a diagnostically mixed clientele and anorexia sufferers would be treated in the company of people suffering from other problems. Another exception to the rule of hospital admission being predominantly for clinical management arises when geography or overall service organisation dictates that inpatient treatment is the only suitable treatment available and the only way to get therapy for someone with severe anorexia nervosa (see Box 7.1).

Whenever possible, the patient's decision to come into hospital should be both well informed and carefully considered. She should feel that she is putting herself into a situation which she has reason to believe may make her feel secure enough to do something which, on balance, she wants to do but would otherwise not be able to bring herself to do. She needs to have enough information about what to expect and what admission would involve. She should know what she is letting herself in for. There will, of course, be plenty of surprises in the personal emotions and experiences which weight gain brings, but the outline of the inpatient regime should be explained to the patient before she opts for it. Time spent explaining and discussing the whole venture before admission takes place is nearly always time well spent. Likewise, neglecting this process of emotional preparation may jeopardise the success of inpatient treatment. It is usually better to slow things down and allow more time for vacillation than to accept a rapidly made panic decision which is then so often just as rapidly reversed.

So how may inpatient treatment help the individual to change her eating and gain weight? There seems to be two kinds of ways in which the situation of the patient may be considered. She may be thought of as wilfully resisting doing what is clearly in her best interest to do – namely, eating adequately and gaining weight. It follows from this that it may be appropriate to try to overcome this resistance and to push the sufferer into eating more, and so on. Alternatively, the anorexia sufferer may be thought of as being caught in a painful and frightening dilemma and dithering as a result. This view leads to attempts to construct a situation in which it feels just about safe enough for her to begin to resolve her dilemma and opt for the difficult path towards weight gain and the chance of recovery. In almost all cases the latter way of looking at things is preferable. The former can lead to battles between the patient and those who would help her. The latter should lead to a situation where the sufferer and the others feel as though they are all on the same side. This does not mean that clinicians should never 'push' a patient at all. It may be essential to do so some 'pushing' at times. But this pushing should be in the context of a shared understanding of the situation in which the patient finds herself – that is, a shared understanding of her dilemma. To invoke yet another image, the situation is perhaps a bit like that of the swimming instructor and the non-swimmer. There may well be a place for the kind of 'pushing' that involves saying 'Go on, take your foot off the bottom. I'll catch you. It'll be OK. Even if water goes up your nose, you won't drown. You can do it.'. That is quite different to pushing the person into the deep end without warning or agreement.

The construction of a safe and supportive atmosphere around the patient is much easier if the ward has a tradition of treating patients with anorexia nervosa and several such patients are being treated at once. A method of working can then grow up which would be difficult to contrive around a single occasional patient. The provision for anorectic patients need not be separated from others, but the regime for those patients needs its own culture.

The goal or endpoint of inpatient treatment may differ according to the indication. For instance, the second indication may at times be managed with a short 'rescue' admission.

Box 7.1   Some Indications for Admission

In all cases, except perhaps emergency admission for life-threatening crisis, the patient should be – on balance – wanting to change and agreeable to admission and what it involves. The indications for offering admission include:

- Failure of outpatient treatment after an adequate trial. Failure may involve deterioration or lack of progress.

- Physical deterioration to a point where health or even life is at significant risk.

- Marked physical comorbidity which notably complicates treatment.

- Notable psychiatric comorbidity and especially suicidal risk of a kind which can be managed and treated better in hospital.

- Lack of available outpatient treatment.

Inpatient Regimes

Most inpatient regimes in specialist units have clear rules and expectations (see Box 7.2).[5] These are beneficial if, but perhaps only if, they are understood appropriately by all concerned. Used properly, rules are a way of making the patient's task seem safer and more acceptable. Rules should take some of the unnecessary surprises out of the venture for both the patient and the staff. It is important that everyone sees them in this way. They are not instrumental procedures which will make the sufferer put on weight or otherwise change. For instance, many inpatient regimes start off with some restriction of the sufferer in terms of movement or access to parts of her hospital environment. Such restrictions may vary from strict bed rest through an injunction to stay in her single room to being restricted to the ward. These may be rationalised as to do with restricting energy expenditure or increasing observation but are usually better thought of as limiting the sufferer's need to make repeated decisions about how to manage herself. She has, of course, already made the big decision to come into hospital and each day she stays constitutes a confirmation of that big choice. The restriction enables her to avoid the smaller hourly decisions such as whether or not to seek out food to binge upon or whether or not to attempt to jog off the calories she has consumed. At best, rules and the patient's compliance with them reflect both her resolve to change and the professional's acknowledgement of just how difficult a task she is tackling.

In the past, strict behavioural regimes were popular. These made access to various rewarding experiences contingent upon eating or weight gain. Sometimes such regimes involved a first stage in which almost all positive environmental stimuli were banned and given back only as the desired behaviours occurred. For instance, the patient might be nursed initially in a bare room and be given access to a television or visitors only if she gained weight. Such management has now largely fallen out of use. This is partly because of evidence that strict behavioural regimes offered no advantage over more lenient management (Touyz, Beumont, Glaun, Phillips & Cowie, 1984). However, perhaps more importantly there has been a growing awareness that such regimes can feel or come to be punitive and that any short-term gains are likely to occur at the expense of lessening the chance of establishing a good long-term alliance with the patient. Behavioural principles of operant conditioning – at least such principles simply applied and understood – are probably not the best way of construing the procedures of most inpatient treatment regimes for anorexia nervosa. As was stated above, regimes are about creating a secure and predictable atmosphere in which an anorexia nervosa sufferer can begin to relinquish some of her own tight internal controls which are likely to be far more rigid and punitive than those of even the most strict regime. Provided that the emotional tone is one of partnership, then rules can be a source of relief to the kind of sufferer who has struggled in vain to escape from the constraints of anorexia by herself.

Such an emotional tone needs to be present in the task of supervision of meals. The role of the supervisor – usually a nurse – is less to make sure that the patient eats but rather to promote an atmosphere of support and expectation that allows the patient to feed herself appropriately. In the earliest stages when each meal is an ordeal, this may involve skilful selection from a palate of skills which include pushing, cajoling, reassurance, advice giving, listening and simply being there. It will rarely involve argument or negotiation. The issues are more emotional than cognitive. However, the supervisor may well need to state repeatedly that which is obvious but too often unsaid. For instance, it may be useful to remind the patient that she will not be allowed to overeat or that the nurse, or whoever, knows something of the terrible dilemma that eating represents. The task of eating is easier all round if both the patient and the person supervising know what should happen. And what should happen is laid down in rules of the regime to which the patient has agreed before admission. These rules may be adjusted somewhat for each patient, for instance, in the matter of likes and dislikes. However, too much variation between patients may make a ward with several anorectic patients more difficult to manage for the staff. Furthermore, too much negotiation and too many exceptions may make the patient feel less secure.

Box 7.2   An Example of an Inpatient Regime

(at Leicester General Hospital at the time of writing)

- Patients are admitted only after detailed discussion with the clinician who is seeing them as an outpatient and at least one visit to the ward for a 'show round'. (The only rare exceptions would be admissions in extreme emergency.) Most patients will be in established weekly therapy at the time of their admission.

- On admission, the patient will be allotted to a key worker nurse. This is in addition to the therapist who will continue to see the patient during and after her admission.

- Patients can name up to five foods which they dislike. (These cannot be chosen to exclude all 'fattening' foods.) Vegetarianism is respected unless it is both recent and clearly motivated only by the eating disorder. There is a rolling recurring menu from which the foods are chosen with the supervision of the nursing staff; otherwise, patients agree to eat the food provided. This is a 'normal' mixed diet. Patients cannot eat extras or food brought in by others except where this is an agreed part of the programme.

- A plateau weight is fixed. This is usually at a BMI of 20 unless there is some good reason otherwise.

- For the first week or so the patient is nursed in a side room. She uses a commode in the room and washes there. She is supervised on a one-to-one basis at meal times. There is no restriction on visitors, television, reading and so on.

- After the first week or so, when the patient is eating adequately with supervision, she will move into a five-bedded room with other anorexia nervosa patients. She will then eat with them in a special dining room with one nurse supervising the group. She will continue to be confined to the ward but can use the ordinary lavatories and bathrooms.

- As soon as she is settled and physically fit to do so, the patient will spend the day, Monday to Friday, in the Eating Disorders Day Programme where there are a variety of group activities and therapies. The midday meal is eaten in the Day Programme.

- The diet is titrated by the addition of increased meal size, snacks and supplements in order to produce an average weight gain of around a kilogram per week.

- As the patient gains weight, she will be allowed to do more, take more responsibility and eventually to go out of the hospital on trips or visits home. Most patients spend two or three weekends at home before leaving hospital. However, local patients who are progressing may become true day patients before reaching their plateau weight. Patients who come from afar tend to stay as inpatients until they have achieved their plateau weight and for a few weeks beyond.

All such issues of rules and so on need to reflect an appropriate balance. Mistakes can be made either way. Applied too rigidly or with the wrong attitude, rules can become the focus of the very insecurity and battles which they are designed to avoid. Sometimes the whole treatment enterprise can come to feel as though it pivots around the issue of whether or not a patient should or shouldn't be allowed to do this or that – even when everyone knows that of itself the issue is trivial. The treatment team may feel that a principle is at stake. The patient may feel that she is being made the subject of an arbitrary decision. Often they are both correct in a sense. The issue may be trivial and the decision arbitrary, but in the strange but special world of the anorexia nervosa treatment regime it may represent an important principle. Usually such situations represent a failure by all concerned to keep an appropriate eye on the big issues, and getting better from anorexia nervosa involves confronting those. There are no neat answers to be looked up in a cook book. Sometimes the staff need to compromise, sometimes not. However, handled well these apparently mundane issues of everyday clinical management can make an important contribution to psychological change and, in that sense, they are a part of therapy. For instance, it may empower a sufferer to confront her own fears and discover her own capacities when, for perhaps the first time within her illness, others stay firm and expectant in the face of her distress and she is not allowed to avoid what is difficult. On the other hand, another patient may be helped to discover that everything is not so black and white as she seemed to have thought hitherto when an appropriate compromise is worked out.

Tight rules and supervision are a means to an end, and that end should be what both patient and professionals are aiming to achieve. But, of course, the end must be clearly specified. A weight of 55 kg or whatever is part of it, but the full aim is for the sufferer to be able to eat in a way that sustains such a weight. Thus, most regimes have some sort of plan whereby external control and supervision are lessened stage by stage until the sufferer is once again in charge of her eating. Again there are things to be said for handing back such control quickly or more slowly. Interestingly, many clinicians feel that their method is just about right until they come across others who do it very differently. Predictability and confidence are probably the key ingredients of a good workable regime rather than any particular procedure.

If weight gain is the primary aim of most inpatient treatment, the issue of how much weight is to be gained is crucial. This is, of course, a part of the wider question of the overall aims of the treatment venture of which the admission is a component. Again this should, in general, be a topic of explicit discussion before the admission takes place. In some cases, the purpose of admission may be no more than to rescue the sufferer from a position of significant physical risk. In others, it may be to help the patient to get unstuck as an adjunct to ongoing outpatient therapy. In many cases, however, the aim of admission will be full restoration of body weight to a premorbid healthy weight, or something like it. Indeed, classically admission would involve also a final time when this weight is sustained whilst the patient is still in hospital. This is sensible but is also, of course, very expensive. An admission which aims to help a sufferer weighing 30 kg to restore a weight of 52 kg and then give an opportunity to sustain that weight for six weeks would usually last for many months and cost a lot of money. That, of course, may well be money very well spent. Indeed, there is an argument that *not* investing in such potentially radical treatment may well be a false economy as well as providing the patient with less than optimal treatment (Baran, Weltzin & Kaye, 1995). However, such arguments – although persuasive – lack clear supporting evidence, although lack of formal evidence does not mean that they are false.

All other things being equal – and, of course, they may not be for financial or other reasons – it does seem sensible for most anorexia nervosa sufferers who start on a weight regaining regime to continue with it until they have reached a normal sustainable weight. The issue of sustainability here refers to a body weight that is sustainable without undue eating restraint and which is likely to support normal hormonal function. (In the terms of Chapter 4, this is a weight associated with a 'spring' near the point of equilibrium.) This is the sort of body weight for which the patient should be aiming. For this reason, it is often referred to as the 'target' weight. However, since attaining such a weight is merely a stage on the road to recovery rather than an end in itself, the image of a target is not ideal. An alternative is the term 'plateau weight'.[6] In principle this weight is perhaps best predicted from the individual's own history if that history includes a period of adult life in which she has had a stable weight that has not been associated with undue restraint. In practice, many and perhaps even most anorexia nervosa sufferers have either not had a time in their lives when this was true, or their recollections are so fogged by their current preoccupations that the truth of the matter is difficult to find. For most sufferers it may therefore be reasonable to agree a weight that is within the normal range and which, for most people, would be sustainable in the sense used above. In agreeing such a weight it is useful to discuss the choice in such biological terms rather than get into unproductive arguments about aesthetics or personal preferences. The point is less what weight the person would want to be but rather the weight that she can be without having to struggle unduly against her own body. Of course, some patients will have been premorbidly obese and the implications of this need to be discussed. Such patients may well have difficulty in sustaining an average body weight without unsustainable restraint. However, it is usually worth suggesting that they have a go at doing so rather than aim from the beginning at restoring what may be their 'normal' weight. Someone who had weighed 80 kg but who now weighs 35 and who has the characteristic fears of anorexia nervosa may shy away from facing any more weight gain than is involved in getting to an average weight of, say, 54 kg.

People who suffer from anorexia nervosa characteristically experience fear of loss of control of their weight and of their eating. For them, letting off their own tight controls is frightening and raises the spectre of sudden uncontrolled change. Thus, weight change within an inpatient regime needs to be predicted, manageable and steady. Likewise, ideally the expectations about what the patient eats should be known about, reasonable and not too different from what most people would consider 'normal'. Too rapid a weight gain achieved by 'artificial' means such as naso-gastric tube or parenteral feeding or by the consumption of very large quantities of food may seem good on paper but tends merely to confirm the sufferer's worst fears. In practice, once the patient has got going, a diet which leads to a weight gain of around a kilogram each week is reasonable. This should be composed of 'normal' foods served at conventional mealtimes, perhaps with some additional planned snacks or supplements. The emphasis should be on predictability. The patient should be expected to eat in the kind of way with which she has agreed in principle before admission. She should eat as she expects and the regime expects her to eat – no less but importantly no more either. She should not be allowed to have sweets or treats or unauthorised snacks unless or until they become part of the programme. Preventing overeating is one of the most important techniques for promoting adequate eating.

Someone who is putting herself through the process of weight restoration within an inpatient treatment regime for anorexia nervosa will characteristically go through a roller coaster of emotion. She will regret coming into hospital. She will feel gross and greedy. She will feel that nobody understands her. She will feel the stirrings of hormonal change. She will feel that others are being petty or fear that she is being so. She will feel dependent on certain people but feel unsafe in doing so. She will feel all over the place. And, with luck, she will also feel all sorts of more positive things and experience a sense of achievement. She needs to be reminded – implicitly and explicitly – that she is engaged in the brave, sensible and 'grown up' process of attempting recovery and escape from the trap of anorexia nervosa. This is the case however 'little', childlike or even childish she may feel at times. Usually it is the nursing staff who have the central role of being with the patient as she makes this journey. It is they who are there day by day and, importantly, night by night. As such they can become embroiled in the patient's feelings and may have to avoid getting caught up inappropriately in roles such as playing the finger-wagging parent to the whinging or 'naughty' child. Things can go wrong but when they go well there is great therapeutic power in these day-by-day, meal-by-meal interactions. Often one nurse may be designated as the key worker or whatever. However, it is important that the whole staff is broadly in tune with the overall culture of the regime. Furthermore, it is important that the ward staff who are there all of the time and those others who, as it were, only visit the ward – doctors, therapists and so on – are seen to be and indeed see themselves as being part of one overall venture with and for the patient. If this is achieved on a special unit with several patients at the same time, the patient group itself becomes an important part of the overall culture. Sufferers support and sustain each other and at times may do so more insightfully and robustly than the staff are able to do. However, things may go wrong if a harmful 'counter culture' arises perhaps around the despair or anger of one or two patients. It is always the staff's role to promote and maintain the culture and in some circumstances to protect and repair it.

Towards the end of inpatient treatment it is usual for patients to go on leave for increasing lengths of time – perhaps first for a few hours then for a day or a weekend. Indeed, some regimes incorporate leaves throughout or even run routinely on a five-day per week basis. Leaves are useful as opportunities for the sufferer to generalise her ways of managing herself and, crucially, to build her confidence in feeding herself appropriately.

If leaves from hospital coincide with recurring slumps in weight, the patient and those advising her are confronted by a dilemma. The expensive business of admission can come up against the problem of diminishing returns. There is the fear that despite all the hard work which the patient and others have put in, her situation will return quickly to how it was before admission. There is a feeling that this can only be prevented if she extends her stay. At the same time, however, there may be a sense that such serial delay in discharge is not achieving much. There is a need to work out what is going wrong. Is it to do with the sufferer's secret aim? Is it to do with the effects of others upon her emotions and motivation? Do practical matters of food choice and the like contribute? Different remedies may be offered but, in the end, weight restoration that can be sustained only by continued hospitalisation may not be worth much. The patient must sooner or later be launched, albeit with continuing outpatient or other support if at all possible.

Day Patient Programmes

Over recent years, a number of centres have set up special day programmes for people suffering from eating disorders, and especially anorexia nervosa. The reasons for doing so are clear. At least a substantial minority of those suffering from anorexia nervosa do not seem to progress with outpatient treatment alone. However, hospital admission, which is the usual alternative form of more intensive management, has real disadvantages. Firstly, it is very costly. Secondly, it can be disruptive, frightening and sometimes unacceptable to the patient. Lastly, there is a suspicion that if it is not done well, the process of full hospitalisation could be harmful.

Day treatment is intended to be a form of clinical management intermediate between outpatient and inpatient treatment. It may represent an enrichment of the former and an avoidance of some of the disadvantages which may be associated with the latter.

Forms of partial hospitalisation other than day care are possible – for instance, staying in hospital for a few days each week or coming to the hospital only at night – but there is little reported experience of these options. What will be discussed here is *special* day provision for anorexia nervosa. This is to be distinguished from a situation where patients with anorexia nervosa attend day programmes or hospitals which are general in character. Such non-specific day treatment undoubtedly happens but there is little or no evidence, even of an anecdotal kind, as to whether or not it is helpful.

The special day programmes that have been described seem to differ widely from each other (Freeman, 1992; Piran & Kaplan, 1990; Gerlingoff, Backmund & Franzen, 1998). There are almost certainly others that have yet to be recorded. Some – perhaps most – cater for anorexia nervosa sufferers along with other eating-disordered people. Some operate as part of a wider service whilst others offer self-contained programmes. Likewise, in some programmes patients may attend seven days each week, although five-day programmes are probably the most common. Hours spent in the programme each day and the number of meals provided also differ. In some programmes, some patients stay in a special hostel which is associated with the hospital in some way or with other local but especially arranged accommodation. Furthermore, there are reported differences in the crucial issue of the management of eating. Some have clear expectations, as would typically be the case for many inpatient regimes, whilst others seek to provide support and a context in which people may eat but leave the details of eating to be largely the responsibility of the patient, as would be the case in most outpatient treatment (Freeman, 1992; Kaplan & Olmsted, 1997). At present, there is no systematic evidence to suggest which is better and the particular style tends to reflect the overall approach to issues of responsibility.[7]

Of course, any programme of day treatment or other partial hospitalisation will be unable to provide as much supervision and support as full admission to hospital. Patients will have greater opportunity to eat too little or abnormally because most will be more in charge of themselves than would be the case if they were in hospital full time. This may be both good and bad. It may mean that what progress they do make may be more self-motivated and in that sense more 'real' and perhaps more lasting. However, progress in terms of weight gain may well be slower. Perhaps the important thing is that it should be significant and sustained. If it is not, and the sufferer becomes stuck or deteriorates despite day treatment, then everyone is confronted with the dilemma of whether or not this can be tolerated. There may be arguments both ways but a facility can become damagingly clogged up if it accommodates too many 'stuck' patients for too long.

At present, the optimal style of provision of day treatment for people suffering from anorexia nervosa is the subject of more opinion than evidence. Several different approaches and regimes have been shown apparently to help some people, or at least to coincide with improvement (Freeman, 1992; Piran & Kaplan, 1990; Kaplan & Olmsted, 1997; Gerlingoff, Backmund & Franzen, 1998). However, no one approach has been shown to be superior in a way that would convince a sceptic. Indeed, the role of day care in general has yet to be established beyond question. Much of the impetus for setting up new programmes is undoubtedly economic and comes from the wish to avoid expensive admissions. However, the existence of a day treatment programme may lead some sufferers who would otherwise have been managed solely as outpatients to be offered more rather than less input. Furthermore, for those who would otherwise have been admitted as inpatients, the probable greater overall length of day treatment may erode the advantages in terms of cost and perhaps even in terms of disruption to life. The issues are not simple. For the present, it does seem clear that not all admissions can be avoided, although perhaps most can be shortened if day treatment is available. Perhaps the best system is one where outpatient, inpatient and day treatment can be offered within the same service as part of a coordinated whole. What is clear is that most sufferers from anorexia nervosa can be – and on a worldwide perspective probably are – managed solely as outpatients.

Outpatient Treatment

Unfortunately, the optimal place and manner of outpatient treatment for anorexia nervosa is as much a matter of opinion as are the other modes of clinical management. Once again there is a paucity of good evidence. However, the quite massive cost differential between outpatient treatment and almost any other form of clinical management means that, in practice, it should usually be the first approach used until other treatments have been shown to be superior. The exception to this rule would be where there are real immediate dangers to the patient which could be contained only by more intensive management. The other main indication for such intensive management is failure to progress with outpatient care. In such circumstances, it is probably optimal when outpatient care can progress to inpatient care without any break in the relationship with the clinician who has been conducting the outpatient treatment – unless, of course, that treatment has not gone well because of some particular difficulty between the patient and that clinician. Some kinds of service organisation make such continuity difficult.

When the sufferer's only contact with the clinician is as an outpatient, the distinction between clinical management and therapy is more blurred than in other situations. The same meetings serve both functions and it is difficult – and perhaps meaningless in many instances – to make the distinction at all, at least when the style of the clinician is well balanced and not extreme. However, not all approaches are balanced in this sense either by default or by design. Thus it is possible, on the one hand, for outpatient sessions to be concerned solely with direct advice and discussion of weight and eating or on the other hand for such issues not to be mentioned at all in outpatient therapy which addresses only other issues. However, either approach would seem to miss the point somewhat. The entanglement of these two sets of issues lies at the heart of the matter. In the absence of evidence to the contrary, it seems sensible that outpatient treatment should seek to address both weight and psychological issues and the entanglement of the two.

Viewed from the perspective of clinical management, the function of outpatient contact is – as with the more intensive forms of management – to make the sufferer feel safe enough to face a change. At the beginning, and often also recurrently during the course of the treatment, individual conversations with a clinician form the setting in which the patient should be enabled to express her fears and clarify her mixed feelings. The clinician needs to behave in a way that allows for such feelings and promotes a sense of safety. At the simplest the clinician should aim to be reliable and predictable. This is usually best done by arranging from the outset a framework of regular meetings. These would often be on a weekly basis but might be more or less frequent. Each meeting should usually be of a predictable duration. The arrangement should explicitly recognise the difficulty and probable length of the task which the sufferer is confronting. She should not be left with the impression that the clinician believes that a couple of chats will get things sorted or that all will be well once she has put on a few pounds. *She* may talk or act as if she believes this but such sentiments are more likely to be a form of self-reassurance rather than her true feelings. It is sometimes a good idea to arrange appointments in 'chunks' with explicit reviews after an agreed number of sessions. This is especially the case if outpatient treatment looks as though it may not be getting anywhere. An arrangement which feels too temporary or contingent either upon recovery or continued problems is unlikely to make the sufferer feel optimally secure.

Whatever conclusions the clinician reaches, he should be honest about what can and cannot be done. It tends to promote confidence in the patient for the clinician to appear to be not only confident and knowledgeable but also accurately empathetic about what the patient is likely to be feeling. He should give space for her to talk and he should listen, but a well-judged guess at her unspoken feelings may be very potent. Issues of responsibility should be discussed, including the responsibility which the passive patient may seem to push upon the worried but in some respects impotent clinician.

The clinician should take whatever steps are necessary to try to monitor the physical state of the patient, including crucially her weight. This issue should certainly be discussed. What the clinician does depends upon the nature of the arrangements that should be in place to deal with the physical state of the patient. Arguably the best arrangement is where one clinician – or at least colleagues in one service – is able to monitor and manage all aspects of the case, including the physical aspects. Sometimes this may not be practicable, and then communication and the construction of a situation in which everyone is truly working together becomes important.

If the patient refuses to cooperate – for instance, with weighing or blood tests – this needs to be discussed as a difficulty in the working partnership which may limit its effectiveness. Battles should be avoided but the issue should not simply be shelved. It is not possible to say what is always the right thing to do because the matter is particular to the relationship between each clinician and each patient. The patient's mixed feelings about the whole enterprise of treatment and recovery need to be addressed. Once again the aim is the promotion of a sense of safety. When things are not going well, threats and dire warnings are rarely helpful although the clinician should be honest about any dangers. Likewise, he should be clear in his advice. The patient needs to be enabled to face up to what she has to do to get out of harm's way. The clinician needs to try to provide her with anything she needs, but lacks, to do this. Only in a very few instances should the matter be taken out of the sufferer's hands, and then only temporarily. In most legal systems, formal compulsion is possible only in conjunction with hospital admission. Outpatient management is, and indeed should always be, a matter of cooperation. The clinician needs to foster such cooperation and to resist the temptation to be heavy handed in a way that makes this less likely. But, of course, managing a sick but less than cooperative patient can be a worrying business.

In the outpatient context the business of eating is in the hands of the patient and there must, of necessity, be more discussion and indeed negotiation of what she can and cannot manage in that respect than would be typical in hospital. In general, weight gain may take a while to get going and is likely to progress at a slower rate than would be typical with inpatient treatment. Even an average of half a kilogram (or one pound) each week would be doing well. Of course, in practice many factors can affect the body weight that is actually measured – everything from hydration status and constipation to faulty scales and deliberate deception. Initial weight gain over the first three or four weeks of attempted change often seems to be surprisingly slow (which can be disappointing to a patient who is trying hard) or surprisingly rapid perhaps because of hydration issues (which can be alarming for the patient). The rate then usually settles down, although unexplained 'jumps' or 'rests' may still occur. It is necessary to take a long view. In outpatient treatment, it is usual to weigh patients every week, but it is often useful to judge weight gains not by weekly changes but by the net change over a longer period, say a month. This monthly weight change can, of course, be calculated every week – rather in the way that the annual rate of inflation is announced each month.

The task of the clinician is to strike the best balance between pushing too hard and colluding with the patient's fears by not expecting enough. Again the particular business of advice about eating has to be considered within the overall context of the wider aim of moving towards recovery. As the saying goes, the proof of the pudding is in the eating – and in this case in the weight change also. If the individual eats in a way that leads her to gain no weight, or even to lose it, this needs to be discussed in terms of that consequence and what this means for her prospect of escape from her present suffering. How much she is trying; how trying makes her feel; how unreasonable the expectations of others are; what her friends eat and so on are relevant with regard to her feelings, but her body – not the clinician – is ultimately the judge of whether what she is doing is adequate. There may be rewards for effort alone but recovery is not one of them. Rather than simply nagging, the clinician will often do well to emphasise repeatedly that he understands how distressing and difficult are both of the options facing the sufferer – these are the options of staying as she is or of doing enough to change.

The matter of precisely what the patient should be advised to eat is rarely a major conundrum in a material sense. The difficult questions concern the correct compromise between what it would be good for her to eat – a substantial balanced diet – and what she can bring herself to consume. The issues are rarely technical except perhaps in the case of a sufferer who is in a truly extreme and physically compromised state. There is a need for the sufferer to eat sufficient calories to get into positive energy balance. How much is enough is difficult to predict and, furthermore, may well change from time to time. Thus the amount that is sufficient to start weight gain may be insufficient to continue it. Also, of course, body weight is a crude index which may change in relation to dehydration, rehydration or fluid retention. It is not possible to say that someone is eating enough unless her is weight is rising steadily at a manageable rate and in a way that is not explained by shifts in fluid. Fortunately, that is exactly the aim of treatment in this respect. So there is a sense in which all that can be said is that enough is enough. In addition to total calorie intake, it is desirable that the diet should contain balanced quantities of carbohydrate, protein and fat. It is probably sensible for the patient to take vitamin supplements and especially thiamine during the first few weeks of attempted weight gain. However, many sufferers take these anyway and, of course, they are no substitute for food.

It is usually best that the food which the sufferer allows herself should be organised into meals and planned snacks rather than 'grazed' throughout the day. This should be the aim as soon as is practicable. Keeping a food diary may be useful, although some patients keep wonderful diaries without benefit whilst others get on very well without. Likewise, making detailed suggestions about what to eat may help many patients but complicates things for others. At the beginning of treatment it may be necessary to tolerate eccentric eating patterns in the interests of increasing intake and shape up a pattern of 'proper meals' only gradually. The sufferer should know both where she is going and the recommended route. She may, however, start off on an idiosyncratic path, but the most important thing is that the sufferer is on the move in the direction of weight restoration and the resumption of a more normal and sustainable pattern of eating.

Fear of eating too much or of bingeing may be an important issue even when this has never actually happened. The patient needs to feel that the clinician is concerned that she should not overeat and will help her if she does. The loss of control fantasies about both weight and eating need to be discussed and revisited as the treatment progresses. In some cases it may be helpful to enlist parents or others in the role of potential helpers in the case that the patient should feel that she was eating excessively. They may support her or sometimes actually take steps to stop her overeating if she is indeed 'losing it'. The very act of discussing this with important others in the presence of the patient may reassure her that her fears are understood. Of course, it may not be easy for a mother who has spent months or years trying to get her daughter to eat more to understand the need for such reassurance – as the saying goes, 'We should have such problems' – but most can come to see the point of it. Sometimes patients do go through a time of allowing themselves to eat excessively, and the emotional tone of this can vary and is sometimes positive. However, the clinician needs to be wary of cheering. The task is to help the patient to resume an appropriate degree of control without slamming on the brakes.

The clinician will inevitably give advice. However, he should always try to be aware of the emotional context in which that advice is being given and received. That context may include immediate issues such as hidden hunger, a sense of greed and fears of loss of control which affect the reception of the message, 'I think that you should try to allow yourself to eat more at lunch time. What about adding a yoghurt?' It may also include more general issues which could be thought about in transferential terms. For instance, the same message about lunch might be experienced by one patient as part of an overwhelming takeover bid for control of something that represents her autonomy and by another as an accurate and heart-warming acknowledgement of her needs and her concerns. The clinician should try to tune into such personal meanings and experiences and attune the style of his advice accordingly. In doing so, he needs to think like a psychotherapist even when he is giving concrete advice about baked beans or whatever. Likewise, the professional who is engaged in psychotherapy with an anorexia sufferer cannot usually afford to be too purist and needs to consider the concrete as well as the symbolic aspects of those same baked beans. Such is the nature of the disorder.

THERAPY

Almost everyone thinks that psychotherapy of some kind is a good thing in the treatment of anorexia nervosa. However, once again it must be acknowledged that this belief rests mainly upon experience and what might be called common clinical sense. It certainly *seems* right that direct attention to the psychological and emotional aspects of recovery should be of great potential value. In order to recover, the sufferer has somehow to trust someone – or 'the world' – sufficiently to risk changing, and clinicians should seek to increase the probability of this happening. Now, of course, that trust and sense of safety may arise from family, friends or from non-treatment experiences or somehow from some other change in circumstance or resolve. Some people get better with no formal treatment; others may use aspects of treatment which are not construed as 'therapy' to achieve the same ends. However, it does seem rational that any treatment programme which sets out to improve the chances of recovery of people with anorexia nervosa needs somehow to provide therapy in the sense of explicit and skilled attention to the psychological aspects of the disorder and the tasks of recovery.

If therapy can do good, then it may be that its potency might also in principle do harm. That is at least plausible and needs to be borne in mind. The nature of the therapy might be important. Once again, opinion and experience have to provide the main guide since there is little hard evidence about what is the best kind of psychotherapy in anorexia nervosa. However, there are some studies which illuminate the issue.

The most ambitious trial of both the therapy and management of anorexia nervosa was conducted at St. George's Hospital in London by Professor Arthur Crisp and his team (Crisp *et al.*, 1991). Within this trial patients were randomised between four treatment conditions: namely, inpatient treatment, asessment only or two differing types of outpatient treatment. Unfortunately, the bold design meant that some subjects were offered more than might have been optimal and others less. Furthermore, there was little control over subsequent therapy and, for instance, many of the 'assessment only' group went on to receive inpatient treatment elsewhere. Consequently, the results of the trial are difficult to interpret. However, the fairly positive results of the outpatient treatment wing of the trial do provide evidence that even rather modest outpatient therapy – and it was less within the trial than would have been usual at St George's – may lead to important improvement (Gowers, Norton, Halek & Crisp, 1994).

There have been rather few trials of pure outpatient therapy. Most have been small and have had insufficient statistical power to have had a chance of revealing other than enormous differences. Thus, for instance, Channon, de Silva, Hemsley and Perkins (1989) studied behavioural and cognitive-behavioural therapy and Treasure *et al.* (1995) compared educational behavioural treatment and cognitive analytic psychotherapy. However, neither of these small trials of outpatient therapies showed important differences between the main treatment conditions although many subjects made progress. Arguably, none of treatments studied replicated the kind of long-term outpatient therapy that is likely to be optimal.

Arguably the best and most influential trials have been the series of larger studies conducted by the group at the Institute of Psychiatry in London (Russell, Szmukler, Dare & Eisler, 1987; Dare & Eisler, 1995). In the first of these, adult patients who had been treated on a weight restoration regime in hospital were randomised on discharge to either individual therapy or family therapy over one year (Russell *et al.*, 1987). At the end of the year, few patients were recovered but there were notably different effects of the two treatments. Patients with an onset of disorder before the age of 19 and history of less than three years did better with family therapy, whereas the reverse was true for those with a later onset and longer history. (Those with bulimia or those with an early onset and long history showed no differential treatment effects.) Remarkably these differences in outcome were still detectable five years after treatment (Eisler *et al.*, 1997).

This result is important but is in need of replication as it was based on one study and the crucial result involved only 21 patients. Interestingly, some further evidence in favour of the use of rather different family treatment with young patients comes from a small study of 'behavioural family systems therapy' compared to 'ego-orientated individual therapy' (Robin, Siegal, Koepke, Moye & Tice, 1994). The Institute of Psychiatry group has gone on to compare the efficacy of their family therapy against what they call family counselling in young anorexia nervosa patients who have not been admitted. Family counselling involves the patient and her family being seen separately, rather than together as would be the case in more usual family treatment. Preliminary results suggest that this new treatment is of similar efficacy to family therapy (le Grange, Eisler, Dare & Russsell, 1992; Dare & Eisler, 1995). Two other studies are being conducted by this group but definitive results have yet to be published (Dare & Eisler, 1995).

The main trial mentioned above examined the efficacy of different therapies given after the patient had restored a reasonable weight in hospital. In a sense, it used a relapse prevention design. This design may have been adopted for a variety of reasons connected with the research. However, some practitioners believe that many patients are not really open to psychotherapy until they have gained at least some weight and moved out of an extreme physical position, and the degree of cognitive impairment that has been demonstrated in some low-weight sufferers may used to support such a view (Szmukler et al., 1992). However, this is questionable as a basis for delaying psychotherapy, at least in a broad sense. After all the sufferer has to struggle with her thoughts and feelings even when she is in an extreme state. She cannot delay doing so and postponing the help she requires does not seem sensible. The evidence about the possibility of impairment suggests modification of technique and content rather than postponement of therapy.

When a patient is treated solely as an outpatient, therapy and clinical management may be joint functions of one relationship. In this case the therapy has to promote the sufferer's determination to change. The role of therapist can be isolated from that of what might be called clinical manager as, for instance, when the issue of weighing or dietary advice is left to others. Nevertheless, for the patient, weight and eating and wider issues are mixed up and there may well be an advantage in one clinician combining both roles whenever this can be achieved with confidence.[8]

When psychotherapy occurs in the context of inpatient care, the therapist may need to emphasise the practicalities of weight and eating somewhat less, but these should not be ignored. They will be on the mind of the patient. The therapy may not have a prime function in promoting weight gain but weight gain will be one of the important influences upon the experience and feelings which the patient brings to therapy.

Any kind of therapy for anorexia nervosa rests crucially upon the treatment alliance between the therapist and the patient. It is that relationship which promotes a sense of security and allows the patient to change. However, establishing such an alliance may well not be easy and straightforward when the patient has anorexia nervosa. After all, mixed feelings are characteristic. In a recent multi-author volume (Brownell & Fairburn, 1995) two authorities, one on the cognitive-behavioural therapy of anorexia nervosa and the other on its psychodynamic therapy, wrote neighbouring chapters. The former, Kelly Vitousek, wrote: 'a substantial portion of the first few sessions of therapy may be devoted to helping the client develop an exhaustive list of both the 'pros' and the 'cons' of her eating disorder, phrased in her own terms' (Vitousek, 1995). The latter, David Herzog, wrote: 'It takes a number of sessions to gather a sufficiently detailed history from the anorexic patient to formulate this complex dynamic. The anorexic is generally private, guarded, and fearful of being controlled. She will need time to develop an alliance with the psychotherapist before revealing her understanding of the symptoms, what kind of therapy she wants, how willing she is to participate, and how ready she is to change' (Herzog, 1995). These quotations reveal different styles but a similar goal. Both emphasise the need to establish a sound working alliance with the patient. Both authors go on to discuss how the therapy of anorexia nervosa is usually a long job.

There is a measure of agreement that the psychotherapy of anorexia nervosa should involve a rather more 'active' technique on the part of the therapist than would be the case in classic psychodynamic psychotherapy. In such therapy, the therapist would often adopt an 'analytic stance' and respond only to material introduced by the patient. However, the evident physical state of the low-weight patient cannot easily be ignored and should not be. Indeed, if it were effectively to be ignored, that lack of attention to something so central would be likely to constitute a form of active neglect and be experienced as such. Someone who is sinking in quick sands may or may not shout out, but the fact that half of their body has disappeared beneath the mud itself constitutes a signal to those on solid ground. As was noted above, those who undertake psychotherapy with anorexia sufferers need to take cognisance of the physical and behavioural aspects of their patients' state just as those, who would be rather more 'physicianly', need to attend to the psychological aspects of their interventions. In practice, most therapists who are experienced in dealing with anorexia sufferers adopt a style of therapy which pays explicit attention both to weight and eating and to wider issues and the relationship between the two domains. Indeed, dietary advice and weight monitoring may well be included in the remit of the therapist. Even when they are not treated directly, the therapist needs to pay attention to these issues and should be in touch with those who are focusing upon them. Importantly, the therapy needs to provide the patient with the opportunity to examine the ideas and experiences which provide the links between weight and eating and wider issues. Such links are in the mind and on the mind of the patient. The therapy provides a secure context in which these ideas can be considered and be challenged or transcended. The theoretical framework within which the therapist does so may vary. As yet there is little evidence which favours one framework over another. Until any such evidence becomes available therapists will continue to follow whatever set of ideas and practices they favour and have been trained within.

The therapist operating within a psychodynamic framework is likely to construe the mental life of the patient in terms of the psychodynamic developmental story and the relationship with the patient in transferential terms. However, as has been stated above, he may need to be more active in giving advice and comments than might be usual in such therapy. The therapist who thinks and practices within a cognitive behavioural framework may well focus on the patient's behaviour and the beliefs and ideas which seem to sustain it. Such a therapist will seek to construct a relationship with the patient which is straightforward, collaborative and organised around the task of achieving change. In contrast to the psychodynamic therapist, in CBT the therapist may have to adapt the therapy in the direction of being more reflective and of giving the patient plenty of opportunity to express and get around her complicatedly mixed feelings about change. Work on basic assumptions and 'self-schemata' will often be required. Each kind of therapist needs to adapt his technique to the particular situation of the anorectic patient.[9]

There is only limited experience with the use of group therapies as the prime mode of treatment in anorexia nervosa (Polivy & Federoff, 1997). None suggests superiority to individual therapy. Indeed there are reasons to think that the difficult business of managing motivation and mixed feelings is likely to be complicated within a group. However, supportive or creative groups as adjuncts to other therapies may well be useful. Indeed, many inpatient regimes and day programmes have group therapies and activities as central components.

Family Therapy

As was mentioned above, the use of some kinds of family therapy for some anorexia nervosa sufferers is supported by evidence. The family therapy used in the first Institute of Psychiatry study involved an attempt to mobilise the parents to feed their daughter (Russell *et al.*, 1987). Great emphasis was placed upon the parents' crucial role in recovery, but this is combined with a parallel emphasis upon avoiding any sense of blame for the illness itself. This explicit relief from and avoidance of blame is important. Many families feel that they are in some way to blame for their child's illness. Some feel rightly or wrongly that they are blamed by others. Such feelings can be promoted by heavy-handed family therapy. Indeed, sometimes the professionals involved may believe that the parents have in some sense caused the illness and that blaming is appropriate. More often perhaps clinicians fail to dispel such ideas which are rarely justified. One way or other, family therapy can be experienced by families as a persecutory and damaging experience when it is not done well. Perhaps even more than individual therapy, the undoubted potency of family therapy carries the risk of negative effects as well as the chance of the clear benefits which have been documented in the trials.

The evidence from the research trials is important. It is supported by less formal accounts of family interventions from other centres (Dare & Eisler, 1995, 1997). However, only the main trial so far makes a direct comparison between individual and family therapy and there is a danger of overgeneralising the result to suggest that *any* family therapy is likely to be superior to *any* individual therapy in younger patients. This is unlikely to be the case. Family therapists with the necessary specific skills to treat anorexia nervosa sufferers in the manner developed by Dare, Eisler and colleagues for the trials may often be in even shorter supply than therapists able to provide adequate individual therapy. Even if the finding that family therapy is best is accepted uncritically, there may be circumstances in which it is important that the best should not be made the enemy of the good. In practice, good individual work may well be better than mediocre family therapy.

Whilst family therapy or family counselling may be employed as the central therapeutic activity in the treatment of anorexia nervosa, family work of other kinds may be a useful adjunct to treatment which is mainly individual. Thus, it is a common practice for parents and others to be supported by a team member during the their relative's treatment. Such 'support' may include more detailed history taking about the antecedents and circumstances of the illness, the giving of information or advice and providing a setting for emotional ventilation and non-directive counselling.[10]

Occasional meetings in which the whole family including the patient is brought together may also be useful. Such meetings may provide the professionals with a valuable opportunity to observe family interactions and gain important insights. They may give the family an opportunity to express their worries and opinions. There can be useful exchanges of information and sharing of views. Lastly, such meetings may sometimes seem to be the occasion of some useful shift in understanding or behaviour. In that case, of course, the activity comes to be a form of family therapy albeit one that is less clear cut than when such therapy is the main form of treatment.[11]

Family work of all kinds is likely to be more important the younger is the sufferer. It may well be central when the patient is a child or in early teenage. The special issues involved in the treatment of these youngest sufferers will be discussed in Chapter 9.

Drug Treatments

Over a century ago, Sir William Gull wrote that he 'had not observed much advantage from the administration of drugs', adding that he 'would rather trust to moral influences and feeding than to medicines, though these might be still be amongst the adjuvantia'. There is surprisingly little to add as a result of the last century and more of experience. Thus there is little evidence that any of the drugs which have been evaluated so far have a specific beneficial effect in anorexia nervosa. Nevertheless, they may indeed be useful as 'adjuvantia"; that is, in the management of particular symptoms and comorbidity. Furthermore, it may well be the case that new drugs will be found to be helpful.

People suffering from anorexia nervosa have, in general, a distorted but undiminished urge to eat which they seek to control. It would therefore not seem rational to prescribe appetite stimulants in most cases. Nevertheless, the serotonin antagonist cyproheptidine, which does have such properties, has been studied and found not to influence weight gain in an inpatient setting except in a small subgroup of patients who showed especially severe disorder of the restricting type (Halmi, Eckert, LaDu & Cohen, 1986).

There have been surprisingly few trials of psychotropic medications in anorexia nervosa. Antidepressants have been tried the most. However, few trials have been of substantial size or power. No antidepressants have been shown to promote recovery, at least as measured by weight gain (Garfinkel & Walsh, 1997). However, preliminary results of a study from the USA, which at the time of writing has yet to be published, suggest that the prescription of fluoxetine may reduce the risk of relapse in patients who have had their weight restored in hospital, although it does not seem to be helpful at low weight. This result is of interest and could be important if it were to be replicated. However, there is no evidence that fluoxetine is helpful in low-weight patients (Attia, Haiman, Walsh & Flater, 1998).

With regard to psychiatric comorbidity, there is once again little evidence. However, someone suffering from anorexia nervosa who is also morbidly depressed or anxious or impaired by symptoms of obsessive-compulsive disorder should be treated in general as would someone of normal weight. Such treatment might well include the prescription of appropriate medication. That having been said, some such symptoms may well be present in many sufferers and someone who is going through a weight restoration programme may well be in a rather changeable emotional state for understandable reasons. Clinical experience suggests that it may often be appropriate to try to support the patient and wait rather than rush in with medication. However, this kind of dilemma concerning how and when to prescribe is not much different to that encountered in other kinds of clinical practice.

A much smaller minority of anorexia nervosa sufferers may develop comorbid psychotic features of a schizophrenic or paranoid kind (Ferguson & Damluji, 1988). These should be treated with neuroleptic medication. However, there is no evidence that neuroleptics are helpful for non-psychotic sufferers. The once fashionable prescription of substantial doses of chlorpromazine as part of weight restoration programmes was not supported by evidence and has been largely abandoned. However, such past regimes did demonstrate that many patients could tolerate surprisingly large doses of neuroleptics. Such drugs may sometimes have a place in helping patients to manage troublesome restlessness.

Drugs may be useful in relieving some of the physical symptoms of anorexia nervosa, especially those associated with re-feeding and weight gain. It is well documented that anorexia sufferers tend to have slow gastric emptying (Robinson, Clarke & Barrett, 1988), and this is likely to explain some of the experiences of bloating and the like which some sufferers then misinterpret as 'fat'. Drugs such as metoclobamide and cisapride might be thought to be helpful and there is some clinical experience that suggests this. However, the latter has been assessed in a double blind placebo-controlled trial with largely negative results (Szmukler, Young, Miller, Lichtenstein & Binns, 1995). However, such drugs may worth a try in patients with more than average gastrointestinal symptoms, especially bloating.

Likewise, constipation may be a genuine issue. In the longer run this can usually be avoided or managed by adopting a diet with plenty of bulk and fibre. However, in the short run, laxatives or even suppositories may be required. The purging anorectic who has become habituated onto large doses of stimulant purgatives may need to reduce her dosage in a stepwise fashion over time. If this is being done in the context of inpatient re-feeding, the dosage could be simply stopped and any resulting constipation dealt with by other means if necessary. If the sufferer is trying to stop herself as an outpatient, then she may be well advised to stop in a similar fashion but may find it difficult to take such advice and a tapering off of the dose may be more acceptable. The length of the weaning-off period will probably say more about her fears than about her bowels. The latter can usually readjust over two or three weeks. Tapering the dose may be required for emotional reasons. Towards the end of any weaning period it may be better to concentrate any purgative the patient continues to take into two or three days each week rather than continuing with a small daily dose. Such a modest but significant dose taken every few days resembles an appropriate use of a laxative drug for therapeutic purposes.

Many patients with anorexia nervosa worry about the effects of their diet upon their physical health. Many take vitamin supplements and minerals in the belief that this may ameliorate such effects. Perhaps surprisingly there is only modest evidence of vitamin deficiency in most cases. Amongst the vitamins which are most relevant is thiamine (vitamin B1) deficiency of which can cause neurological and neuropsychiatric complications. At least one study has shown that a substantial minority of anorexia nervosa sufferers have measurable depletion of this vitamin (Winston, Jamieson, Madira, Gatward & Palmer, 1999). The implications of this are not as yet clear. However, taking vitamin supplements in normal dosages probably does no harm and may be helpful. It may often be a good idea to incorporate such a prescription into a therapeutic regime where its place can be discussed in a rational manner. Resumption of a good balanced diet remains, of course, the best remedy.

PHYSICAL CARE AND COMPLICATIONS

Anorexia nervosa may be best thought of as a psychological disorder in its origins but it is unequivocally physical in many of its manifestations. Its mortality is amongst the highest from psychiatric disorder and around half of these deaths are from physical causes rather than suicide (Patton, 1988; Sullivan, 1995). Furthermore, there is much physical morbidity and suffering. Any programme of help for people suffering from anorexia nervosa needs to take account of this. Physical issues must be addressed. For some clinicians and services this is not difficult; for some it is a major problem which requires cooperation with others and this may not be easily achieved. Thus although the chief thrust of the therapy, and even of the clinical management, of anorexia nervosa is to be thought about in psychological terms, many of the consequences are clearly physical and not amenable to psychological understanding. It goes without saying that the experience of having the physical symptoms, or indeed of taking the risks which anorexia nervosa involves, is individual and open to empathetic understanding. The meaning of slow gastric emptying or of a vertebral collapse due to osteoporosis may be different for the individual sufferer. In turn that meaning may lead to different behaviour and different outcome. Nevertheless, remedies or interventions relevant to the particular problem are still crucial. Some of the complications of anorexia nervosa seem to arise through low weight and malnutrition. Others are the consequence of abnormal weight control behaviours such as self-induced vomiting or laxative abuse. Some probably arise through a combination of these and other factors. The physical complications which may arise through bingeing, vomiting and purging will be discussed mainly in the next chapter.

Fortunately, most, but not all, of the physical problems associated with anorexia nervosa are reversible upon recovery. Nevertheless, some may present real dangers when they are present and others may contribute to vicious circles which make progress toward recovery even more difficult than would otherwise be the case. Furthermore, although many physical complications are evident some may be hidden until they declare themselves with some calamity. The following account is merely a summary of some of the more common or important issues.[12]

As was stated in the chapter on assessment, a commonsense view of the stability and apparent health of the sufferer is an important although not infallible guide to her actual physical health. If an individual looks fairly well, is active and has few physical complaints, it is likely that she is not at great immediate risk. Likewise, absolute levels of weight or particular symptoms may be less significant than rapid change or deterioration. It may be more appropriate to be worried about a young woman who has lost 15 kg, weighs 36 kg and is still losing, than about a woman of the same height who has been stable but stuck at a weight of 30 kg for the last three years. Even non-medical clinicians can develop a feel for physical deterioration or major problems. The value of such a 'feel' should not be underestimated, and nagging worries should be investigated. The clinician needs to listen for and ask about physical symptoms which may signal significant or remediable problems. Furthermore, he needs to be aware of the serious problems which may remain hidden and for which a more proactive approach may sometimes be indicated. The important physical complications of anorexia nervosa are set out in Box 7.3. They are arranged not by organ system but by the ways in which they may be manifest.

Very Low Weight

The severely affected patient at very low weight may experience symptoms or limitations of function which arise simply through low weight and malnutrition. Indeed, at extreme weights – for instance with a BMI in single figures – the body's capacity to maintain homeostasis may be

---

BOX 7.3   Some Important Physical Complications of Anorexia Nervosa

(*N.B.* This list is not comprehensive. See text and reviews.)

Symptomatic Complications

Bloating and gastrointestinal symptoms
Acute dilatation of the stomach
Seizures

Complications Evident upon Enquiry or Examination

Dehydration
Oedema
Myopathy
Bradycardia and hypotension
Parotid enlargement

Complications Detectable on Investigation

Osteoporosis
Abnormal electrolytes especially hypokalaemia
Cardiac problems - prolonged QT interval and arrhythmias
Anaemia, neutropenia and thrombocytopenia

---

compromised and lack of body mass and 'fuel' may directly threaten death. However, perhaps surprisingly, these issues do not usually impinge except when the sufferer is extremely ill in a way that does not need a skilled physician to detect, although the involvement of a physician in the management would be important. When such matters arise the patient is clearly 'at death's door'.

At a somewhat less extreme position a patient may show tiredness, lack of energy and muscle weakness. A particular form of weakness arises from a specific myopathy which tends to particularly affect the proximal muscles of the legs. The sufferer may experience great difficulty in climbing stairs. A useful test to reveal this problem is to ask the patient to attempt to squat and then rise again to an upright position. Being unable to do this is a sign of significant myopathy (McLoughlin *et al.*, 1998). In this state, the sufferer is running significant risks of collapse or worse.

Fortunately, this problem seems to be reversible. It is an indication for further physical assessment and for greater effort to reverse the weight loss perhaps by hospital admission. The sooner the patient is enabled to come back from the brink the better.

Severe anorexia nervosa may also affect the heart muscles. When weight loss is severe or there are any relevant symptoms such as tiredness or palpitations, examination of cardiac function should be arranged. Pulse, blood pressure and electrocardiogram (ECG) would be a reasonable minimum. Any anorexia nervosa sufferer at very low weight may show low blood pressure, bradycardia (an abnormally slow pulse) and be vulnerable to fainting attacks. Again such features are indications that the sufferer needs to reverse her weight loss if she is not to run increasing risks. Any abnormality of heart rhythm or prolongation of the QT interval on the ECG would be an indication for a suitable specialist opinion (Cooke *et al.*, 1994). Drugs such as some antidepressants and neuroleptics which may increase the QT interval may be best avoided.

Gastrointestinal Problems

Most anorexia nervosa sufferers experience some physical symptoms and notable amongst these are gastrointestinal symptoms. Not surprisingly, constipation is common as are feelings of bloating and 'indigestion'. These issues were touched upon in the previous section on drugs. Sometimes abdominal symptoms may reflect the onset of ulcer disease which may need treatment in its own right. On the whole, the criteria for action in relation to abdominal complaints in anorexia nervosa patients are similar to those which would be appropriate in other people. If it would usually be a cause for concern or treatment, a symptom should be a similar cause for concern with an anorexia patient. This would be the case with the rare but painful and dangerous complication of acute dilatation of the stomach (Abdu, Garritano & Culver, 1987). This presents as an acute abdominal emergency and needs to be managed as such. Find a surgeon and get the patient into hospital.

Electrolytes and Fluid Balance

Sufferers who vomit or abuse laxatives or diuretics may become dehydrated or otherwise have their internal chemical environment seriously deranged (Mitchell, Pyle, Eckert, Hatsukami & Lentz, 1983). They should have their blood taken for electrolyte estimations. If abnormalities are found or the behaviours persist, such investigation should be repeated at regular intervals. The most common and significant abnormality is a low potassium level (hypokalaemia). Hypokalaemia is potentially dangerous in two respects. Most immediately it may lead to cardiac arrhythmias which may – fortunately rarely – lead to sudden death. An ECG is an important investigation both as an assessment of this risk and as an indicator of intracellular electrolyte status. Chronic hypokalaemia can lead to renal disease. Often, but not always, hypokalaemia occurs together with general signs of dehydration. The seriousness of electrolyte disruption depends upon the weight of the patient and whether the state is thought to be acute or chronic. On the other hand, it seems to be common clinical sense to worry about someone who has abnormal electrolyte levels and also has her health compromised by a very low or rapidly declining weight. However, at least some people who vomit or abuse laxatives over years seem to be able to tolerate a degree of hypokalaemia that would be very alarming if discovered in others. In someone who is newly ill in some way, a potassium level of, say, 2.4 mmol/l would be thought of as a medical emergency. Hospital admission under a physician and intravenous replacement might well be indicated. In contrast, a sufferer from chronic bulimic anorexia nervosa may run levels of this kind over months without catastrophe, although presumably she is at some risk. However, she should perhaps be protected from the overzealous interventions of those who would treat her as if she, too, was experiencing a new medical emergency. In particular the rapid intravenous replacement of fluid and electrolytes in such a compromised person can itself have its dangers.

The best treatment of electrolyte disturbance is for the individual to stop the vomiting or other behaviours which have promoted it. If that happens, all other things being equal, the body's own homeostatic mechanisms will sort out the internal environment within hours or days. Abnormal blood findings can be used to encourage a patient to change but heavy-handed scare tactics can be counterproductive. Likewise, admission to hospital may be useful as an additional means to the end of controlling behaviour, but it would be naive to assume that any admission in any circumstance will stop potentially dangerous behaviour. Whilst the patient struggles to change it may be appropriate to prescribe oral potassium supplements. This should be discussed with the patient and described merely as first aid. It is rather like trying to fill a bucket with a hole in it. It makes much more sense to repair the bucket. The clinician should beware of giving the impression that vomiting is now acceptable if the patient takes her tablets.

Oedema may be a manifestation of disturbance in fluid and electrolyte imbalance in anorexia nervosa. It is present to some degree in a substantial minority of cases and in a few may be a major feature. The mechanism is often unclear, but oedema is a regular feature of malnutrition in general ('famine oedema'). Low plasma proteins are sometimes evoked as the cause for some cases but more often than not they are normal.

Whatever the cause, oedema can complicate the management of anorexia nervosa if only through making the assessment of true core body weight difficult. Thus an oedematous patient who is improving in every respect, including gaining body substance, might seem to be losing weight as measured on the scales because of loss of excessive fluid.

A particularly mysterious and problematic type of oedema occurs in a minority of patients in the early stages of re-feeding. This can sometimes be quite dramatic with the appearance of substantial swelling over a few days with associated gain in measured body weight which may go up by several kilograms over a week. The patient is often distressed by this both as a symptom in its own right and as the apparent fulfilment of all of her fears that eating a little more will lead to sudden massive weight gain. In general the symptom is self-limiting and can be ridden out. However, if it is severe and troublesome the prescription of potassium sparing diuretics may be appropriate. The mechanism of re-feeding oedema is not known. Clinical experience suggests that it is most common in patients who habitually abuse laxatives. It may be a good idea to predict the phenomenon to such patients if they are about to embark on a re-feeding programme. If nothing happens then little is lost. If they do get oedema, they may be able to cope with it rather better if it has been so anticipated.

Menstruation

Of course, one of the defining features of anorexia nervosa is the absence of menses (amenorrhoea) in females. That is a physical feature to which sufferers have differing attitudes. In general, it is not a feature that requires treatment, but it is a signal that all is not well physically and many sufferers see its return as an index of recovery. Indeed, it is usually as progress occurs with weight restoration that demands for intervention arise. Return of spontaneous menstruation occurs early in some patients but in some it is delayed for months after full weight restoration, or even longer. Sometimes this may be explained by continued dietary chaos but sometimes it is mysterious. In the main, there is little to said for early intervention with drugs or hormones and it usually seems best to await a natural return of periods. When patience runs out it is possible to kick start menstruation with drugs such as clomiphene, but such interventions are best left to specialists in the field of gynaecological endocrinology.

Of course, amenorrhoea is primary in young girls who develop anorexia nervosa before their menarche. The active management of such matters in very young sufferers is an even more specialist business. However, as ever, the prime task of the eating disorder specialist is to help the individual to get back to the normal track of development in terms of body weight and eating as soon as possible. Growth and development will usually resume if this can be achieved, although an individual who has experienced a major episode of anorexia nervosa in her early adolescence may never gain the stature that might have been expected otherwise. Her growth may be permanently stunted in this sense.

Osteoporosis

The effect of anorexia nervosa upon the bones is important because it is one feature that does not seem to be readily reversible by weight gain. A significant minority of anorexia sufferers develop detectable thinning of the bones (osteoporosis) and some experience major problems in relation to this (Serpell & Treasure, 1997). For instance, they may suffer pathological fractures or vertebral collapse (Rigotti, Neer, Skates, Herzog & Nussbaum, 1991). Often, however, the problem is silent and represents an ongoing physical vulnerability. It may be useful to detect the problem and the best method is by a DEXA (dual energy X-ray absorptiometry) scan. This allows the patient to know the state of her health in this respect and may motivate her to change. It should provide yet another good reason for the patient to seek to recover, and for some it will be experienced in that way. Recovery with restoration of weight will halt the progress of osteoporosis and probably lead to the chance of some recovery of bone density. This prospect provides a rational reason for weight gain but, of course, the whole business of facing recovery is not a calmly rational one. Some sufferers may react to the possible permanence of the problem with stoked up despair and a feeling that recovery is not worth while. They should perhaps be told that bone is not dead tissue that has no capacity to recover. The problem is that at present it is not entirely clear how best such recovery may be promoted. The prescription of calcium supplements seems to be rational. However, the routine use of hormonal preparations is more problematic since there are some reasons to believe that they may not be helpful and at present there is no definitive evidence in their favour (Serpell & Treasure, 1997). It is at least possible that some future therapeutic advance may radically change the current somewhat gloomy picture. This argument could be very real for a woman of 25 with osteoporosis. Some new treatment which becomes available in 20 years' time might still lessen the risks of complications in old age.

NEUROLOGICAL PROBLEMS

Another form of covert physical change may occur in the brains of some anorectic subjects. This might be thought to be especially relevant in such a disorder. There have been a number of studies which have demonstrated evidence of changes in brain anatomy using various kinds of imaging techniques (Ellison & Foong, 1998). The most consistent findings are of apparent cerebral atrophy with ventricular enlargement and sulcal widening. However, although these changes have been observed repeatedly they are of uncertain significance. The relationship between the changes in structure and any impairment in function is uncertain. Furthermore, it is not clear to what extent the changes are fully reversed on weight restoration. Once again, perhaps, the message is that anorexia nervosa is a state in which it is best not to linger. However, if some degree of such abnormality is found on a brain scan in an anorectic patient it should not necessarily be taken as a sign that some additional pathology is at work.

Peripheral neuropathy may occur in anorexia nervosa (Patchell, Fellows & Humphries, 1994) and may be the result of nutritional deficiency. Prominent amongst these deficiencies is that of thiamine. The more dramatic neuropsychiatric manifestations of such deficiency, Korsakoff's psychosis or Wernicke's encephalopathy, have been reported only rarely in anorexia nervosa. However, it could be that the milder forms of cognitive impairment associated with thiamine deficiency might play some part in promoting the non-specific symptoms of the disorder (Winston et al., 1999). There is a case for routine supplementation with thiamine in severe disorder. Prescription of adequate doses should be tried if patients complain of symptoms suggestive of deficiency.

A proportion of anorexia sufferers experience seizures (Patchell, Fellows & Humphries, 1994). Of course, this is also true for a proportion of the general population. Nevertheless, there probably is an excess of fits amongst those with eating disorders. It seems likely that some of the behaviours and consequences of eating disorder may tip some people who perhaps have a somewhat low ictal threshold into having frank seizures. New fits occurring in those with anorexia nervosa should be investigated in the same way as with others.

MANAGEMENT OF VERY SEVERE DISORDER

The management of anorexia nervosa with very severe physical manifestations is a complicated business. It presents a problematic mix of issues. On the one hand, the psychological problems, fear, mixed feelings and their interpersonal manifestations in terms of difficulty in trusting others are likely to be at least as prominent in the very severe case as in the less severe. However, the physical problems add their own pressures to the situation for both the patient and the clinician. The patient is at risk of death and yet problems of cooperation may still occur. The mix of skills required to manage such situations is unusual and particular. This is a very specialised business. It takes time and a special service to build experience in dealing with what are fortunately rather rare patients. The team of clinicians involved – psychiatrists, nurses, physicians – need to have confidence in each other if they are to manage optimally the risks involved. The psychiatrist – or whoever – needs to be able to rely on his own knowledge and to know when to turn to the internal physician. However, in many circumstances the physician, although knowledgeable about dealing with very sick patients, may not be very experienced in managing the reluctant anorectic. The ideal situation is one where a group of people build up both trust and experience together by handling a series of such patients.

Some of the psychological traps and dilemmas will be discussed further in Chapter 10 which is entitled 'What may go wrong?'. What follows is a very brief discussion of some of the physical problems and issues that may be encountered in dealing with very severely ill patients. They will assume a moderately cooperative patient.

In general, people with anorexia nervosa should be able to cope physically with eating a normal diet if they can allow themselves to do so. However, a person at very low weight – say BMI 13 or below – may be importantly weakened in some respects. Her heart may be affected and find it difficult to manage a sudden increase in its workload. A way in which this may happen is if a notable sodium (salt) load is given too quickly and overloads the circulation. This can occur if a dehydrated patient is rehydrated rapidly with salty fluids, and the danger is greater if this is done intravenously. In such circumstances the heart may fail and pulmonary oedema and death may follow. In most cases it may be safer to rehydrate even a severely ill patient by mouth or via a naso-gastric tube, thus allowing the gut to act as an additional buffer to the circulation. In such circumstances the patient's fluid balance, circulatory state, ECG and blood electrolyte levels need to monitored carefully until she is stable. A low salt diet may be a useful precaution in beginning the re-feeding of emaciated patients when this is done entirely by mouth. In general, once the patient has been eating and gaining weight for a few weeks the low salt diet may be relaxed.

The use of a naso-gastric tube as a means of feeding may sometimes be justified as a way of reliably delivering nutrition to a patient who is in extreme physical need and for whom the burden of decision and effort involved in feeding in the usual way is temporarily so difficult as to place her at risk. However, it should almost always be done with the explicit cooperation of the patient and as a short-term measure over a few days only.[13]

The management of nutrition in this way is an instance of a case where the technical advice of a dietician can be of great value.

Rapid re-feeding in an emaciated state may precipitate hypophosphataemia. This may be associated with a variety of symptoms including weakness, delirium and cardiac arrhythmias and can be serious or even fatal (Beumont & Large, 1991; Birmingham, Alotham & Goldner, 1996). It seems to arise through a lack of reserves being exposed by the needs of re-feeding. Once again the risks are probably lower when re-feeding is by mouth. Hypoglycaemia may occur, but is perhaps surprisingly uncommon as a clinical problem. Likewise, hypocalcaemia, hypomagnesaemia and low levels of zinc have been reported but seem to rarely cause problems in practice.[14]

MANAGEMENT OF THE TRULY CHRONIC CASE

Most people who suffer from anorexia nervosa eventually improve and recover. However, some do not. The particular needs of those who remain stuck within the condition for many years are often neglected. Whilst it is true that no patient should be written off as having no chance of recovery, some patients are not well served by the kind of treatment offers and interventions which are aimed at those who are less stuck. Thus, someone who has been ill for 15 years and has perhaps been admitted to hospital on several occasions is unlikely to benefit from another attempt at weight restoration in hospital unless she is clearly stating that she wants to aim at full recovery. Too often people with chronic anorexia nervosa are recycled through treatment regimes which do not really address their particular needs. However, it is not always clear what these needs are. The following are some suggestions based upon clinical experience but the issue has not received the systematic attention that it deserves.

One thing that chronic sufferers seem to need is a lasting relationship with a clinician – or team of clinicians within a service – who can provide a context in which to consider their difficulties and options for their amelioration. One option which should always be kept open is the option of radical recovery. The clinician needs to keep this possibility alive as an option whilst not pressing it too hard or playing down the difficulties. Indeed, there needs to be consideration of the difficulties of living a life *without* anorexia nervosa were recovery to occur against all the odds. To some sufferers anorexia nervosa and the accommodations it requires become a way of life. If a woman is now 43 and has lived this way of life since she was a teenager, 'recovery' is almost a misnomer since getting out of anorexia nervosa would place her in a position which she has never before occupied. She may have almost no experience of being anything like a healthy adult and none at all of being a middle-aged woman at normal weight. Other chronic sufferers lead a busy life around their anorexia. For them, getting rid of it may involve opening themselves up to all sorts of emotions and distress. Again the cost of losing this way of being may be considerable. Such a change may seem to threaten much that they value. And yet, escaping from anorexia nervosa must always be there as a possibility. The clinician needs to be receptive to both sides of the dilemma. If he pushes too hard for change, he risks both being insensitive to the difficulties and provoking resistance. If he accepts things as they are too much, he risks seeming to write the sufferer off as a hopeless case. The role which I have described may be occupied appropriately by a member or members of an eating disorders service or other specialist mental health team. However, it is important that such a lasting role should be occupied by one of the more 'chronic' – in the sense of long-lasting – members of the team. Otherwise, the patient's contact may feel like an endless series of fresh starts with new team members each of whom brings her own style and agenda. Often this role can be accomplished with only occasional outpatient contacts at, say, two or three monthly intervals. An alternative is for this role to be occupied by the general practitioner or family doctor who may well be able to provide the necessary long-term contact.

The person with chronic anorexia nervosa is likely to have significant associated problems of physical and mental health. The issue of osteoporosis has been discussed above. There may be many less specific physical symptoms and problems which require assessment and possibly treatment. Likewise, depression, anxiety or obsessional problems may need attention. All of these need to be looked at within the context of anorexia nervosa, but not dismissed as its inevitable consequences. What can be done should be at least offered. It should be remembered that many of the deaths in anorexia nervosa are suicides.

Lastly, the person may need help in making the most of her life within and around her condition. How this is best achieved is likely to vary from person to person. For some, special groups or self-help organisations may provide support and social encouragement to an otherwise isolated sufferer. For others, their wish may be to build up social contacts which have nothing to do with their illness. Even some people who suffer from severe and chronic anorexia nervosa manage to sustain a successful working life. They may have good social skills in that respect but great fears about some other aspects of life. Again the trick for them, and those who would help them, is to try to build on their strengths whilst not totally neglecting what they find difficult. Few specialist services make good provision for those with truly chronic anorexia nervosa. There is need for more thought and innovative practice in this area. A framework of ideas from rehabilitation may be useful. The issue of chronicity will be discussed again in Chapter 10.

SERVICE ORGANISATION

The business of helping people with anorexia nervosa is complex. The two overlapping elements of clinical management and therapy need to be combined with appropriate physical care. Furthermore, in general, all of these are personal matters in which individual clinicians, therapists and practitioners cannot be substituted one for another without detriment to the relationship with the patient upon which their effectiveness often importantly depends. A problem of service organisation is how to square the circle of providing all of these elements in practical ways which preserve this personal quality and continuity as much as possible. Some of the difficulties of service organisation and some of the possible solutions for them will be discussed in Chapter 11.

NOTES

1. An image I have used elsewhere is of someone who can walk with ease along a plank placed upon the ground but who would be terrified to do so if it were suspended high in the air. The task is the same. The fears and circumstances are quite different. To the anorexia nervosa sufferer the act of eating a meal must at times feel like the walk across the high plank. To those around her it seems such a simple business; to them it is as if the plank were on the ground. Their exhortations and reassurances fall on ears deafened by fear. Of course, this analogy misses something of the complexity of the sufferer's dilemma. It ignores the fact that, in general, a woman with anorexia nervosa has a big urge to eat. Perhaps the picture requires that there is a crock of gold at the other end of the plank. But images that get too complex lose their point.
2. Like any metaphor, this talk of building, damage, repair and scaffolding expresses only part of the matter. At best, the relationship between the patient and professionals who would help her needs to be expressed in much more human terms such as trust, respect and so on. Indeed, negative emotions may also be involved, and even these may have their role. Moving on from 'help' may involve a sense of both loss and relief.

3. It seems to me that it is only a modest play on words to describe the treatment of anorexia nervosa as a kind of confidence trick. The sufferer needs to do difficult things if she is to recover. She has to put herself through it. In order to do so, she borrows confidence and some sense of safety from the clinician who would help her. The clinician in turn needs to have some faith in what he is offering. He needs to believe in it for this purpose although, of course, unbridled faith can lead to rigidity and error.

4. I dithered a good deal about how best to arrange the issues in this chapter. I found that whatever way it was done, there was a way in which the emphasis felt wrong and there was scope for misinterpretation. The problem with the present arrangement is that it puts inpatient treatment first and management before therapy. Things that are put first tend to be thought more important. The problem is that recovery from anorexia nervosa involves several tasks and, in practice, they are best done together. Likewise, attempts to help involve both what I have called management and therapy, and these are also better done together. So where do you start? The order which I have adopted may well not be the best. I hope that it will do as well as any. It will serve provided that its arbitrary nature is borne in mind.

5. The account that follows inevitably reflects my own views, practices and indeed prejudices with regard to inpatient treatment. These are based upon my own experience and intuitions and upon my reading of the views of others. In the absence of evidence that is hard and neat, it cannot be otherwise. However, I recognise that other clinicians approach things differently, at least in detail. My justification in presenting mainly my own views is that it would be perverse not to do so and that I have at least flagged up their fallible and provisional nature. Box 7.2 gives some particulars of the inpatient regime which operated at the Leicester General Hospital at the time of writing. Like many regimes it has evolved slowly and will probably change further with time.

6. We coined, and now use, the term 'plateau weight' in Leicester to emphasise that reaching a satisfactory weight is only a stage in a long process. Hitting a target conjures up images of something having come to an end, whereas a journey may be only just beginning when a plateau is achieved after a climb. Furthermore, climbing is usually a constrained and arduous business, whereas travel on the plateau may be full of opportunities – if you keep away from the edge. After all, most people live on the plateau. In Leicester, the plateau weight is defined in most cases as the weight corresponding to a BMI of 20. (See Box 7.2 for further details of the Leicester regime.) The patient is expected to reach such a weight and then sustain that weight within a

kilogram or so. If, in the longer term after having reached such a plateau, an individual seems 'naturally' and without restraint to sustain a healthy weight which is above or below this, that is fine. The plateau weight is essentially a best guess and a tool for starting a life without undue restraint.

7. In Leicester, in line with our general approach, we have clear expectations of what the patient should eat. Patients attend the Day Programme five days each week and have two meals on most days. The details of these meals are arranged as for inpatients. Indeed, current inpatients attend the Day Programme from the ward, which is in the same building, after the first two or three weeks of their admission. When individuals have reached plateau weight there may be some self-catering, preparation of packed meals, visits to restaurants and so on. People who do not progress because they cannot bring themselves to eat adequately are, in due course, confronted with the choice of seeking more security and supervision by opting for full admission or moving back to being simply an outpatient. Hanging around the Day Programme without making progress is not an option for long.

8. I am aware that some people would take a precisely contrary view and base it on similar grounds. They would argue that because weight and eating and wider issues were so entangled it is helpful that they are separated off as the concerns of different clinicians – for instance, one acting as a 'psychotherapist' and one as, for instance, a 'dietician'. (The inverted commas are meant to convey the idea that in this context these words refer to roles rather than professions.) Doubtless, such an arrangement can work. However, personally, I am unconvinced that it is optimal. It is not usually the best way to sort out a tangled ball of wool to get hold of either end and pull. It usually involves a lot more than that. In practice, the 'psychotherapist' is likely to have to think a lot about weight and eating and the 'dietician' a lot about beliefs and emotions, so why separate the roles?

9. There is not room here to do justice to the rich literature on the way in which different psychotherapies and psychotherapists have thought about and treated anorexia nervosa. The point that I am making is that in our present state of ignorance about what is best, experienced psychotherapists should probably stick to the broad framework with which they are most comfortable. They need to adapt it to the circumstance rather than adopting some other framework just because they are dealing with an anorectic patient. However, an open mind is required. Therapists need to read the contributions of those who write from within their own favoured orientation but may be able to learn from reading more widely also. Some key references are included at the end of the chapter as entry points into the literature.

10. In the past in the United Kingdom within the National Health Service, such a role was often taken by a specialist social worker. Such workers were employed by Local Authority Social Services Departments but attached to the Health Service. The best were very knowledgeable and skilful practitioners. They made a valuable contribution. However, over recent years redefinition and reorganisation of social work services have led, almost universally, to such professionals being withdrawn at least from services for adults. Seniors such as myself bemoan the passing of this group of specialised professionals.

11. In my own practice, we tend to arrange family meetings every few weeks for those anorexia nervosa sufferers who are in our inpatient or day patient programmes. The meeting brings together the sufferer, her family, the therapist, the key worker from the ward and myself as consultant. The first meeting tends to follow a pattern in which the purpose of the meeting is explained as one of sharing the views of key people involved one way or other in the difficult business of the patient's attempt at progress towards recovery. The past is defined as important only inasmuch as it illuminates or still influences the present. The focus is explicitly on things that help to promote progress now. An important function is to try to modify any unrealistic expectations that the patient is likely to feel and be 'better' as soon as weight is restored. I find myself repeating at many a meeting that 'if things go very well' when the patient reaches a normal weight she will feel 'mixed up, unhappy, uncertain and full of difficult feelings'. I suggest that through negotiating this emotional obstacle course lies the prospect of true recovery. This often seems to come true and it is better that everyone should expect this than that such emotional turmoil arrives unexpectedly and is seen as failure. If things go more smoothly than expected, having predicted otherwise is no problem.

12. In writing this account, I have tried to strike a balance between merely producing a brief list of major complications and trying to be inclusive of all of the things that can go wrong. I have tended more towards the former for four reasons. Firstly, the list of potential problems is very long indeed and is certainly too long to discuss each in detail in a book such as this. Secondly, there are a number of reviews available. Thirdly, I am no expert myself on all of the physical complications and how to manage them. Fourthly, the role of the clinician treating someone with anorexia nervosa is to have suitably informed clinical nous and to know when to ask for the help of others. The extent to which the clinician needs to enlist others will depend upon his professional background but all will need to involve others sometimes. However, every clinician needs to know something of the range of problems, how they

may be manifest, what to do or what to ask others to look at. That is what this section sets out to do for the more common or important problems.

13. Some clinicians use naso-gastric feeding rather more readily than this. I respect their judgement. I have used it in only two or three cases in twenty years or so of practice in the field of eating disorder. In each of those cases, there were unusual features. Most patients, even those with very severe disorder, manage to eat and drink sufficiently by mouth.

14. Zinc deficiency as an issue in – if not the cause of – anorexia nervosa had a brief popularity as an idea a decade or more ago after some claims by a scientist were widely reported in a Sunday newspaper. For a while many sufferers took zinc supplements bought at health shops. They did not seem to offer much benefit. The idea seemed simplistic to the majority of clinicians and did not gain much credence amongst professionals. However, there is one trial that suggests that zinc supplementation may be beneficial (Birmingham, Goldner & Bakan, 1994). All of these rarer complications of severe anorexia nervosa occur, but as the old saying goes, 'rare things are rare'. In my own practice, or in consulting with others, I have come across all of the problems mentioned in this chapter except those mentioned in this last paragraph. However, it is clearly important to know about these issues and to be on the look-out for them, especially when dealing with severely ill patients who are not doing well.

FURTHER READING

van Furth, E F (1998) The treatment of anorexia nervosa. In: Hoek, H W, Treasure, J L & Katzman, M A (Editors) *Neurobiology in the Treatment of Eating Disorders*. John Wiley & Sons, Chichester and New York.

Garner, D M & Garfinkel, P E (Editors) (1997*) Handbook of Treatment for Eating Disorders* (second edition). Guilford Press, New York.

Sharpe, C W & Freeman, C P L (1993) The medical complications of anorexia nervosa. *British Journal of Psychiatry*, **162**, 452–462.

Szmukler, G, Dare, C & Treasure, J (Editors) (1995) *Handbook of Eating Disorders: Theory, Treatment and Research*. John Wiley & Sons, Chichester and New York.

8

WHAT HELPS PEOPLE WITH BULIMIA NERVOSA?

Someone who has sought help from a professional for bulimia nervosa or a closely related state and who has gone through some process of assessment is likely to want to escape from her condition. She is likely to be willing to invest her time, effort and, in some systems, her money in the endeavour. However, this does not mean that all of her fears and mixed feelings will have been resolved. She may well underestimate what is involved in recovery and overestimate the potency of the therapy or the clinician who provides it. Attention to the process of engagement in the tasks of recovery must continue beyond assessment. Many sufferers drop out even of established therapy.

GENERAL ISSUES

Most treatment of most cases of bulimia nervosa in most countries takes place on an outpatient or 'office' basis without the sufferer being offered admission to hospital.[1] Hospital admission is usually reserved for those sufferers whose state includes a substantial risk of suicide or self-harm or who have notable comorbidity. Sometimes admission may be suggested for those who have failed to respond to outpatient help and for whom residential treatment is thought to offer a better chance.

Certain elements are likely to be common whatever therapy is offered for bulimia nervosa. These need to be explained to the patient even when they may seem obvious to the clinician. Thus, within most kinds of professional therapy, meetings are likely to be held by appointment and the appointments are likely to be at predetermined and predictable times. Indeed in many of the short-term therapies the whole programme of treatment may be fixed from the outset. The type of therapy may dictate the style of interaction to some degree, but most treatments require an explicitly collaborative approach in which both the patient and therapist are active in the common task of overcoming the disorder and any issues which are thought to perpetuate it. However, although the interaction may be friendly and in some cases informal, the relationship between the clinician and the sufferer needs to be, in the best sense, 'professional' and contained by appropriate boundaries. The broad nature of the treatment and the 'rules of the game' need to be explained to the patient at the outset and an agreement reached.

The physical state of the patient is another general issue. Assessment of physical issues was emphasised in Chapter 6. If there is cause for concern at assessment, then some mechanism needs to be put in place to reassess this as treatment progresses. The most common need would be for the monitoring of serum electrolytes – especially potassium – in patients who have abnormal results at the outset or who are continuing to engage in frequent vomiting or substantial laxative or diuretic abuse. Within many treatment settings this monitoring can be comfortably encompassed within the therapeutic relationship. In others, some special and parallel system may need to be put in place. However, even in patients whose physical state is not a cause for undue concern at the outset there needs to be continuing vigilance and thought about possible physical deterioration. Arguably the most important part of this is simply the clinical common sense of the clinician who is in regular touch with the patient.

What may be called the therapeutic alliance is the relatively little discussed but central 'carrier wave' of all psychological interventions and, indeed, it is the basis of the trust that sustains compliance in drug treatment. Just as with the therapy of anorexia nervosa, expectations and attitudes derived from earlier experiences may affect the sufferer's behaviour. Such experiences may be general or distant, as with issues which would be construed as transferential within a psychodynamic vocabulary. On the other hand, they may be more recent and particular as when a sufferer has had a bad time in previous treatment or has been poorly received when she has talked with family or friends about her problems. The therapeutic alliance needs to contain all of this. Of course, the psychodynamic concept of countertransference is also relevant here. The clinician's expectations and attitudes may have powerful and unexpected effects. Therapy of all kinds can best be kept on track if the clinician is clear about the limits of the therapy and delivers what he says he will and does not say that he will deliver things that he cannot or does not intend to deliver. All of these matters need to be thought about. However, such particular issues which differ from patient to patient will largely be neglected in the following discussion of what has been found to be helpful to people seeking to recover from bulimia nervosa in general.

PARTICULAR TREATMENTS

Gerald Russell's first paper on bulimia nervosa named the condition as an *ominous* variant of anorexia nervosa (Russell, 1979). This carried the inference that it was especially difficult to treat. This may have been true –

and indeed may even remain true – of the kind of case that was described. Russell's cases were collected from patients referred to a tertiary treatment centre with a high reputation. Such centres tend to attract patients who have disorders which are especially severe and difficult to treat. However, the concept of bulimia nervosa has found broader application over the years and more and more people have presented for help with the condition. The typical patient has changed and there has been a widening in the range of severity and complication. Most are at normal weight and have never had anorexia nervosa, which may have made the therapeutic task more straightforward on average. Certainly, most clinicians would now think of bulimia nervosa as *typically* – although, of course, not always – more responsive to treatment than typical anorexia nervosa. Perhaps the change in patient characteristics has been important but there has also been major progress in developing and evaluating particular treatments for bulimia nervosa. At present, not only is the treatment of bulimia nervosa better researched than that of anorexia nervosa, it is better researched than that of many psychiatric disorders. It seems that this happy state arose through certain key individuals responding to the uncluttered therapeutic challenge of a 'new' condition with great gusto and to great effect. A bandwagon rolled. The progress has been remarkable. However, as will become clear, the presently available treatments are not universally efficacious and, indeed, even in the best hands, leave a substantial proportion of patients still suffering from the disorder.

The treatments for bulimia nervosa which have been most researched, and for which there is the best evidence of efficacy, are psychotherapeutic. This is itself unusual and is certainly not the case for most psychiatric conditions. Psychotherapy research and evaluation tends to lag behind the easier business of examining drug treatments. However, the emergence of bulimia nervosa coincided with the rise of cognitive behavioural therapy (CBT) and its associated research emphasis. The new enthusiasm met the new problem. A specific variant of CBT came to be the 'gold standard' treatment for the disorder. However, other psychotherapies have also been shown to be of benefit, as have some drug treatments and forms of 'self-help'. The following is a summary of the present state of the art.[2]

Cognitive Behavioural Psychotherapy

The term 'cognitive behavioural' refers to a general orientation to psychological treatment which puts dysfunctional beliefs at the centre of its model of disorder and change. Characteristically the style of therapy is described as one of active collaboration and experimentation in which the therapist and patient together explore and seek to change beliefs which are thought to importantly underpin problems. There may be some attention to the past development of the disorder but the chief focus is on ideas, behaviours and modes of thought which may be currently perpetuating the disorder. The archetype of much such treatment is the cognitive therapy of depression devised by Aaron Beck (Beck, Rush, Shaw & Emery, 1979). Recording and monitoring often play a central role in therapy. Such continuous evaluation – both of the progress of the particular patient and of the efficacy of interventions – greatly facilitates research. CBT seems often to be the best form of psychotherapy for a variety of disorders. It is nearly always the best evaluated. This is the case for the cognitive behavioural therapy of bulimia nervosa.

The use of CBT for bulimia nervosa was pioneered in the early 1980s by Christopher Fairburn of the University of Oxford and it has subsequently been developed and refined (Fairburn, 1981). It has also been extensively evaluated both by Fairburn's own team and by others (Wilson, Fairburn & Agras, 1997). The treatment is based around an aetiological model which postulates a series of highly plausible links between low self-esteem, beliefs about the importance of body size and shape, eating restraint, bingeing and vomiting. (This is set out in diagrammatic form in Box 8.1) This model of the disorder is used explicitly within the treatment and is shared with the patient. It is the rationale for the treatment and forms the practical framework within which the particular interventions are construed.

The standard form of CBT is that devised by Fairburn and described in the treatment manual co-authored with Marcus and Wilson (Fairburn, Marcus & Wilson, 1993). The outline of the treatment is set out in Box 8.2. It is a highly structured treatment both overall and within each session. Its originators and advocates would argue that it should be applied routinely in the way that is closely specified by the manual. They advise that there is no good reason to deviate from the prescription of the manual in order to try to tailor the therapy to the individual patient, and indeed to do so risks losing efficacy (Wilson, Fairburn & Agras, 1997). Some experienced therapists find the thought of following the prescription of a therapy manual uncongenial and would argue from principle that, when faced with a particular patient, they should know better than any manual what to do. Such a view has intuitive appeal although human hunch is often in error and we should be humble enough to put such matters to the test. In this case, the evidence favours the manual, although it must be recognised that the collection of evidence is likely to be biased in that direction. However, it is certainly arguable that this is a treatment better given 'off the peg' than 'bespoke'. This does not mean that it should be delivered mechanically. Indeed, when done well the treatment is a very human collaboration between patient and therapist. Furthermore, there is scope for the exercise

Box 8.1 Fairburn's Cognitive Model of Bulimia Nervosa

The disorder is seen as perpetuated by a viciously circular set of influences in which low self-esteem is associated with an over-valuing of weight and shape and attempts to slim. Eating restraint then leads to break-out bingeing and compensation with a renewed drive to eat and further impaired self-esteem.

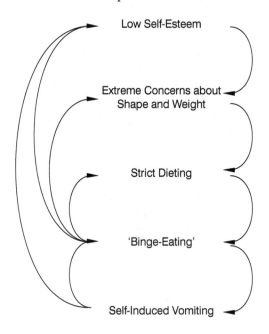

The cognitive view of the maintenance of bulimia nervosa (From Fairburn, Marcus & Wilson (1993). Copyright: Guilford Press.)

of considerable therapeutic skill, not least in preserving a good working alliance throughout the treatment.

As its name implies, CBT focuses upon both beliefs and behaviours and uses techniques which include cognitive restructuring and problem solving as well as behavioural monitoring and homework. More purely, behavioural treatment has been shown to be less efficacious. In the major Oxford trial, a treatment which omitted the cognitive elements of CBT

Box 8.2 Outline of Manual-based CBT for Bulimia Nervosa

The therapy is delivered as an outpatient and usually involves 19 sessions over 20 weeks. Sessions are twice weekly for the first week or two, weekly for the subsequent sessions and then fortnightly from session 16 onwards. Each session lasts up to 50 minutes. The style is collaborative and a good therapist–patient relationship is important.

Stage 1: First 8 Sessions

Involves establishment of the therapeutic relationship. Education of the patient in the cognitive view of the disorder and its effects (see Box 8.1). Establishment of a pattern of weekly weighing and of regular eating. From the first session self-monitoring is introduced. The keeping of a diary to record eating, purging and the context of these behaviours becomes central to the therapeutic enterprise.

The patient is helped to use self-control strategies to regulate her eating and to manage her feelings. For instance, she may be encouraged to use alternative activities when she is at high risk of bingeing or to 'urge surf' to avoid vomiting.

Stage 2: Sessions 9 to 16

In these sessions the self-monitoring continues as do the activities of stage 1. In addition, the eating restraint and the ideas which perpetuate the disorder are addressed.

The therapist seeks to help the patient to reduce and eliminate 'dieting'. The pattern of eating which has been established in stage 1 is shaped up to include more appropriate quantities of food and more foods which have previously been 'forbidden'. The patient may be asked to produce a list of such foods arranged in order of difficulty and to work up this hierarchy, incorporating such foods in her pattern of regular eating. She may be encouraged to eat with others in circumstances such as restaurants where she has less control over what is on offer. The aim is to expose the patient to the consequences of behaviours which had previously been avoided. Behavioural techniques may also be used to expose the patient to fears associated with her beliefs about her body, for instance, by encouraging her to go swimming and to note the characteristics and 'imperfections' of others, especially those who are in general rated as attractive.

In this stage also, the therapist helps the patient to examine and change some of her extreme views on weight, shape and eating (cognitive restructuring) and to find new ways of coping with emotionally demanding situations which might habitually lead to bingeing (problem solving).

Stage 3: Sessions 17, 18 and 19

In these sessions the focus is on consolidation of improvement and relapse prevention. There is discussion of future vulnerability, how to cope with lapses and how to manage times of anticipated risk and vulnerability.

(The above is a brief summary of the treatment which is described in full in Fairburn, Marcus & Wilson, 1993.)

was both less immediately effective and had much less sustained benefit than full CBT (Fairburn et al., 1991; Fairburn, Jones, Peveler, Hope & O'Connor, 1993).

Some workers have advocated particular behavioural techniques either as components of a CBT approach or as treatments in their own right. One technique is that of exposure and response prevention (Rosen & Leitenberg, 1985; Leitenberg, Rosen, Gross, Nudelman & Vara, 1988). This involves the sufferer being encouraged to eat in a binge-like fashion and then to avoid the vomiting which would be the usual consequence of such eating. This treatment can be delivered as an outpatient but requires unusually long sessions, and an alternative is to use a brief intensive admission (Tuschen & Bents, 1995). The rationale is that vomiting is seen as reinforcing bingeing through reducing the fear of weight gain which would otherwise follow. The procedure is aimed at extinguishing this link. However, exposure and response prevention is not an easy treatment. It is a time-consuming business and many patients may be reluctant to cooperate. The evidence seems to be that it adds little or nothing to standard CBT (Agras, Schneider, Arnow, Raeburn & Telch, 1989; Wilson, Eldridge, Smith & Niles, 1991). Likewise as an alternative component added to an abbreviated CBT it has only transient superiority to a relaxation control treatment (Bulik, Sullivan, Carter, McIntosh & Joyce, 1998). Response prevention has had its enthusiasts, but on balance it does not seem to deserve a place in the canon of usual techniques (Carter & Bulik, 1994). It should probably be relegated to the box of tricks that may be raided when therapist and patient feel thoroughly stuck.

There is now evidence from many trials that manual-based CBT is an effective treatment in bulimia nervosa (Wilson, Fairburn & Agras, 1997). Indeed, the extent of this formal evaluation and its positive results have made CBT the standard against which other treatments should be judged. It has been shown in a number of clinical trials that the benefits of CBT in bulimia nervosa tend to be lasting. Most notably a major trial demonstrated that CBT treatment effects were sustained at one year and six year follow up (Fairburn et al., 1993, 1995). Where it is available, CBT is likely to be the treatment of choice to be recommended to most people suffering from bulimia nervosa. However, it is neither universally efficacious nor without its disadvantages or limitations (Schmidt, 1998). Even in the best hands it seems to lead to complete or nearly complete remission of symptoms in only about half of cases whilst being somewhat helpful in rather more. This is impressive but leaves perhaps a quarter to a third of those treated still suffering from significant eating disorder. Furthermore, standard CBT is a moderately demanding and expensive treatment in that it requires around 20 hours of contact with an appropriately trained therapist. Such therapists are not always and everywhere available. There are other treatment approaches.

Standard manual-based CBT sets out to shape up a new pattern of eating and to help the sufferer to change the beliefs that have sustained the old one. In the terms of the tasks of recovery outlined in Chapter 5, it places most emphasis on tasks one and two. Problem-solving skills are developed which may be relevant to task three – progress in wider issues – but as applied within the treatment these skills tend to be focused on situations where eating symptoms have occurred or are likely to occur if some new way of behaving is not found. (Of course, it is possible to take a cognitive behavioural approach to such wider issues, but this is not part of the standard treatment.) By contrast, the other psychotherapeutic treatment for which there is impressive evidence of efficacy in bulimia nervosa – namely, Interpersonal Psychotherapy – concentrates largely on the wider personal issues, that is, upon the third task of recovery.

Interpersonal Psychotherapy (IPT)

Interpersonal Psychotherapy (IPT) is a particular brief psychotherapy which, like CBT, was first developed as a treatment for major depression (Klerman, Weissman, Rounsaville & Chevron, 1984). It was originally the creation of the late Dr Gerald Klerman and Dr Myrna Weissman – a psychiatrist and a psychologist respectively. They designed their new therapy for use within a research project and until recently IPT has been better known and more used in research than in clinical practice. Indeed, the same

Box 8.3 Interpersonal Psychotherapy (IPT) for Bulimia Nervosa

IPT is a brief outpatient therapy which typically involves about 15 to 20 sessions which occur weekly, except for the last three or four which may be offered fortnightly. The whole treatment therefore lasts around five months or so. Each session lasts for up to 50 minutes or some similar fixed time. The focus in general is on the here and now and in particular is on the current interpersonal relationships of the patient. Indeed, one or two particular problem areas are made the focus of treatment. Furthermore, the discussion and exploration is in terms of the interpersonal rather than the intrapsychic world of the patient.

The first three or four sessions constitutes the initial 'assessment' phase. Sessions are taken up with explaining the rationale of the treatment, identifying the current interpersonal problems of the patient and choosing a focus for the therapy. The explanation of the treatment may include the idea that interpersonal problems perpetuate bulimia nervosa and that studies have shown that changing these can lead to improvement and recovery. The therapy is presented as an opportunity to change. During these initial sessions there is an exploration of links between the patient's eating disorder and interpersonal issues. Subsequently, the focus is on the latter and the patient is told that the focus will change in that way.

Interpersonal problems are classified for the purpose of IPT as falling into one of four types: namely, 'grief', 'role disputes', 'role transitions' or 'interpersonal deficits'. An issue or set of issues corresponding to one of these categories is chosen as the focus of therapeutic work and attempted change.

In the second phase of treatment – say, from the fifth to the twelfth session – this focus is discussed and the patient is encouraged to try to make changes in relation to the problematic area. The style of interaction with the therapist is collaborative and non-directive except that the therapist actively urges the patient to try out new ways and strategies for change. The therapist tries to keep the patient focused and will use techniques such as clarification and facilitation but not, in general, interpretation or advice.

In the final three or four sessions, the emphasis is on reviewing progress, anticipating future changes and discussing the management of lapse or relapse. Such discussion may include telling the patient that evidence shows that improvement in symptoms characteristically continues after the end of therapy and that the aim has been to improve her competence at dealing with difficulties in her life and that that should continue. The treatment is time limited from the outset, and although the patient should be encouraged to talk about her feelings about ending, IPT should rarely, if ever, be extended beyond the agreed time, although of course other interventions might be indicated immediately or in the future.

(See Fairburn, 1997a, for full account.)

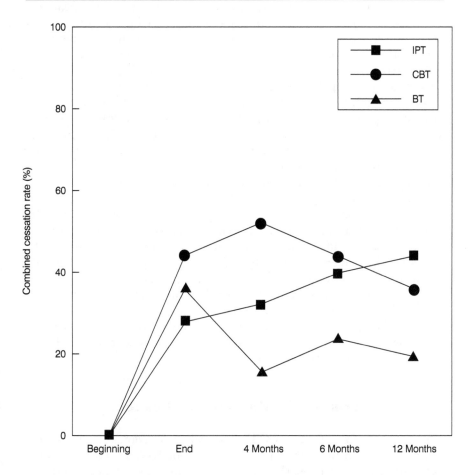

Figure 8.1: Proportions of patients who met strict criteria for a good outcome following CBT, behaviour therapy (BT), or interpersonal psychotherapy (IPT). From Fairburn, Jones, Peveler, Hope, and O'Connor (1993). Copyright 1993 by the American Medical Association. Reprinted by permission.

pattern has been followed with respect to its use in bulimia nervosa. Once again, Christopher Fairburn has played a central role. He chose IPT as a comparison treatment in a trial of CBT (Fairburn *et al.*, 1991, 1993). The idea was to compare CBT with a treatment which did not focus directly on beliefs or symptoms involving weight or eating. IPT was chosen because, as its name implies, it is concerned with examining and promoting change within the current interpersonal world of the sufferer (see Box 8.3). Although some attention is paid to symptoms, especially in the initial assessment phase, the main focus of the therapy is the current pattern of the relationships and problems within them.[3]

The results of the Oxford trial showed that at the end of the 19 treatment sessions delivered over four months, the subjects who had received IPT were doing less well in terms of their symptoms than those who had received either behaviour therapy (BT) or cognitive behavioural therapy (CBT). However, at four months after the end of treatment the patients who had had BT had relapsed somewhat, but the IPT patients were still improving. Indeed, they continued to do so and at eight months they had reached a point where their average state was indistinguishable from those who had received CBT (see Figure 8.1). Remarkably these differences between treatment groups were maintained at one year and six years after treatment (Fairburn *et al.*, 1995). These results have now been broadly replicated in a further major study comparing CBT and IPT (Agras, Walsh, Wilson & Fairburn, 1999).

It would seem that IPT is a psychotherapy with a similar overall efficacy to CBT in bulimia nervosa. However, it clearly has a different time course of response and is likely to work through different mechanisms. The continued improvement after the end of active treatment, together with the focus on issues other than weight concern and eating, suggest that it may work less directly than CBT. Perhaps improvement in life circumstance, relationships, self-esteem and confidence allows the sufferer to test out and relinquish the maladaptive entanglement of these wider issues with weight and eating control. By contrast, CBT may work on this tangle more directly and from the other end as it were.

Doing it by the Book or Bespoke

The evidence for efficacy of CBT, IPT and so on comes from research studies in which these therapies have been delivered according to the relevant therapy manuals. They have quite literally been done by the book. It is, of course, necessary in a comparative research trial to be clear about the treatments being given. This does not mean that the therapy has been given by rote or in an impersonal way, but it does mean that it has been confined within certain predetermined limits which are the same for all the patients. It will not have been adjusted or changed outside of these limits. The treatment is, to use the jargon, 'programme led'. By contrast, in many cases outside of clinical trials therapy tends to be 'therapist led'. This means that the therapist may well change methods and do things differently according to what he judges to be the needs of the particular patient. This is what might be called bespoke therapy. There is a debate about which approach is more effective (Wilson, 1996b). Those who favour programme-led approaches have evidence to back up their claims for efficacy, but have to fall back on anecdotes to support their contention that bespoke approaches are less effective. However, in general, those who advocate bespoke or 'therapist-led 'therapy have to rely entirely on informal tales of their success. In principle, it might be possible to compare the two in a formal way but there would be major difficulties in making such a comparison in practice.

It is likely to be the case that more patients are treated by therapists who do not closely follow any form of manual-based treatment. A kind of conservatism combined with a necessary belief in their own judgement leads many clinicians to create their own styles of therapy rather than follow the prescriptions of others. However, most such therapies are variations on the themes set by the better researched therapies. In the treatment of bulimia nervosa these will usually involve attention both to the issues of lessening the background of eating restraint and examining the ideas that link this with wider issues of self-esteem and the like. The interesting idea that emerges from the CBT and IPT research is that it does seem that therapies which concentrate upon either end of the entanglement may be efficacious. That does not mean, of course, that just any applied therapy will be effective. However, therapies other than CBT and IPT have been studied.

Other Psychotherapies

One of the first psychotherapeutic approaches to bulimia nervosa was described by Hubert Lacey of St George's Hospital Medical School in London in the 1980s (Lacey, 1983). It combined an essentially behavioural approach to symptom control with a more psychodynamically informed therapy for the emerging personal and interpersonal issues. In the original form of the treatment, the former was delivered on an individual basis and the latter in a group, although the two components took place in parallel on the same day. The treatment sessions took place weekly over ten weeks with subsequent follow up. In the first description the patients did well. The treatment has since been modified for delivery on an entirely individual basis although there has been little formal evaluation of it in this form (Lacey, 1992). Furthermore, the treatment has, perhaps surprisingly, not been taken up and evaluated outside of its centre of origin. This may be because it resembles in many ways the better researched CBT approach. Thus, it involves the use of a diary for dietary monitoring. However, there is less shaping up of the diet because the broad outline of an eating plan, rich in carbohydrate, is prescribed and the patient is required to agree to this at the outset. The thoughts and feelings that arise as the patient follows the diet and has fewer binges are the subject of the wider therapy. In practice, within this treatment the therapeutic approach to these wider issues can vary somewhat according to the style of the therapist. It is in this sense less highly specified and more 'therapist led' than CBT. This may make it more congenial for some therapists but probably means that it is more varied and perhaps more variable in outcome. There has been no 'head to head' comparison between this therapy and classic CBT.

Of course, many therapists adopt a psychodynamic approach to the treatment of bulimia nervosa (Johnson, 1991, 1995). The documented efficacy of IPT has supported the idea that treatments for bulimia nervosa may be helpful even when they pay little direct attention to the eating symptoms. However, there is little systematic evidence of the benefits of psychodynamic therapy although, of course, there are many anecdotes and opinions. This is unfortunate and may in part be due to the regrettable tendency for skill in psychodynamic therapy to be associated with a lack of enthusiasm for systematic research and treatment evaluation. This is the reverse of the association which tends to prevail in the world of cognitive-behavioural therapy.

In principle, psychodynamic psychotherapy might well be thought to provide useful insights into the meanings which accrue to the experiences and behaviours of the bulimia sufferer. It certainly seems to be the case that the causes and consequences of eating restraint and of bingeing and purging are likely to be both complex and personal from the outset and to be further complicated by the progress of the disorder. However, in an unmodified form, the psychodynamic stance may tend to overemphasise the symbolic and play down the concrete. At worst such a stance may lead to the lengthy examination of meaning without direct discussion of the option of changing the situation by action in the here and now. Thus, for instance, purging behaviour might be thought of – in a particular case – as reflecting a rejection of any sense of need and a triumph over appetite and dependency. Indeed, such a formulation might accurately reflect the experience of the sufferer and be linked meaningfully with significant issues in her current and past life. Such is the nature of entanglement. However, the same purging behaviour and its consequences may also drive the very experiences – appetite and so on – which, within such a formulation, are thought to drive the urge to purge. Such is the nature of vicious circles. The sufferer is missing something if she does not consider the option of changing her experience through changing her behaviour as well as the other way around. Behaviour and biology can hype up experience and their force can be missed if mechanism is ignored and the focus is exclusively on meaning.[4] Very prolonged examination of the meaning of things as an end in itself can come to be collusive. (See Chapter 10.)

Feminist ideas may also provide a framework for psychotherapeutic work with bulimia sufferers. This framework may involve new ways of attempting to understand the particular disorders, a critique of what are thought of as the traditional power relationships involved in treatment and a tendency to emphasise particular cultural issues as central to aetiology (Wooley, 1995). Ruth Striegal-Moore has written that feminist scholarship tends to be 'relatively uninterested in the question of differential diagnosis and has considered it of greater importance to understand and change the conditions that contribute to psychopathology in general' (Striegal-Moore, 1995). Such scholarship can be illuminating. However, once again, as with psychodynamics, there may be a tendency for the symbolic and archetypal to take over. If the stance of this scholarship constrains the scope of therapy so that the focus is entirely on the cultural dimension, important issues may get left out. It may indeed be liberating for an individual to understand the wider social roots of her desire to be thin and that to dare be otherwise may be to take an important stand for herself and her sisters. However, the particularities of her trapped position may involve vicious circles which contain crucial elements which are personal or biological and outwith this analysis.[5]

Feminist analyses have much to say that is of importance. The most interesting issues concern the way in which particular social forces, aspirations and oppressions come to be – literally – embodied in particular sizes, shapes and body images. In the language of Chapter 5, these are the roots of the entanglement which comes to be central to the eating disorder. Escaping from an eating disorder is in general a positive thing, as is escaping from and changing a position of social, cultural or political oppression. However, doing one does not entail or guarantee the other. Something similar could be said about the kind of entrapment which may arise through family or other relationship issues. Again, therapy which is focused upon and carried out with the family group or the couple of which the sufferer is a member may be useful in defining and changing problems in the sufferer's life. However, assuming that the wider personal issues which have become entangled with weight and eating are necessarily of a kind which are best addressed in this way, involves a conjecture that may not be justified. The evidence in favour of the use of family therapy in the treatment of bulimia nervosa is neither extensive nor impressive (Schwartz, Barrett & Saba, 1985). Furthermore, the better outcome for younger anorexic subjects in the Institute of Psychiatry trial did not apply to bulimia nervosa sufferers (Russell, Szmukler, Dare & Eisler, 1987).

Some people advocate the use of non-verbal therapies for the treatment of bulimia nervosa. Often this is as an adjunct to more conventional treatment but may also be offered as the prime therapy. A rationale can be made for such an approach. It is plausible that a sufferer might be helped to escape from her state by experiencing herself, and especially her body, in a new way through dance, massage or whatever. There is a modest literature on the subject although much of it is either descriptive or theoretical and it provides little evidence for the efficacy of these approaches. Intuitive appeal alone is a poor justification for the use of a therapy in clinical practice. However, it is a good reason for a therapy to be tried out in a circumstance that allows it to be systematically evaluated so that conclusions can be drawn and comparisons made.

GROUP TREATMENTS

Almost all of the treatment approaches mentioned above have been adapted for delivery in small group form (Fettes & Peters, 1992; Polivy & Federoff, 1997). Thus, there is a literature on the group dynamic therapy of bulimia nervosa (e.g. Roy-Byrne, Lee-Benner & Yager, 1984), group CBT (e.g. Schneider & Agras, 1985) and even group IPT (Wilfley et al., 1993). However, in general, these treatments have been somewhat less evaluated than their individual counterparts. What evidence there is suggests that group treatments are rarely if ever better and may tend to be less effective. Nevertheless, there are arguments in favour of group approaches. They may be thought of as providing wider support and as countering the shame and isolation which are not uncommonly experienced by bulimia nervosa sufferers. However, the commonest argument in their favour is that they are thought of as being cost effective. Whether this is truly the case in practice depends upon the numbers in the group, the length of the group, the amount of preparation time that is involved and so on. A group that has six members and two therapists and lasts for 90 minutes per session will be likely to use more time in practice than would the alternative strategy of offering each patient a 30-minute individual session. This is because groups take more organisation and coordination time. Furthermore, running groups requires that there is a sufficient flow of suitable patients for an individual not to have to wait too long for the others to come along. Differential efficacy may also be relevant to cost, because if a greater proportion of patients do not respond, they may eventually require further treatment and consume more resources in the long run. The whole cost-effectiveness argument needs to be examined carefully and it is simplistic to assume that groups will always win out. However, groups can provide valuable training for a junior clinician who acts as co-therapist with a more experienced colleague. There are all sorts of pros and cons of groups. Sometimes they may be the better choice.

Psychoeducation

One form of group approach to the treatment of bulimia nervosa is to adopt an essentially didactic or educational style. A number of such 'psychoeducational' programmes have been described (Olmsted *et al.*, 1991; Olmsted & Kaplan, 1995). They tend to include talks and handouts on such topics as the effects of dieting, social pressures and the components of a healthy diet. Some may also include discussion of self-esteem and emotional issues. If homework is set and individually monitored, there may be little gap between psychoeducation and some other group approaches. However, psychoeducation 'classes' do allow more people to be included than would be the case in an ordinary therapy group. As a treatment of itself such psychoeducation is probably adequate only for those with mild problems (Olmsted *et al.*, 1991). However, psychoeducation may be useful as a first step therapy and as a component of other treatments (Garner, 1997).

'SELF-HELP'

The term 'self-help' is ambiguous. It can mean help deriving from groups of sufferers and perhaps their families meeting together for mutual support and more. (This will be discussed more fully in Chapter 11.) However, that is not the sense in which the term is being used in this section. Here 'self-help' means attempts to recover in which the sufferer uses books or other materials to organise her efforts without the aid of a therapist. If a professional is involved but plays a relatively minor part, the process may be called guided self-help. There is evidence that self-help in these senses may be of significant benefit in a proportion of cases of bulimia nervosa (Fairburn & Carter, 1997).

Over the last few years a number of books have been published which have set out to provide the basis for such self-help (Cooper, 1995; Fairburn, 1995b, Schmidt & Treasure, 1993). These have usually followed a broadly cognitive-behavioural approach. Some have been subjected to formal evaluation with bulimia nervosa sufferers and others with binge-eating problems (Cooper, Coker & Fleming, 1996; Carter & Fairburn, 1998; Treasure *et al.*, 1994). The evidence to date suggests that following a self-help programme is importantly helpful to a least a minority of suffers. Even the use of a book alone seems to be better than nothing and, of course, in some places that may be the alternative. Furthermore, some sufferers may actively avoid professional help because of embarrassment or for other reasons. However, the use of a self-help book with the guidance of a generally but not specifically skilled professional seems to be a promising approach when there is no specialist help at hand. For instance, Cooper, Coker and Fleming (1996) found that about a third of patients given self-help with sessions by a professional who was not specifically trained seemed to benefit in a substantial and sustained way. Indeed, it could be that such guided self-help might be a reasonable first step in many cases presenting for the first time. Guided self-help could involve just a few sessions with the 'guide' or could be delivered with the same number of sessions as full CBT. It is as yet unclear how such an intervention would compare with full CBT delivered by a trained therapist. Overall, the optimal place of self-help books in a comprehensive array of help for bulimia nervosa and binge eating disorder has yet to be defined (Fairburn & Carter, 1997).

DRUG TREATMENTS

Not unexpectedly a wide range of drug treatments have been tried in bulimia nervosa (Mayer & Walsh, 1998). However, many have been evaluated only inadequately in small trials, open studies or case reports. The drugs which have been best evaluated and with positive results are various antidepressants. By the term 'antidepressant' is meant drugs which have proved efficacy in the treatment of major depression. This could be taken as meaning that the actions of such drugs are essentially antidepressant and, furthermore, that any efficacy in bulimia nervosa would indicate that some sort of 'depressive' mechanism was being revealed in that disorder. However, this may well not be a valid conclusion even though it has been argued that bulimia nervosa may be thought of as a variant of affective disorder. Indeed, a plausible case can be made that bulimia nervosa and major depression are somewhat related disorders based upon a number of similarities and overlaps (Swift, Andrew & Barlage, 1986). Some such argument may well have motivated the early trying out of antidepressant drugs in the disorder. However, the common efficacy of antidepressant drugs in the two conditions may not add much to this proposition. There does seem to be fairly consistent evidence that the beneficial effects of antidepressant drugs in bulimia nervosa are not confined to those patients with comorbid major depression or even to those with depressive symptoms (Walsh, 1995; Goldstein, Wilson, Ascroft & Al-Banna, 1999). Any 'antibulimic' effects seem to be largely independent of effects upon lowered mood. Furthermore, the time course of beneficial effect may be different for bulimic symptoms and mood symptoms, as may the dosage required to produce it. It is likely that if the antibulimic effects of these drugs had been discovered first and bulimia nervosa had been as common as depression, then they would be known as 'antibulimics' rather than antidepressants. Perhaps then the debate would be about whether major depression was best thought of as variant of eating disorder or appetitive disorder. Doubtless an argument could be constructed to support such a view involving the commonly observed changes of weight, appetite and eating in what we would call affective disorder.

Most, but not all, of the antidepressant drugs that have been adequately assessed in bulimia nervosa have shown positive effects. Exceptions include mianserine (Sabine, Yonance, Farrington, Barratt & Wakeling, 1983) and perhaps surprisingly, in a yet to be published study, fluvoxamine, the serotonin reuptake inhibitor (SSRI) . The drug which has been most widely used and advocated for bulimia nervosa is another SSRI, fluoxetine (Fluoxetine Bulimia Nervosa Collaborative Study Group, 1992; Goldstein, Wilson, Thompson, Potvin & Rampey, 1995).[6] There are reasons why drugs which act predominantly on the serotonin system might be especially likely to benefit bulimic symptoms. Serotonin, which is also known as 5 hydroxy tryptamine, or 5HT, is a neurotransmitter which seems to play an important part in satiety, and persistent variations have been found in bulimic subjects (Kaye *et al.*, 1998). However, some drugs which act mainly on other neurotransmitter systems have demonstrable antibulimic properties. For instance, desipramine is a tricyclic antidepressant drug which seems to act mainly on noradrenergic systems but has nevertheless been shown to be more effective than placebo in the treatment of bulimia nervosa (Walsh, Hadigan, Devlin, Gladis, & Roose, 1991). Likewise, there have been a number of studies of the oldest antidepressant of them all, imipramine, which is not predominantly a serotonergic drug (Agras, Dorian, Kirkley, Arnow & Bachman, 1987).

The antidepressants which are helpful in bulimia nervosa have real but modest efficacy. The demonstrated effects of fluoxetine may be taken as an example. In the major trials of that drug the group which was treated with placebo showed less improvement in symptoms than was the case with the active drug. However, this effect was evident only in those subjects receiving doses of 40 or 60 mg per day. The usual antidepressant dose of 20 mg daily had no demonstrable benefit. Furthermore, even at this higher dose, in the longer term study, in which treatment was studied over 16 weeks, the rate of full remission of bingeing was only 18% compared to 12% on placebo (Goldstein *et al.*, 1995). Enthusiasts for drug treatment point out that in clinical practice better results may be obtained by changing from drug to drug until there is an adequate response. However, there is little evidence on the long-term use of antidepressants, and clinical impressions suggest a high relapse rate after discontinuation. Furthermore, many patients are reluctant to take drug treatments.

The proper place of antidepressant drugs in the treatment of bulimia nervosa may depend upon a variety of local or particular factors. In general, there is no doubt that psychotherapeutic interventions, particularly CBT, are more effective than drug therapy (Schmidt, 1998; Whittal, Agras & Gould, 1999). However, the psychotherapies require appropriately trained therapists and these may not be available. Pharmacotherapy also requires an appropriately trained therapist but the training here may be less particular. A medically qualified generalist may be available where a specialist psychotherapist is not. However, confidence in dealing with eating disorders is likely still to be important even if the main mode of therapy is the prescription of a drug. Placebo effects have been noted to be markedly different across trials and this may represent, at least in part, differential therapist effects (Mayer & Walsh, 1998).

There has been some debate as to the relative cost of short-term psychotherapy and drug treatment. The latter looks as though it should be cheaper but the need for some monitoring appointments and the high cost of medical input and sometimes of the medication itself makes this less clearly the case. Overall the verdict would seem to be that drug treatment alone is not the treatment of choice in bulimia nervosa.

COMBINED TREATMENT

There is some evidence about the results of combining drugs and psychotherapy in the treatment of bulimia nervosa. Overall, the results of the few studies of this type suggest that there is, in general, little to be gained from the addition of antidepressant drugs to otherwise adequate psychotherapy (Schmidt, 1998). Nevertheless in clinical practice, faced with a patient who is not responding, the offer of additional drug treatment is one of the options. Indeed, in many circumstances it would be a sensible thing to do. Of course, if the patient is comorbidly depressed, drug therapy may well be indicated from the outset. The combination of drug treatment with guided self-help might be more effective than either given alone, but the combination has yet to be evaluated.

BINGE EATING DISORDER

There is less evidence about the appropriate treatment for binge eating disorder (BED) than there is for bulimia nervosa. However, CBT, broadly as for bulimia nervosa although in group format, has been found to be somewhat helpful (Marcus, 1997; Levine & Marcus, 1998). Likewise, a group form of IPT has been shown to be beneficial in one trial (Wilfley *et al.*, 1996). Antidepressants have some efficacy and in that proportion of sufferers who present to services, comorbid depression is likely and the prescription of antidepressants may often be appropriate for that reason (Marcus, 1997; Levine & Marcus, 1998).

Thus, therapy so far has followed the pattern of that for bulimia nervosa. However, this may not be optimal since there are at least hints that the two disorders may differ in pathogenesis. Furthermore, BED is often complicated by some degree of obesity. A central issue would seem to be the role played by eating restraint in the two disorders. Restraint is probably crucial in the perpetuation of most cases of bulimia nervosa but its role, if any, is not nearly so clear in BED. Stopping or limiting eating restraint is part of most approaches to bulimia nervosa but may be difficult to achieve in the treatment of many people with BED. Giving up restraint may well not be acceptable to someone who is very obese. (It is commonly difficult enough for someone who just *feels* obese.) But is it necessary? There is some evidence that suggests that it may not be. Thus, weight control programmes which encourage restraint and cognitive-behavioural treatments which incorporate calorie restriction have both been shown to benefit obese binge eaters (Wadden, Foster, & Letizia, 1992; Marcus, Wing & Fairburn, 1995; Marcus,1997). Overall, BED remains a poorly charted territory with unclear borders. Indeed, further mapping may lead to it being meaningfully subdivided. It seems likely that there might be various biological or indeed psychological states which might have this behaviour as their common manifestation. More rational treatment may follow their discovery.

STEPPED CARE

The range of treatments available for the bulimic conditions and their different costs and efficacies has led to much discussion of the idea of so-called stepped care (Fairburn & Peveler, 1990). The basic idea is that treatment interventions should be offered according to a heirarchical sequence with lesser and cheaper treatments being offered before more elaborate and expensive interventions. In practice this might mean that group psychoeducation or individual guided self-help with minimal professional input might be offered first, and full psychotherapy, for instance CBT, would be reserved for those patients who failed to respond. There might be a further treatment 'step' for those who did not respond adequately to CBT or other mainline treatment.

Stepped care sounds sensible since a proportion of people do seem to be able to escape from bulimia nervosa with less than standard treatment, and others certainly need more. Moreover, most services are short of resources and getting away with offering the least expensive treatment, provided it is efficacious, allows the total resource to be used to the best effect overall. However, real life tends to be messier than such neat schemes allow. People drop out; some have comorbid depression; others seem to cry out for more than minimal treatment from the outset. Furthermore, even in principle there seems to be a possibility that stepped care demands of the most severely ill or least treatment responsive that they survive failure – perhaps repeated failure – before being offered the interventions that might help them. It is probable that some will fall by the wayside and possible that some might become, as it were, inoculated against the very treatments which might have helped them had they been offered at the outset. For instance, someone who had genuinely struggled to use a self-help manual based on CBT might have a 'here we go again' response when offered full CBT. These are objections in principle to a rigid stepped care approach although there are as yet few data to show that they actually occur in practice. However, both in principle and in practice it would be preferable if it were possible to predict which sufferers would respond to lesser treatments and which would be likely to need greater treatments. We all, as clinicians, think that we can make these judgements but we rarely put ourselves to systematic test. Once again there is as yet little research with which we can bolster our hunches.

UNRESPONSIVE PATIENTS

What is clear is that at least a substantial minority of patients to not respond fully or even at all to standard therapies such as CBT. What should be offered to these people? Broadly speaking, offers of further treatment could be subsumed under the headings of 'more of the same' or 'something different'.

The 'more of the same' approach would involve a lengthening or resumption of therapy after the standard 'dose' has been delivered. Of course, such an approach would be usual with some therapies, such as psychodynamic treatment where the number of sessions is not specified at the outset. However, what have come to be the standard treatments for bulimia nervosa are time limited and so the concept of a standard or a greater 'dose' does have meaning. Although there have been experiments with shortened treatment, there has been little systematic study of offering many more than the usual number of sessions, although undoubtedly it happens in practice. Furthermore, the authorities in the field seem to give somewhat mixed messages (Wilson, Fairburn & Agras, 1997; Wilson, 1996a).

In the main the advice would seem to be to give the standard treatment and then to have a pause for thought. Standard treatment is doubtless sometimes extended in practice, but there is also a widely held view that if a patient has not shown significant response by about the eighth session of standard CBT then pushing on further may well be a demoralising waste of time. Perhaps, the upshot may be that it is worth continuing CBT beyond its usual span when the patient has not responded fully but has responded to some extent. If the treatment is extended in such circumstances it may be that the parts that receive more emphasis are those that address the patient's beliefs and problem-solving skills. Indeed, it may be that continued therapy within a framework of CBT might move on to self-schema work and an examination of ideas that are less directly involved with weight and eating. These might include issues concerned directly with negative affect and interpersonal problems (Wilson, 1996a, 1999).

Moving on to an emphasis on wider issues and shifting the focus away from weight and eating is the essence of the 'something different' approach. This may certainly be the case where manual-based CBT has been the first treatment. Then a shift to a less eating-focused therapy might well be rational and IPT a sensible choice if an appropriately trained therapist is available. However, the evidence that this is effective in practice is lacking (Agras et al., 1995; Wilson, 1999). An alternative would be therapy that was psychodynamically informed. This could be arranged on a short-term focal basis or as more long-term therapy. Unfortunately there is little evidence about what is the most rational choice in these circumstances. Admission to hospital may sometimes help people to change, although the idea that this may simply 'break the cycle' of bulimia is rarely as effective in practice as it may seem to promise in prospect to the hard-pressed patient and her therapist. Admission may be indicated for the more vigorous treatment of comorbidity or the containment of suicidal behaviour.

When following on from unsuccessful short-term therapy, it may often be sensible to allow a break before other treatment is offered. Sometimes people change without treatment. Furthermore, therapy may have delayed effects. Certainly, delayed effects have been clearly demonstrated after IPT for bulimia nervosa in the Oxford trial (Fairburn et al., 1995). It may well be appropriate to have a gap of a few weeks or months, although distressed and symptomatic people may need some supportive holding appointments during this time. Such a period may allow time for reflection and reassessment.

Reassessment of the stuck patient should include careful review of the presence and significance of any comorbid conditions such as major depression. A trial of antidepressant drugs may be indicated if the patient is depressed and could be useful even if she is not when such drugs have not been recently tried. The presence of major relationship or social problems should also be reassessed since they might be contributing to the sufferer's lack of response. Getting better from bulimia nervosa is a personally demanding and challenging enterprise at the best of times. If the individual is in the midst of the worst of times, it may be better for her to be supported or otherwise helped through these before she makes another attempt at escape from her eating disorder. Such decisions have to be based on the judgement of the clinician and the opinion of the patient. Sometimes the time is just not right. However, the sufferer should always be assured that this does not mean that the time to escape will never come. She should not feel 'written off'.

Reassessment should also include consideration of the issue of personality and personality disorder – so-called axis II comorbidity. Some people do have problems in their view of themselves and their relationships with others and do show relatively consistent but maladaptive ways of managing these. In any kind of therapy, the therapist becomes an important other person and these general difficulties become manifest within the therapy and may disrupt it. People who show these problems may need special therapeutic techniques to hold them if they are to use therapy successfully.

'MULTI-IMPULSIVE' BULIMIA NERVOSA AND BORDERLINE PERSONALITY DISORDER

The term 'multi-impulsive' bulimia nervosa has been proposed by Hubert Lacey and colleagues at St George's Hospital in London to draw attention to a group of sufferers who show additional self-damaging behaviours which are construed as impulsive in nature (Lacey & Evans, 1986). These behaviours may include self-cutting, overdosing, stealing and drug or alcohol abuse. Such 'multi-impulsive' people also typically show notable emotional lability and have marked problems of self-esteem and relationships. Most would fulfil criteria for borderline personality disorder. There is some debate as to whether such people are usefully thought of as constituting a distinct subgroup of bulimia nervosa. There is even more debate about what is the best approach towards trying to help them. Most clinicians will recognise the challenge that these unhappy people present.

One approach is to offer initially the kind of short-term psychotherapy that would be the usual treatment for more straightforward cases of bulimia nervosa. This may be justifiable because some may do well even if the chance of a good outcome is less than would be the case in uncomplicated bulimia. What evidence there is suggests that comorbid personality disorder reduces the chance of treatment success but does not support therapeutic nihilism (Rossiter, Agras, Telch & Schneider, 1993; Wonderlich,

Fullerton, Swift and Klein, 1994; Steiger & Stotland, 1996). Sometimes people with chaotic behaviour change in surprising ways if they manage to improve their bulimic symptoms.[7] However, the clinician must not be surprised if things go wrong. Treatment may be disrupted by all sorts of crises and complications, in which case the usual patterns of help may need to be supplemented with or replaced by other interventions. For instance, the sufferer may need to be offered extra support or even hospital admission at times of increased self-harming behaviour or extreme distress. Then the whole treatment enterprise may be difficult to sustain in its usual form. Both patient and clinician may come to feel that they are just lurching along from one crisis to the next – and that, indeed, may be the case.

The concept of borderline personality disorder was developed in an attempt to describe people who tended not to do well in relation to psychological treatments in general. One view of the nature of the problem is that people with such characteristics are by temperament highly emotional but have not had experiences which have validated this tendency in ways that enable them to use it adaptively (Linehan, 1993). They tend to expect invalidation and to get it. Their behaviour may provoke both overinvolvement and rejection. Such difficulties may be recapitulated in therapy. It is difficult for all concerned to maintain the boundaries upon which good therapy depends. Such people tend to burst the banks of many therapeutic relationships. Rejection may sometimes be dressed up in the guise of referral on to some more expert setting. Also, because the patient may have many problems it is sometimes only too easy to convince oneself that problem X is the more important problem – if, that is, one is a specialist in problem Y. Such patients do the rounds. The comments about the utility of trying standard treatments notwith-standing, it may be useful to construe the borderline personality disorder itself as central when considering what to do in such circumstances.

The special therapy of borderline personality disorder is a demanding and uncertain business. There is little consensus and no easy answers. In the case of the bulimia nervosa sufferer with borderline disorder the specific eating disorder features may come to be overshadowed by the many other symptoms and difficulties which the person experiences. Likewise, the proportion of most overall management strategies which relate especially to the bulimia may well be fairly small. Nevertheless, people with bulimia nervosa and borderline personality disorder often suffer dreadfully and may consume large quantities of helping resource with little apparent benefit. There is a need for new approaches and special programmes have been developed. For instance, the St George's Hospital group have developed a complex treatment package which involves assessment, a four-month inpatient stay, a similar time as a day patient and then follow up (Lacey, 1995; Lacey & Read, 1993). Others have used predominantly outpatient approaches (Dennis & Sansome, 1991).

There are other approaches which have been devised for borderline problems in general which might be adapted for use with eating-disordered patients although few have been evaluated adequately (Kisely, 1999). Dialectical behaviour therapy (DBT) is a treatment devised by Marsha Linehan of Seattle for borderline personality disorder (Linehan, 1993). It has been shown to be effective in such patients where the main associated behaviour is recurrent self-harm (Linehan, Armstrong, Suarez, Allman & Heard, 1991). It is an intensive outpatient therapy which combines individual therapy sessions with skills training in a group and out-of-hours telephone contact. It seems to have some promise as an approach for those with both borderline personality disorder and bulimia nervosa.[8] Likewise, there are more psychodynamic approaches which have been advocated, although again these have not been evaluated with bulimia nervosa sufferers (Higgitt & Fonagy, 1993; Kerberg, Selzer, Koenigberg, Carr & Applebaum, 1989; Stevenson & Meares, 1992).

For the present, the best available option for most patients and most clinicians is likely to involve some kind of 'bespoke' therapy created individually with the patient in the light of whatever knowledge and experience is available. However, any clinician, of whatever seniority, engaged in therapy with a patient with severe borderline problems is well advised to use any kind of supervision or forum for regular case discussion that is available. Trying to avoid making things worse is a good start, although even this minimal prescription may not be easy in some cases.[9]

PHYSICAL COMPLICATIONS

Many of the physical complications discussed in the chapter on anorexia nervosa may occur also in bulimia nervosa at normal weight. Thus, gastrointestinal symptoms are not uncommon, deficiencies may occur and even osteoporosis has been reported (Mitchell, Seim, Colon & Pomeroy, 1987; Mitchell, 1995; Newton, Freeman, Hannan & Cowen, 1993). Amenorrhoea may occur but is less common than irregular menstruation, although there seems to be an interesting association between bulimia and polycystic ovaries (Copeland & Herzog, 1987; McCluskey, Lacey & Pearce, 1992). However, the chief particular complications of bulimia nervosa are those which arise from bingeing and the various compensatory methods which the sufferer may employ.

Bingeing may sometimes be fatal. This happens when the frantic eating leads to choking or the inhalation of vomit. Bingeing is almost always a solitary activity and this may increase the danger since no one is likely to be at hand if such calamities occur. Fortunately these events are rare. More usually the dangers arise through the vomiting or purging that follows.

Self-induced vomiting may directly cause tissue damage. Thus, it is not uncommon for sufferers to bring up blood and this should be questioned. Specks of fresh blood are usually the result of superficial abrasions in the throat caused by the very act of inducing vomiting. However, violent vomiting may also lead to more serious damage – so-called Mallory–Weiss tears – in the oesophagus and to significant or even dangerous haemorrhage. Sometimes such tears require surgical intervention, although this is rare. Actual perforation of the oesophagus is a surgical emergency. Less extreme is inflammation of the oesophagus due to acid reflux. This may be associated with peptic ulceration and treatment with antacids and proton pump inhibitors may be helpful.

Vomiting can also lead to acid damage to the teeth. People who habitually vomit often develop erosion of the dental enamel and may lose teeth although the association is not as clear cut as is sometimes thought (Milosevic, 1999). They should seek dental advice and tell their dentist about the vomiting. However, the only real remedy for recurrent problems is to stop vomiting.

The mode of vomiting may be significant. Regular use of the hand to induce vomiting sometimes leads to one of the few physical signs of psychiatry, namely Russell's sign. This is a callous on the back of the hand where the teeth regularly impact when it is thrust down the throat. More significantly, the practice of 'washing out' after vomiting may exacerbate electrolyte disturbance. In this, the individual not only vomits until she believes that she has thrown up everything which she has eaten but also then drinks copious amounts of water until the vomitus is clear. This leads to a greater loss of salts than would usually be the case. Likewise, the use of emetics may have similar effects. Ipecac has been abused as an emetic by bulimia sufferers and is associated with a risk of cardiomyopathy which has been fatal on occasion (Pope, Hudson, Nixon & Herridge, 1986). Patients should be warned of the dangers of this practice. However, even this obvious advice to warn patients of potential dangers needs to be qualified at times. Thus, it is not unknown for patients to engage in behaviours *because* they are dangerous. In such a case, it would still seem appropriate to give information about danger but also to focus upon the relevant psychological issues which drive the risk-taking or self-destructive behaviour. Just occasionally, the routine feeding back of blood test results and the like may come to feel counterproductive if abnormal results immediately trigger behaviour aimed at increasing the danger. Such behaviour is most likely in sufferers with comorbid borderline personality disorder.

Any method of vomiting or purgation which leads to the loss of fluid and salts can have a bad effect upon the individual's internal environment.

The loss of water leads to dehydration and the loss of salts to efforts by the body to maintain homeostasis. The net effect of these may be to preserve the internal environment within normal limits but sometimes the power of the body's regulatory mechanisms to do so are exceeded and the levels of extracellular potassium tend to fall. The low potassium levels may have bad effects on the heart and cause cardiac arrhythmias, which could be fatal. More chronically, hypokalaemia can cause kidney damage which, in turn, impairs the regulatory mechanisms upon which the body relies to counteract the effects of the individual's behaviour. These issues have been discussed above in relation to anorexia nervosa. The same need arises to monitor electrolyte levels, initiate ECGs and give supplements when indicated. However, even more than with the person with low-weight anorexia nervosa, the need is to help the bulimia sufferer to regain some measure of order in her eating and to give up vomiting. If she able to do this, her biochemistry will usually return to normal within days if not hours.

NOTES

1. As I make this confident assertion, I am assailed by some doubts. It is certainly true in the United kingdom where I work. However, I am aware that in some countries people with bulimia nervosa are often treated within inpatient programmes. For instance, this is the case in Germany where there are major – indeed statutory – divisions between inpatient and outpatient services. In other countries it may be that geography dictates a greater use of inpatient treatment. If you live far away from any source of specialist treatment, it may be necessary to accept that treatment in a distant hospital may be the best available option. However, even here something less than full-time hospitalisation may be on offer – for instance, staying at a guest house whilst attending a day patient or outpatient programme.

2. The most that a book such as this can do is to note and describe briefly the various treatment approaches. Most of them require particular training for their implementation. Furthermore, such particular training needs to be grafted on to appropriate general training. Unfortunately, special training is often not easy to obtain. However, at the very least, clinicians need to read the full accounts of the therapies before trying out the treatment approaches mentioned. I have tried to include the best references to each approach in the text, and key references are included in the recommendations for further reading at the end of the chapter.

3. So concerned was Fairburn to make IPT very different from CBT, that if, within the main body of therapy, patients started talking about eating,

therapists within his trial were required within seconds to try to get the conversation off that subject and back to talking about relationships. Surprisingly, they could usually manage this. However, this rule produced a therapy which seems to differ from what might be called 'classic' IPT as it has been used in the treatment of depression. In such 'classic' IPT there is much reviewing of depressive symptoms and time is spent relating these to the interpersonal issues. Of course, the evidence for the efficacy of IPT in bulimia nervosa currently comes from Fairburn's studies and is evidence of efficacy of IPT as it was performed within that research. It is just about plausible that it is the combination of attention to interpersonal matters with a concerned inattention to weight and eating that is the potent therapeutic factor in Fairburn's version of IPT. However, if IPT done in this way is thought of as importantly different from what one might call 'classic' IPT, which pays more direct attention to symptoms, then we must conclude that there is currently no actual trial evidence of efficacy of the latter treatment – 'classic' IPT – in bulimia nervosa. Some would say that the latter treatment resembles more closely the treatments used in depression although perhaps the difference could be thought of as subtle. However, for what it is worth, colleagues in Leicester who are trained in 'classic' IPT have obtained good results in bulimia nervosa, although so far in usual clinical practice rather than within a research project.

4. Those of a more exclusively psychodynamic persuasion may feel that my comments are unfair or misrepresent their stance. However, to modify the well-known phrase, 'some of my best friends – and most respected colleagues – are psychodynamic therapists' and, indeed, I was myself brought up professionally within the broader reaches of such ideas. I still think that much of the psychodynamic framework is one of the best ways of thinking about human experience and interaction. However, like other systems of ideas, when used too narrowly it can ignore whole swathes of the biological and the social in favour of an exclusive concentration on the subject's inner mental life. This is strange when one considers that Freud's original project seemed to be about reconciling particular inner experience with universal biological imperatives.

5. In writing about this topic I am wary of seeming to take too neutral a stance. When one thinks of oneself as having a view which has risen above the culture and perspectives of one's own particular position, then that is the time when one's prejudices may be most evident to everyone but oneself. Images of hot air ballooning come to mind. The view is wonderful but the precarious nature of the position and what is sustaining it is most evident to those below.

6. This drug is better known in lay circles by its trade name Prozac. In the late 1980s and 1990s, it became not only one of the most widely prescribed drugs of any kind but also some sort of icon in ideological battles about the nature of mental illness and the place of drug treatments. To me all this brouhaha seemed at times to be a rather excessive reaction to an antidepressant which was merely one amongst several dozen available drugs. On the whole it does seem to be a usually well tolerated and effective medication but it is perhaps exceptional only in the success of the hype and marketing it has received and the flak that its prominent position has attracted.

7. The concept of personality disorder is not without its difficulties. There are those in clinical psychology and psychiatry who doubt its utility. Indeed, there is a critique of the concept of personality itself. For the present it is enough to say that it is sometimes difficult to know how best to think about the wider problematic behaviour of many bulimia sufferers. To put it in stark terms, is such behaviour 'part of the illness' or an aspect of 'personality' or 'personality disorder' – or is the distinction not useful? Someone, now aged 22, who has been caught up in the truly vicious circles of bulimia nervosa for, say, the last six years has had little chance to develop characteristic adult patterns of behaviour which have not been importantly shaped by the disorder. What is her 'usual personality'? If she can escape from bulimia nervosa, she may be able to progress rapidly in other ways. However, she may not if through this experience or perhaps through earlier experience she has formed a notably maladaptive view of herself and her relationships with others. There is much scope for muddled and circular thinking. And in practice prediction is difficult. Beware of people who are too confident in saying that a particular person will do badly. It is said that 'blessed are the pessimists for they shall have some pleasant surprises', but if pessimism leads to a treatment not even being offered, there may be little or no chance of such surprises.

8. In Leicester, a team of us have undergone the training and have been trying out DBT for a few people with eating disorder and borderline personality disorder. We have added a specially devised 'Eatingness' module to the skills training component. At the time of writing, the programme seems to be of benefit to the patients who are self-harming much less and to the therapists – including myself – who are feeling more positive and confident. However, it is too soon to draw any conclusions.

9. I sometimes wonder whether less intensive therapy or sometimes just less therapy or therapist's time may be advantageous for some people with borderline personality disorder and bulimia nervosa. Sometimes the readily established intensity of the therapeutic relationship may be

tantalising to the therapist who feels that real progress is just around every corner. This very intensity can, however, lead to difficulty and even to harm to the patient as well as to progress. Certainly it may at times feel right to stage a 'tactical retreat'. It may be better to back off but to remain available rather than to recapitulate what may have been a cycle of previous rejections. For instance, it might be worth while offering some guided self-help. Of course, offering less in the face of high distress and risk of self-harm may not be easy either emotionally or from the perspective of defensive practice. Nevertheless, it may be one way of moving on from a position of therapeutic trench warfare. However, I would warn the reader that this suggestion is merely an opinion and is unsullied by any real supporting evidence.

FURTHER READING

Fairburn, C G (1997a) Interpersonal psychotherapy for bulimia nervosa. In: Garner, D M. & Garfinkel, P E (Editors) *Handbook of Treatment for Eating Disorders* (second edition). Guilford Press, New York and London.

Fairburn, C G, Marcus, M D & Wilson,G T (1993) Cognitive-Behavioural Therapy for binge eating and bulimia nervosa: a comprehensive treatment manual. In: Fairburn, C G & Wilson, G T (Editors) *Binge Eating: Nature, Assessment and Treatment.* Guilford Press, New York and London.

Garfinkel, P E & Walsh, B T (1997) Drug therapies. In: Garner, D M & Garfinkel, P E (Editors) *Handbook of Treatment for Eating Disorders* (second edition). Guilford Press, New York and London.

Marcus, M D (1997) Adapting treatment for patients with binge-eating disorder. In: Garner, D M & Garfinkel, P E (Editors) *Handbook of Treatment for Eating Disorders* (second edition). Guilford Press, New York and London.

Schmidt, U (1998) Treatment of bulimia nervosa. In: Hoek, H W, Treasure, J L & Katzman, M A (Editors) *Neurobiology in the Treatment of Eating Disorders.* John Wiley & Sons, Chichester and New York.

Wilson, G T, Fairburn, C G & Agras, W S (1997) Cognitive-Behavioural Therapy for bulimia nervosa. In: Garner, D M & Garfinkel, P E (Editors) *Handbook of Treatment for Eating Disorders* (second edition). Guilford Press, New York and London.

9

UNUSUAL EATING DISORDERS

Some people who suffer with eating disorders present unusual problems. They may do so because they have disorders which are markedly different from the average or because they are different from the average sufferer, or both. For instance, a young female may suffer from a disorder in which she is preoccupied with her body and loses weight through eating restraint although the motivation for that restraint seems to have nothing to do with a desire to control weight. Her ideas are unusual. On the other hand, a male may be considered an unusual sufferer simply because he is male even though, in other respects, his disorder is typical. A third group comprises those sufferers who present special problems because of notable physical or psychiatric comorbidity. This chapter will discuss briefly each of these broad groups with particular reference to any special problems which may arise in treatment. It will start with the issue of unusual sufferers, although many of these will also have unusual features.

EATING DISORDERS IN MEN

In clinical practice and in most published series, males constitute only a small minority of adult sufferers from both anorexia nervosa and bulimia nervosa, although this is probably not the case for binge eating disorder. For the main eating disorders, the proportion of males varies but is rarely higher than 10% and is commonly less than half this rate. The relative lack of males in clinical samples could reflect a low number of sufferers in the community. However, it may also be the case that male sufferers are even more reluctant to come forward for help than their female equivalents, and that if they do their disorder may not be appropriately recognised, diagnosed or treated. Eating disorders are thought of as 'female problems' and men may miss out.

When a disorder is so skewed in its distribution, the factors which seem to be related to this skew by their absence are of interest. The most obvious issues here would be the different social meanings attached to body size and shape for men and women. Many men wish that they were bigger and bulkier, but this is rarely the case for women. The lesser emphasis upon the meaning of weight and so on is a plausible factor explaining at least some of the relative lack of vulnerability of males. Some men who develop eating disorders have been premorbidly obese. However, a significant proportion of young men of normal size nevertheless wish to lose weight and attempt to slim, and it may be that this proportion is growing.

Can much be said about the characteristics of those men who do develop anorexia nervosa or bulimic disorders? The age distribution of adult sufferers seems similar to that of females. Most are young. It has been suggested that, of those who present to services, a disproportionate number are homosexual and/or have major doubts or uncertainties about their sexuality (Andersen, 1995). Such doubts may be about their sexual orientation or about their gender identity. It has been suggested that to be male and gay may make body size and shape a loaded issue for some in a way not dissimilar to that which is the case for many women (Williamson, 1999). Furthermore, some gay men in a society in which there is widespread prejudice against homosexuality may develop negative attitudes towards themselves and their bodies. Men with gender identity problems are another group who are likely to have complex feelings about such issues as body shape. However, hetero-sexual men with no doubts about their gender do develop eating disorders. Presumably, motivated eating restraint and undereating have to begin somehow and something has to begin to tangle up weight and shape with self-esteem and wider issues. Anecdotally, some men seem to get into the disorder via concerns about health and fitness. Body building and training – and presumably often its failures and disappointments – seem to be able to promote the necessary entanglement for some. Some develop fairly typical eating disorders; others may get caught up in other patterns of entanglement. Such patterns have been referred to as machismo nervosa (Connan, 1998).

Clinical experience suggests that a significant proportion of male sufferers have atypical disorders in the sense that their beliefs and ideas may be less centred around weight, as such, in the way that would be required by the diagnostic criteria that are based around the beliefs of the typical female sufferer. However, most male patients do have beliefs and behaviours which closely match their female counterparts. Likewise the hormonal changes which, in the female, would result in amenorrhoea also occur in males and tend to be associated with loss of sexual drive. In general, the similarity of the illnesses in males is more striking than any differences. Most males have 'typical' disorders in this sense. Most should therefore be offered 'typical' treatment although clearly the psychotherapy needs to take their maleness into account. Male sufferers do not seem to have strong opinions about the sex of the therapist.

Some sense of embarrassment may be present in some men who find themselves suffering from this 'woman's disorder'. If this is accompanied by any doubts about sexuality in general – and arguably such doubts are common – then these issues may need careful handling. However, such careful handling should not be too heavy handed or it may exacerbate by emphasis the very worries it is designed to allay. After all, although most sufferers are female, there are many hundreds of men and boys who have suffered and do suffer from eating disorders. Each individual male needs to know that he is not alone, even though he may not know someone else with the same problem. Likewise, services need to avoid being so tuned into the female majority as to put off the male minority.

EATING DISORDERS IN CHILDREN

One group of eating disorder sufferers in which the skew towards females is less is that of the youngest sufferers. Such young sufferers in general may have particular clinical characteristics and special needs. It has been suggested by Lask and Bryant-Waugh (1996) that the term 'childhood onset eating disorders' should be used for sufferers whose illness starts before the age of 14. This brief section is about these individuals and especially about the ways in which their treatment needs should be thought of as different from their older counterparts.[1]

Bulimia nervosa at normal weight is rare before the age 14 and exceedingly so in children under 12 (Stein, Chaloub & Hodes, 1998). It will be interesting to see whether this remains the case in future. Bulimia nervosa seems to be the eating disorder that varies most in prevalence with social pressures to be slim. There is evidence that such pressures are leading to weight concern and slimming behaviour in younger and younger children (Hill, 1993; Hill & Pallin, 1999). This might be expected to lead to the appearance of bulimia nervosa in pre-teens, although clearly other issues are involved.

Most younger patients suffer from anorexia nervosa. In the main they show the same symptoms and preoccupations as older patients. However, as with men, there may be rather more for whom the ideas which entangle weight and eating control with wider issues are not quite as the diagnostic criteria would suggest. There are perhaps more atypical disorders and the relationship between anorexia nervosa and what is called 'food avoidance emotional disorder' seems less than clear cut (Higgs, Goodyer & Birch, 1989). As its name implies, the latter term is used for apparently emotionally driven states with food avoidance as a prominent symptom but which lack some or all of the necessary features for a diagnosis of anorexia nervosa. Such patients often have a history of strange or picky eating and this is not usually the case with anorexia nervosa. These food avoidance emotional disorder patients are perhaps equivalent to the adult Eating Disorder Not Otherwise Specified (EDNOS) sufferers who are discussed below.

Even where children and early adolescents have typical anorexic ideas, they may talk about physical symptoms, true loss of appetite or other explanations which they may feel are more acceptable. Eliciting the young person's true beliefs and feelings may require skilful interviewing by someone experienced in the task. Likewise the whole business of engaging the patient and making her feel secure enough to change may be the same in principle whatever the age of the patient, but what the clinician actually says and does is going to be different if she is 12 rather than 22.

One important difference is that younger patients have families – or at least carers – who are closely involved in their lives, including in their contact with clinicians. Of course, issues of autonomy and privacy arise with children but their parents, or whoever is in locum parentis, have a right to be informed and involved in a way which is not the case with relatives of adult patients. The adult patient may decide whether or not she wishes her family to be involved in her assessment and treatment. Others may request or advise, but at the end of the day she decides and has the right to exclude others and accept or reject advice. This is not so with children. Their parents have rights too. Should there be disputes between the different rights involved, most countries have some kind of legal framework in which they can be resolved. Child care laws may be more relevant than mental health legislation. In the main such legal frameworks are designed to foster the 'best interests of the child' but the child alone is not left to be the arbiter of her own interests, as would be the case with an adult except in extreme circumstances.

In most cases, the law does not enter explicitly into the matter and the child's parents are incorporated into the treatment process as a matter of course and without fuss. However, the crucial issues of responsibility are different when the patient is a child. In adult cases, there would usually be a mainly dyadic relationship between the patient and the clinician or team of clinicians, but with the child patient there is more a three-way relationship in which the parents – or parent substitutes – play an essential role. For instance, in some forms of family therapy with children and adolescents there is an emphasis upon the parents taking explicit responsibility for getting their child to eat (Dare & Eisler, 1995; Lask, 1996). This is in marked contrast to what would be usually regarded as the optimal stance with adults, where the patient's own responsibility for doing something about her state would be emphasised.

Another difference between the adult and the child is that the latter is still developing physically. Semi-starvation may lead to retardation of growth and a thwarting of puberty. Furthermore, the reserves of fat and energy in children and early adolescents may often be proportionately less than those of their older equivalents (Fosson, de Bruyn & Thomas, 1996). They tend to get more ill more quickly. When they do, their management is a complex business requiring expert treatment and skilled nursing (Glendinning & Phillips, 1996; Lask & Fosson, 1996). There is more frequent recourse to naso-gastric tube feeding.

The task of treatment in physical terms is to help the patient get back on to a developmental track rather than to regain some previously attained state. Inasmuch as 'target weights' are relevant it is something of a moving target. Something similar is true of psychological and educational development. Inasmuch as is possible, the child needs to continue her education even in the midst of what may be a prolonged and severe illness and its disruptive treatment.

The typical age of onset of anorexia nervosa spans what is often the traditional divide between services for children and adolescents and those for adults. This is a problem of service organisation. Some patients may need to graduate from one service to another and the two may have rather different styles. A change of style can sometimes be helpful. However, overly rigid rules about acceptance criteria and so on can hamper the rational care of some sufferers. Clinical pragmatism should prevail over bureaucratic principle.

One solution to the child–adult boundary dilemma is to have services which are focused upon 'young people' and to allow this to include individuals well into their twenties. However, this may then exclude that other minority, those older people who suffer from eating disorders.

EATING DISORDERS IN OLDER PEOPLE

Eating disorders are characteristically found in adolescents and young adults. This means that the term 'older' tends to be applied to sufferers who are in their thirties and forties and who would not, in other contexts, be thought of as especially old. Nevertheless, any service needs to be aware that provision which is too focused upon the needs of youth may risk a substantial minority of its patients to feel awkward and out of place. Furthermore, occasional patients may be older by any standard. The literature contains reports of sufferers in their ninth decade (Gowers & Crisp, 1990) and most clinicians will have come across individuals with unequivocal eating disorder who are in their fifties and sixties. Most such patients give a history of having had the disorder for much of their lives.

However, sometimes there is a history merely of weight concern or, at most, subclinical disorder. Occasionally, there really does seem to have been an onset many years after what would be typical (Joughin, Crisp, Gowers & Bhat, 1991).

The management of older sufferers need not differ much from that of their younger colleagues. However, as with males, they may sometimes need reassurance that although they may be unusual they are not unique. In patients with long-standing disorder the comments made elsewhere about truly chronic illness may apply. The complications of long-term disorder, and especially osteoporosis, may be looming and need assessment and management. However, there may be interventions which are relevant to the post-menopausal sufferer which are not advised in younger women. Referral to a clinician expert in osteoporosis may well be worth while. Physical illness of all kinds is more common in older people and the clinician needs to be vigilant and take care not to dismiss new physical complaints as an aspect of the eating disorder without proper scrutiny or investigation.

There is a clinical impression that older sufferers may more commonly have significant comorbid psychiatric disorder and especially depression. This should be treated but their eating disorder should not be dismissed and needs consideration and therapy too.

EATING DISORDERS AND PSYCHIATRIC COMORBIDITY

Older sufferers are not alone in sometimes showing notable psychiatric comorbidity. Issues such major depression, obsessive-compulsive disorder and social phobia are common. However, sometimes, eating disorders may coexist with bipolar disorder, schizophrenia or substance abuse.

There can be no hard and fast rules on how to approach such complex cases. In general, much comorbidity may be thought of as reflecting a complex response to some of the same personal and social issues, as is the case for the eating disorder. As has been outlined above, both of the main eating disorders seem to share many risk factors with many other psychiatric disorders.

Where broadly psychotherapeutic treatment would be the best approach of all of the disorders present, then the answer may be to adapt a single therapeutic relationship to carry help for all aspects of the patient's difficulties, perhaps organised and prioritised according to some agreed understanding of what would be best.[2] It is usually a false hope to think that one part of a complex set of problems can be entirely 'got out of the way' before the others are approached. However, any psychotherapy is demanding, and a problem which of itself undermines the individual's capacity to work at her problems may need to be addressed first. For instance, it is difficult to get to grips with other problems if you are grossly intoxicated with drugs or alcohol. Where one or more of the psychiatric states present may be responsive to medication or other instrumental treatments, it is probably worth trying to tackle these first. Thus, an individual may be in a much better position to work at her eating disorder if her mania or severe depression has been adequately treated. Sometimes hospital admission may be useful when eating disorder is mixed with psychosis or severe affective disorder. However, high levels of distress associated with personality disorder in the absence of clearly treatable mental illness may be complicated by the process of admission and its associated regression and distortion of issues of responsibility.

EATING DISORDERS AND PHYSICAL COMORBIDITY

There is some evidence to suggest that physical illness is a risk factor for the development of anorexia nervosa (Patton, Wood & Johnson-Sabine, 1986). Certainly, there may be major clinical problems when an eating disorder coexists with significant physical illness. This is especially so when that illness itself affects weight or eating, as, for instance, with gastrointestinal disorders such as Crohn's disease or ulcerative colitis. Sometimes, the eating disorder may seem to emerge out of the other disease. A not uncommon story is of a somewhat weight-concerned individual who loses weight as a result of a physical illness with true loss of appetite. As she partially recovers and regains her urge to eat she may try to preserve the weight loss which may to her seem to be the only positive aspect of her condition. She then restrains her eating and adds an eating disorder to her other problem. Sometimes this may present the clinician with a difficult diagnostic problem, but this is not usually the case provided that it is appreciated that two disorders are present rather than one. In general, both disorders need to be treated but the more psychotherapeutic management of the eating disorder needs to take account of the effects of the other disorder. When the 'other disorder' is itself a problem which lies in murky territory between the physically and the psychologically determined – for instance, irritable bowel syndrome or chronic fatigue – then the therapy may become complex. Especially with chronic fatigue, the clinician needs to avoid getting caught up in disputes about the nature of the disorder. However, even in the simpler case of comorbidity of eating disorder and unequivocal physical illness, the experience of the patient needs to be thought of as a whole and her particular and personal situation acknowledged. Therapy may need to be bespoke rather than 'off the peg' although the clinician should not lose sight of the simple things such as the necessary although not sufficient status of weight gain in recovery from anorexia nervosa.

One physical disorder which may form an especially difficult combination with the eating disorders is insulin dependent (type I) diabetes mellitus. One might expect diabetics to be especially likely to develop eating disorders because eating for them is a loaded issue although there may also be a countervailing tendency for their dietary control to be better than average. However, there seems to be little evidence in favour of the idea that the two disorders are associated to a degree that is greater than chance (Neilsen & Molbek, 1998). However, when they do coexist, each may aggravate the other and together they may be difficult to manage (Peveler, 1995). Diabetes sufferers with eating disorders tend to develop complications sooner, especially retinopathy (Neilsen & Molbek, 1998).

Diabetics with eating disorders have at their disposal the ability to omit their insulin and thus induce glycosuria with consequent loss of fluid and some calories. This may produce a gratifying loss of weight albeit at the expense of courting ketosis and coma. They can also, of course, take too much insulin as a suicidal act or as a miscalculation in the midst of a meagre or chaotic diet. Especially in bulimic states with a highly variable net intake of food and a variable motivation to cover intake with insulin, diabetic control may become wildly disrupted along with their mood. The insulin requirements of the anorexia nervosa sufferer may also be difficult to work out. Treatment needs to be along the lines of that for any eating disorder, but with the added issue of diabetic 'control' dealt with alongside the issue of helping the patient to exert less 'control' of a different sort over her weight and eating. Peveler and Fairburn (1989, 1992) have written accounts of how the usual treatment may need to be modified.

EDNOS

EDNOS, Eating Disorder Not Otherwise Specified, is the category to which states of eating disorder of clinical severity are assigned if they do not fulfil diagnostic criteria for either of the two main disorders. Strictly speaking, binge eating disorder (BED) is a variety of EDNOS but the diagnosis, although still provisional in DSM-IV, has won sufficient acceptance for it to be usually excluded. However, there is plenty left. Again, strictly speaking, most cases of EDNOS will be what might be called mild cases or partial syndromes; that is, they closely resemble one or other of the main disorders except in respect of the degree of one of the symptoms. An example would be a woman who fulfilled criteria for bulimia nervosa except in respect of the duration or frequency of the bingeing behaviour. In the main, such cases do not give rise to significant treatment problems. They are likely to respond about as well or better to conventional treatment approaches as do people with full syndrome disorders. The chief conundrum may be as to whether they need full treatment or whether within some systems of third party funding they will be eligible for it. There is some evidence that mild disorder responds to lesser treatments such as psychoeducation in a group (Olmsted *et al.*, 1991). However, full syndrome status does not always map neatly onto distress or overall severity. Diagnostic criteria should not be used rigidly to exclude people from treatment who have significant clinical problems.

This principle applies even more to people with unusual disorders which do not fulfil the criteria but are by no means mild. Thus any clinical practice in the field of eating disorders will include people with a variety of states which, for one reason or another, must be classified as EDNOS. They are a mixed bunch.

Some have disorders which seem to be based around eating restraint but differ in their behaviour. For instance, an important group are those who have weight concerns similar to people with bulimia nervosa and who seek to control their weight in the normal range by regular self-induced vomiting but do not binge. Another behaviourally defined group is composed of individuals who claim to eat nothing at all and survive on calorific drinks. Other EDNOS sufferers differ in their motivation and thinking from typical disorders. Thus, as has been mentioned before, there may be individuals with behaviour more or less identical with bulimia nervosa or anorexia nervosa who restrain their eating for reasons other than weight concern (Palmer, 1993). Both of these broad categories of EDNOS sufferers have disorders in which eating restraint plays a part. In treatment, their needs may closely resemble those of people with more typical disorders, although the different behaviours or ideas need to be acknowledged. In particular, when the ideas are different it can be irritating if the therapist continues to assume a knowing scepticism beyond a certain point about the patient's denial of weight concern. Whilst it is true that some sufferers from eating disorders hide or deny the true nature of their fears and feelings about body weight, it does seem also to be true that some have different concerns.

Other people present unusual problems because of their special lifestyles. In this respect female athletes may be especially challenging in that they may have partial or full syndrome disorders which, however, may be valued in some of their aspects but not others. Furthermore, the ideas involved may be unusual and complex and involve performance pressure and a precarious sense of self-worth which is dependent upon getting things just right in the face of competition, coaching and the ever-present risk of injury (Brownell, 1995). The 'female athlete triad' of disordered eating, amenorrhoea and osteoporosis is well recognised, as is the wish of some athletes to keep their weight low but not too low whilst sustaining the lack of menstruation but somehow avoiding risking the bony changes. The management of the true casualty of athletics who develops a full eating disorder and has to give up her sport may be complex but often presents no special challenges. The case of the still competing partial syndrome sufferer may be full of real dilemmas for both patient and clinician.

Other EDNOS sufferers seem not to be restraining and give other accounts of their over or undereating. Thus, some may eat very eccentrically and in that respect resemble a group which is well recognised in child psychiatry. Others claim to be addicted to sugar or some other food. Others have long-lasting avoidance of adequate eating which seems to be based upon fear of vomiting or some other illness. Others seem to have something very like anorexia nervosa except that they claim to have no appetite or that they are prevented from eating adequately by various physical symptoms. They may say that they wish to put on weight but cannot force themselves to eat sufficient to do so. This last group is of especial interest since it seems that in some cultures they form a significant proportion of all of those suffering from what would otherwise be confidently diagnosed as anorexia nervosa (Lee, Ho & Hsu, 1993). The treatment implications are not especially clear but presumably any psychotherapy must start from attention to how the patient views her own state. All of these states present a challenge to skilled clinicians who wish to construct bespoke therapies from first principles.

Lastly, of course, eating disorders without the classic psychopathology and without a plausible alternative must raise the question of whether some other psychiatric or physical disorder is present. Thus, partially masked depression with true loss of appetite may sometimes present as an apparent eating disorder, as may psychotic disorder with delusions around food. Furthermore, although the diagnosis of a typical eating disorder, or one of the more clear-cut atypical disorders, should always be made on positive grounds, the 'diagnosis' of a truly atypical and mysterious EDNOS cannot be so confidently made. The wary clinician will always keep open the possibility of an as yet to be diagnosed physical disorder. 'Something we haven't thought of yet' should always remain on the list of diagnostic possibilities. Furthermore, if the context is that of a consultation with a puzzled physician who has called in the psychiatrist, or whoever, as the last resort in a case with serial negative investigations, the clinician who is being thought of as yet another investigation should feel free to come back negative. It may be appropriate to act pragmatically but preserve some diagnostic doubt rather than accept a state as 'psychological' as a diagnosis of exclusion.

NOTES

1. I am an adult psychiatrist and this book is written from a notably 'adult' perspective. It is for this reason that childhood onset disorders are tucked away in the chapter on 'unusual' disorders. Of course, for some clinicians such patients are in the foreground. If that is the case for you then the present book can provide only background information and discussion of issues which are common to eating disorders occurring at any age. Fortunately there are accounts which are more focused on younger sufferers. The book by Bryan Lask and Rachel Bryant-Waugh is recommended at the end of the chapter.
2. I am personally wary of the kind of team approach to such mixed problems which involves X seeing the patient for her eating disorder, Y for her post-traumatic stress disorder and Z for her alcohol problem. Team work is often a good idea but such carving up of a case seems often to be asking for complication and trouble. The patient is likely to be bemused and feel like a set of 'problems' rather than a person.

FURTHER READING

Lask, B & Bryant-Waugh, R (1996) *Childhood Onset Anorexia Nervosa and Related Disorders*. Psychology Press, Hove.
Lask, B & Bryant-Waugh, R (2000) Anorexia nervosa and related eating disorders in childhood and adolescence (2nd edn). Psychology Press, Hove. — This is a substantially changed second edition of the 1996 book.

10

WHAT MAY GO WRONG?

Thus far the chapters about treatment have described mostly what is known about the kinds of interventions that have been found to be helpful in general to people with the two main eating disorders and some of their variants. However, even in the best of circumstances things not uncommonly go wrong. Other chapters have included discussions of complications of the disorders as such. However, sometimes what goes wrong may be better thought of as the treatment process itself getting off track. This chapter will discuss some of the ways in which this may happen. It will be something of a mixed bag of topics. The common theme will be the need to foresee troubles, avoid them when that is possible and get through them when it is not.

THE MANAGEMENT OF MIXED FEELINGS

Mixed feelings are characteristic of people presenting with eating disorders. This is especially so with anorexia nervosa. Such feelings have been touched upon in earlier chapters but there has been little discussion of the major difficulties which may arise in relation to them. The following sections will discuss some of these, but first it may be useful to outline again the nature of these mixed feelings and what seems to be the best way of dealing with them.[1]

The person suffering from anorexia nervosa is faced with a dilemma. This dilemma – or set of dilemmas – may be experienced in all sorts of ways. However, it often boils down to something like the following. The sufferer may be frightened, uncomfortable and distressed as she is, but she is also frightened by the prospect of change. She feels that changing is a risky business. What is at risk is a sense of being in control of her life – albeit in a tenuous, unstable and painful way. Any move forward leads to an increase in a fear of losing this control and usually to a retreat. She is stuck and feels trapped. The person who would help her to move forward cannot do so directly but only by helping her to find a way through her dilemma. If she is not moving – or indeed is retreating – the would-be helper is also faced with a dilemma as to how much to allow the sufferer to dither and how much to push, cajole, insist or otherwise take charge of a situation which may seem to be out of hand or even dangerous.

Any dilemma involves confrontation with a painful choice. The basic dilemma belongs to the patient. The clinician may be unsure what to do but his dilemma is secondary. And these two dilemmas need to be kept separate. There are issues which are the responsibility of the patient and there are issues which are the responsibility of the clinician. His role is to act as honest broker in these matters of responsibility and not to mix up the different roles. The basic task for the helper is to support the sufferer in facing up to her dilemma and to help her to feel that she can move forward. She needs to feel just about safe enough to do so. The clinician needs to give information, support and the opportunity to clarify the issues. Sometimes this may also involve the provision of the means of, or the circumstance for, safe change as when hospital admission is proposed. What the clinician should not do is to take over the dilemma of the patient. He should certainly not do this in order to relieve his own worry and concern or even those of third parties such as relatives. That way leads to battles.

BATTLING

The anorexia nervosa sufferer who is confronted with offers of help can respond in a number of ways. She may feel able to form some sort of working alliance aimed at recovery. She may go along with behavioural change but with inner reservations. Or she may resist. If she resists, she may find her thinking and experience strangely changed in a potentially hazardous way. Instead of having to struggle with complicated mixed feelings she may find herself simply opposing the efforts of those who would have her change. Others take over from her the voicing of the need to escape from her present painful position. She leaves this to them. She resists change. They push the case for change. She feels pushed about and resists more strongly. She is left experiencing only her fears of change since others have taken over the case in favour of change. She can now speak of her fears more wholeheartedly. The more a person asserts a belief the more strongly is she likely to hold it. There is a real danger in circumstances like these that the sufferer becomes more and more single minded in her anorexia nervosa. And the more single minded her resistance, the more those around her may worry and push her to change. They have come to be the repository for all of what were previously the sufferer's own positive feelings. What had been an internal struggle has become largely an external battle. Often, of course, the sufferer may give way to the forces both inside her and outside her which are pushing for change. She may then allow herself to put on weight, albeit perhaps with reservations. Then she may indeed be moving onto safer ground and if her state had been extreme this is a good thing. However, if this does not happen the interaction between the sufferer and those around her can turn into an escalating struggle with tragic results. The whole thing can become a desperate poker game in which the 'ante' is increasingly 'upped'. It is a game that can be played out to the death.

Such battles are true tragedies because all of those involved are likely to be acting from the best of motives, but nevertheless together they may construct a disaster. The sufferer is caught up in the web of anorexia nervosa. She may want to escape but is trying to hang on to some sense of autonomy. The clinician – and the family – want to rescue her and save her from harm. The more extreme and dangerous her situation appears to be, the more it feels appropriate to try to force the issue. The stakes are high. Desperate situations seem to justify desperate remedies. Furthermore, the personal pressure experienced by the clinician tends to increase. Something must be done. He, too, becomes emotionally involved and the fears and frustrations promoted by the situation may at times provoke responses which owe a lot to what the clinician brings to the situation. He may feel thwarted, angry, impotent or provoked into a need to win at all costs.[2] The situation may get more and more complicated and feel more and more like trench warfare.

AVOIDING BATTLES

If a clinician finds himself in the midst of such a battle, he should remember that the aim is to win the war. This may well involve tactical retreat, which will usually be the best option when the urgings of those who would help her seem to be undermining the sufferer's own capacity to experience the dilemma which faces her and to be in touch with the possible advantages of change. She needs space and often she should be given it. However, it is important that the clinician should remain available and, indeed, be active in remaining in touch with the patient even when it seems best not to push more active intervention. For instance, he may, if the sufferer is an outpatient, continually make appointments and write letters to the reluctant patient even if she does not always attend or respond. The idea is to seek to be steadfastly alongside the sufferer in her dilemma but not to take it over. It may even be proper for the clinician to be somewhat pushy in reminding the person of her mixed feelings, her uncertainty and her suffering and of the fact that those around her know something of this even when she says little or seeks to reassure them that she is all right. She may be bombed with sympathy about her dilemma but it should remain hers. The clinician should not seek to take it over. There are dilemmas enough in the role of the would-be helper.[3]

Staying alongside someone with severe anorexia nervosa – and it is usually anorexia nervosa rather than bulimia nervosa in which these situations arise – can be worrying. It is a sweaty business. There is a constant temptation to take charge, but to do so is usually a mistake. However, just occasionally this may be the right thing to do when the sufferer seems to be signalling her genuine inability to decide what to do and her exhaustion with the task of trying to make up her mind. However, any taking over – for instance, by strongly urging hospital admission – should be explicit, temporary and accompanied by discussion of the patient's longer term dilemma which will not be resolved by such action.

What Might Have Happened to Faith – Another Version

When she was offered a first outpatient appointment with the local psychiatrist, Faith felt frightened that she was going to be pushed into hospital in the way that she had read about in a magazine. She feared that if this happened it would end all hope of her going to University in the following autumn. She also felt that she would be forced to put on weight and that once this started she would 'lose it' and would never again be able to exercise that self-control that she felt would be necessary to manage. So when the time came she refused to go along to the appointment and her parents were angry with her. She tried desperately to prove that she was all right but the harder she tried the more her mother and father worried about her. She lost more weight and began feeling faint and weak when she climbed the stairs. After a further month or so, her family doctor, urged by her mother, arranged for the psychiatrist to do a home visit. The arrangement had been made behind Faith's back and she was told only minutes before the doctor arrived. Faith was upset and angry. She refused to talk to the psychiatrist. However, the diagnosis and the extremity of the situation were clear enough and he suggested emergency admission to hospital that day. In the end Faith agreed to go in on a voluntary basis although there had been hints about the possibility of legal compulsion if she did not do so.

On admission to hospital, Faith weighed 32 kg and was somewhat dehydrated. Encouraged by the nursing staff who were kind but firm she began to eat and drink a little more. She was scared but also secretly comforted by the care she was receiving. However, when she was weighed again after a few days she had put on over 3 kg and felt that all her fears of sudden and unstoppable weight gain were coming true. She was not reassured when it was explained that the change in her weight was almost entirely due to rehydration. She felt unsafe and out of control and refused to eat. Her doctor was worried and frustrated by her state and repeatedly explained the dangers of her situation, saying that he would have to compel her to eat if her resistance continued. However, he did not explain exactly what he meant by this and Faith imagined all sorts of frightening interventions. The nursing staff told her that she might be detained under the Mental Health Act and mentioned that a treatment order could last six months or even longer.

For a while Faith entertained thoughts that she would rather die than put on weight. However, a day or two later, everyone around her was relieved when Faith started to eat everything that was offered to her. Indeed, her mother was puzzled but delighted when Faith asked her to 'smuggle in' extra chocolate bars. Faith herself was in a complicated emotional state but was secretly resolved to get out of hospital and do things her way. After three weeks, her weight had risen to 40 kg and she insisted on leaving hospital saying that she was now 'better'. Her doctor advised her to stay but said that compulsion was now not on the agenda. Her parents had mixed feelings about her coming home but wanted to believe that things would be all right. They too had been distressed at the thought of their daughter being 'forced' to eat.

The hospital offered follow-up appointments with a clinical psychologist but Faith refused these. Once out of hospital she cut back her eating drastically but occasionally had binges. She resumed her frantic exercising. Her weight fell back to 36 kg. Although she agreed to see her family doctor every month and to be weighed every week by the practice nurse, she declined all other offers of help.

This whole episode left Faith no further forward and, indeed, less trustful of those who might offer to help her in future. She had become somewhat inoculated against professional help and treatment. If she had not decided to eat her way out of hospital and had chosen to increase the stakes, the outcome might have been more extreme and tragic.

The sufferer's physical state is, of course, highly relevant. When this is causing real concern the facts, as the clinician sees them, should be shared with the patient. Any risks are part of her dilemma. However, the clinician should avoid using such information simply to scare the patient and – in poker terms – to up the ante. A statement along the lines 'if you don't do X then Y will happen therefore you *must* do X' often tends to provoke a denial of the possibility of Y and a contemplation of the awfulness of facing up to doing X. A better approach may be to discuss the enormity from the sufferer's point of view of *both* X *and* Y as options and the real difficulty of deciding between them. This should be accompanied by offers of genuine help and support should she opt for X. Patients may need time to ponder – to dither painfully from the perspective of those around them – but few will finally opt for a dreadful Y alone if they feel that real help and understanding are available if they go for X.

The family and important others in the patient's life have strong feelings too. In extreme situations they are likely to be very worried. These worries should be recognised and the people supported. However, this should not be at the expense of the relationship with the sufferer herself – at least when she is an adult and thus ultimately in charge of her own decisions. It is all too easy for the situation to become one in which the patient feels ganged up against and cornered. In general, it may be best for all discussions with relatives to take place in the presence of the sufferer, or at least with her explicit permission. She should not be given grounds to feel that she is being talked about inappropriately behind her back. On the other hand, she should not be protected from the fact that different decisions may have different consequences for others and that some may cause great distress and worry. Being treated as a grown up works both ways. However, being treated as an adult *tends* to help people to behave in an adult manner and to take responsibility for themselves. Being treated as a child tends to have the opposite effect. There are parallels between the state of being a child and that of being a sick person. Both involve the individual in being thought of as less able to take on certain kinds of responsibility. However, the sick adult is usually thought of as having to undertake, in return for relief from some other usual duties, the responsibility for taking appropriate steps to become well again. In the case of a child, such responsibility tends to fall upon the parents – for instance, it is they who have to consent to operations and so on. When a young adult with anorexia nervosa seems to be behaving *like* a child and her state is a worrying one for all concerned, then there is a real temptation to treat her *as* a child. Then issues of illness and immaturity may get mixed up. Furthermore, the issue of lack of competence to take responsibility through *mental* illness may also raise itself.

COMPULSORY TREATMENT

Most countries have laws which allow mentally ill people to be admitted to hospital without their consent and often also to be treated against their will if their state is sufficiently alarming. The gist of such legislation is usually the requirement that the person's safety or that of others should be at significant risk before such drastic steps against personal liberty can be considered. Although there are those who object to all such compulsion, in general the involuntary treatment of people suffering from major psychosis is not controversial. This is not the case with anorexia nervosa.[4] The difficulty would seem to be two-fold. Firstly, is anorexia nervosa to be considered a mental illness in the relevant sense? Secondly, is it truly amenable to treatment without consent?

The first question appears to be one of principle. Is anorexia nervosa a mental illness? However, to be able to answer the question in terms of principle would require there to be an adequate definition of mental illness against which anorexia nervosa could be judged one way or another. Unfortunately, such a definition tends to be elusive. Typically legislation avoids the issue and does not attempt to provide one.[5] Clinicians and others are left to make a practical judgement without explicit criteria upon which to make the decision. However, most would consider that severe anorexia nervosa can be construed as a mental illness and, therefore, given the relevant circumstances of sufficient risk, compulsory hospital admission or treatment *could* be justified and used where the law allows this for other mental disorders. The more practical question then arises of when and if such compulsion *should* be used.

Although it may be appropriately thought of as a mental illness, anorexia nervosa is not really amenable to what might be called instrumental treatments. There are no drugs or other procedures that may be applied without the cooperation of the sufferer which will predictably produce cure or radical change. A surgeon may operate upon the body of someone suffering from bowel cancer, and this will have personal consequences for the patient. However, broadly speaking, the success of the operation as such does not depend upon the attitude of the patient. But interventions aimed at rescuing the physical state of someone with anorexia nervosa affect her person in a more profound sense. Her body is in its present condition as it is as the result of her personal fears and her personal strivings. This whole section has discussed the disorder in terms of the dilemmas which it poses for the sufferer. Elsewhere these dilemmas have been depicted as understandable as complex vicious circles. Any intervention which is imposed upon the sufferer will impinge upon these dilemmas and vicious circles. The clinician who acts without the cooperation of the patient is intervening in a complex system and the results are unlikely to be simple.

When the decision has been made to detain in hospital a patient suffering from severe anorexia nervosa, the dilemmas do not end for either the patient or for the clinicians involved. As the old saying goes, you can lead a horse to the water but you can't make it drink. Detention is not a guarantee that the situation is radically changed. However, 'forced feeding' is rarely required. Faced with legal compulsion and skilled nursing, most patients will at least acquiesce and begin to take food and drink. The emotional atmosphere which is created around the patient remains the most important factor. Nurses experienced in this task can combine firm persuasion with patience and kindness. Such skill and confidence are most easily promoted in a specialist unit which treats a steady stream of severely ill patients of this kind. It is difficult to contrive on a one-off basis around a single patient in a general psychiatric or medical ward.[6]

If such persuasion is unsuccessful, resort may have to be made to more drastic means if the relevant law allows this.[7] This would mean the use of feeding via a naso-gastic tube or even an intravenous drip. Either *can* be given without the consent of the patient and even without her cooperation. However, such feeding in the face of active opposition is not an easy business. Furthermore, when a weak and emaciated patient is fed or even just rehydrated intravenously, great care must be taken not to overload the circulation. It is all too easy to precipitate cardiac failure and pulmonary oedema in such patients in this way. It is likely to be safer to use a naso-gastric tube rather than an intravenous drip in most cases. In dealing with the patient who is very severely ill but uncooperative, there may be real dilemmas about what is the better setting – that of the psychiatric unit or the medical ward. Each may have advantages and disadvantages. Whatever the setting, the psychiatrist may often benefit from the advice of the internal physician and vice versa. And if the cooperation is regular and has been established before the particular case, so much the better.

If the situation has got as far as the consideration of the use of an intravenous drip or naso-gastric tube under conditions of legal compulsion, it is in a sense already out of hand. The patient is likely to be frightened or angry, or both. The clinicians, too, may be experiencing similar emotions albeit in more muted forms and beneath a veneer of professional resolve. There is a need for calm reassessment of the situation although that may not be easy to achieve. All available options should be reviewed, including that of a temporary tactical retreat which lets everyone off the hook even for a few hours. Sometimes that may be enough for the patient to opt to cooperate. Any kind of cooperation is to be cherished because even if the battle is joined and won, the patient and those who are treating her have to get on to the same side eventually if the 'victory' is to have lasting significance. Indeed, the decision of when and how to *end* compulsion may be as full of difficulty as that of its starting. If the intervention has been made in the midst of what feels like a battle of wills, then the act of taking off the legal order may provoke a renewal of the battle or a rupture of the clinical relationship which it has sought to secure. The patient may feel that she *should* now leave or stop cooperating now that she is free to do so. The same issues that were present before the compulsion was used are likely to be present again with full force unless the intervening time has been used to good effect to talk about them and move towards some resolution. Compulsory treatment may buy time – and arguably sometimes does so by saving life – but it does not make the problems of building a usable treatment alliance go away. Patients for whom detention is even considered are a high-risk group. The limited evidence about the outcome of compulsory treatment suggests that the short-term effects are often favourable but the longer term problems, including an elevated risk of premature death, remain (Serfaty & McCluskey, 1998; Ramsay, Ward, Treasure & Russell, 1999).

There is real room for debate about the place of compulsion in the treatment of anorexia nervosa. It should certainly not be used except as a last resort when all else has failed and the patient is in danger. Clearly, different clinicians may make different judgements about when this time has come.[8] However, most would agree that it is a major decision to seek to deprive an individual of her usual rights and liberties. And in the case of anorexia nervosa, the decision is hedged around with fears that the intervention may not always enable the clinician to make matters better and, indeed, could itself sometimes make matters worse. The possibility of making things worse should give pause for thought to anyone who is tempted to invoke legal compulsion too readily when the management of anorexia nervosa becomes difficult. The situation may become more complex and difficult for the clinicians involved as well as for the patient. The imposition of a legal order does not directly change the situation. It may open up some options for intervention which would otherwise be illegal but it may also close off others.

SPLITTING AND RIVALRY

The successful treatment of anorexia nervosa, and indeed of the other eating disorders, depends upon the creation and maintenance of an adequate treatment alliance between the sufferer and the clinician or clinicians who would seek to help her to recover. This is the case whatever the particular mode of treatment. When the treatment is psychotherapeutic, or when the patient is very ill or both, the therapeutic alliance may have to withstand complex pressures. The clinician may come to be ambivalently invested with the hopes, expectations and fears of the patient and such investment may serve a positive purpose. It may help the sufferer to feel safe enough to confront the rigours of recovery. However, the clinician should be aware of the downside of high positive investment. When there is a 'goody' or 'goodies', there are usually 'baddies'. The sufferer may have produced a false resolution of some of her wider uncertainties and dilemmas by splitting her world in this way. The unwary clinician may preen himself inwardly at the implication that he alone truly understands and can help the distressed damsel but such false constructions can rarely bear much weight – almost literally so in the case of anorexia nervosa. Unmitigated goodies are destined to fall from their pedestals and can cause damage as they do so. Furthermore, there will inevitably be those who are cast in the role of outsider in such dramas. Sometimes when treatment is a team effort, these others will be the various colleagues of the clinician who is positively invested.

Different clinicians have different roles in a team effort. Inevitably some will be preferred by the patient from time to time or be seen as more important or as more understanding. However, the team should see itself as a team and be aware of the problems which may arise when differences and preferences become splitting and subversion of the various roles. A sense of common purpose and a mutual respect between team members is crucial. These need to be cherished. If this has been done when things are going smoothly then the team can withstand the difficult times which will always come sooner or later.

There are things that can be done to make problematic splitting less likely. These include regular discussion between the team members and an active attention to the interpersonal aspects of care in good times and bad. The team member whose good work has been acknowledged will be more able to take on board comments about the way that things might be going awry at other times. The team leaders should not be immune from comment since they may be especially vulnerable. However, so may the most junior or those with the lowest status on the team. For instance, in an inpatient setting for the treatment of anorexia nervosa, either the designated therapist or the inexperienced nursing assistant may be led to feel that he or she alone really understands the patient and that the rest of the team is crude and crass in their efforts merely to feed the patient. In either case complex issues of status may compound such difficulties. The therapist may feel that the nursing staff are not so well equipped or trained to understand the subtleties of the patient's feelings. The nursing assistant may identify with the patient's perception of the senior staff as distant and uncomprehending authority figures – or simply as 'old' – and as people who are unable to empathise with her feelings and understand her dilemmas. Of course, there may be grains of truth in any such perceptions but if mismanaged they will tend to grow into weeds which clutter the field. Viewing all of this from what he feels is his all-knowing perspective, the team leader may pontificate and pronounce and he too may from time to time find himself out on a ludicrous limb. A team that has a – perhaps unspoken – appreciation that these kinds of issues are likely to arise is more than half way to managing them well when they do.[9]

When members of the family of the patient come to be construed as the 'baddies', the clinician or team must be wary. They may find themselves in a complicated position. The first move is to try to understand it – to develop a workable story about what is going on. At the simplest it may be that the relationship between the patient and her family has been temporarily damaged by the difficulties of the disorder and its consequences. The family that has spent months or years trying to induce a distressed daughter to eat, will be enormously relieved when she begins to do so. However, they may also experience some irritation that she is doing now for *others* what she so determinedly refused to do in the recent past for *them*. Such irritation is understandable but may be difficult for the family to acknowledge even to themselves. It may emerge in an implicit expectation that the clever clinician should now sort out *everything*, including things that are certainly beyond his power. There is covert hostility in this and the ambivalent hope that the limits of his potency will be revealed. The unwary clinician may fall headlong into a trap by trying to do the impossible or inappropriate when asked or expected to do so by an apparently relieved family. The dangers of this will be the more if the patient is indeed investing excessively in the clinician or working out negative feelings on the family at the same time. As usual the remedy – or, better still, the prophylactic – is to emphasise the idea that it is the sufferer who is the active agent in the enterprise of recovery and it is she who is confronting her dilemmas. The clinician should portray his role as that of providing some of the means and the circumstances for change but not its motive power. Furthermore, he should gently point out that it is his very lack of historical and essential importance in the life of the patient that sometimes gives him the edge and the ability to provide the patient with something to hang on to.

Of course, at times it will be the case that what seems to be the best 'story' about the sufferer's past or current situation includes issues for which the parents or others may justly be criticised from her perspective. Furthermore, it may that the wider process of recovery – the third task in the terminology of Chapter 5 – may involve the patient asserting herself, being critical of or even, in a few cases, cutting herself off from her family. However, once again, it is the sufferer who is the agent of these changes and the role of the clinician is to help her to clarify her thoughts and feelings and to support her appropriately in what she decides to do. It is not to take over. If there are fights between the patient and her family, the clinician may sometimes undertake the role of sympathetic ring holder but should not usually become a protagonist or even a coach. There may be exceptions to this principle; for instance, when a young person has been the victim of abuse or criminal behaviour by members of her family it would be appropriate to take a clear stance on her side. However, in general, a kind of sympathetic neutrality is best. Such neutrality extends to the family also although the relationship is different. It is a legitimate part of the clinician's role to talk in confidence with the patient about her family – behind their back as it were. The reverse does not apply. To that degree the clinician is on the side of the patient.

COLLUDING

The opposite of battling is colluding. This occurs when the clinician responds to the sufferer's fears by allowing her to believe that there is a way forward that does not involve confronting such fears – that there is a way forward that is easy or, if not easy, not frightening in the same way as weight gain. Such collusion may take the form of smothering the sufferer with so much sympathy and apparent understanding that there is no room for bravery. Anything that smacks of change involving pain is deemed too much for the patient, perhaps because the clinician feels that the sufferer has been through so much already. The dynamic is one of protection and often it seems that the professional is out to shield the patient not only from harm but also from difficulty. Especially when enacted over time within a therapeutic relationship, this type of collusion may lead to an unproductive dependence upon the therapist, who comes to occupy a position in which he must ultimately fail. Then for the patient, there is inevitable disappointment and perhaps a recapitulation of past let downs. In such a circumstance the therapist has made the error of thinking of his role as that of providing a substitute or compensation for the deficiencies of the sufferer's life. In truth, of course, that is at most a small and hopefully transient part of the process. Therapy should be mainly about enabling the sufferer to experience herself as able to deal effectively with the demands of life, including the difficulties of recovery. A certain courage is necessary if someone is to escape from a severe eating disorder. The therapist needs to convey an appreciation of that need for courage, a supportive confidence that the sufferer can come to find it within herself and an appropriate cheering from the sidelines as she does so.[10]

Another form of collusion may involve a therapeutic situation in which there is a lot of talk but no action or expectation of action. This may involve an implicit redefinition of the problem as having nothing to do with weight or eating and everything to do with all sorts of issues and feelings that need exploration and discussion *before* any symptomatic or behavioural change can be reasonably expected. The therapist may respond to the patient's implicit fears by taking off all pressure for weight gain or whatever. Such a view may be bolstered with sophisticated theorising and a belief that only 'deep' issues are worthy of attention. Of course, it may sometimes be the case that a deal of talking – exploration and clarification – does indeed need to proceed behavioural change, but such change should always be acknowledged as an essential part of recovery. Fears should be discussed as fears, but most fears need also to be confronted if they are to be overcome. It is rarely the case that they can be talked away entirely and thus avoided. Such avoidance often leads fears to grow. When this kind of collusion really gets going, the sufferer and therapist may come together literally for years in a shared enterprise which both believe will eventually lead to radical change but which runs a real risk of becoming almost a way of life. When both kinds of collusion are present together, the chances of real recovery become remote.

STALEMATE

Such collusion is one way in which a therapeutic endeavour can become stuck. However, sometimes progress may grind to a halt for reasons that are unclear. This may have the feeling of stalemate. Both clinician and patient are making their respective moves but to little or no effect. In such circumstances it is important in the first instance to discuss the situation as a phenomenon of the therapy and as a part of the process. This will be easier to do if the form and process of the treatment have throughout been something that has been both discussable and discussed. Thus, if the patient has been encouraged to talk about her mixed feelings about change when she was making progress, such issues will be much easier to address when there is none. The clinician and the patient both have a responsibility to try to work out what is happening. However, it is usually best to avoid the language of blame. The clinician should think what he might do differently but should not feel that he has necessarily done anything wrong. On the other hand, he should not simply castigate the patient for lack of effort or motivation. Both must think about how things can be made to move forward if that is what the patient wants and thinks she can manage. If she wants it but cannot manage it then the question is: 'What further help or means does she need in order to move?' The answer may be all manner of things from an explicit acknowledgement and discussion of how difficult it feels to her, to a radical change of circumstance such as hospital admission. Or it may seem that there is something about the very nature of the current therapy that is stuck and may even be impeding progress. Sometimes this can be worked out and worked through. If no answer is forthcoming, it may sometimes be worth while slackening off for a while and allowing both parties to let themselves off the hook as it were. For instance, a weekly outpatient therapy that has come to have the feel of stalemate might benefit from a break for a few weeks or a change to a pattern of monthly meetings. Sometimes such manoeuvres can ease things and allow subsequent progress even if the nature of the snag remains obscure. Sometimes a temporary break can be a prelude to a more lasting disengagement from a therapeutic exercise that has become sterile. It is important, however, that the sufferer feels that continuing low key contact is an option and that more intensive treatment might be available again in the future when and if the time seems right. The resolution of a stalemate should never lead to the patient feeling written off by the clinician as an hopeless case and an irredeemable person.

DROP OUT

Sometimes a therapeutic endeavour may end with the patient dropping out. This happens often although the precise rates reported vary with the definition of drop out and the circumstances. It is an issue which receives less attention than it deserves. Perhaps studying our 'failures' has limited appeal. Furthermore, the results of what research there is are far from emphatic (e.g. Vanderycken & Pierloot, 1983; Merrill, Mines & Starkey, 1987; Blouin et al., 1995; Clinton, 1996; Waller, 1997). In general, simply defined variables have not been found to have much predictive value although there is a tendency for those who drop out from treatment for bulimia nervosa to be younger and to have less severe disorder than those who stick to their treatment programme. In anorexia nervosa, one study found that high expressed emotion – especially critical comments – in the family predicted failure to stay in family therapy (Szmukler, Eisler, Russell & Dare, 1985b).

As ever, in the absence of illuminating data, speculation based upon clinical experience must inform practice and future research. One perspective which may prove enlightening is to think of the breakdown or failure to establish a working therapeutic alliance with the patient as an attachment phenomenon. Attachment theory, as developed in the work of John Bowlby, suggests that there are patterns of secure and insecure attachment which may characterise a person in his or her dealings with important others (Bowlby, 1988; Holmes, 1997). Such patterns arise in childhood development but are not entirely immutable in adult life. Individuals may change for better or worse in relation to events, circumstances and relationships. It is difficult for some individuals to muster the trust to establish any working alliance with a therapist. Others may seem to do so readily but the bond is not robust and fails at the first setback or challenge. Of course, the clinician also has a characteristic attachment style, and it takes two to tango. Certainly, it is too easy to attribute drop out to lack of motivation as if motivation were simply an attribute of the patient. Arguably motivation is better thought of as something which is a result of the immediate interaction between the patient and her circumstance, most notably the relationship with those who would help her. Drop out from treatment must, in most cases, involve some change in motivation which has arisen in the therapeutic situation. After all the individual has come along asking for help – albeit perhaps with mixed feelings – but something has changed her mind. It is the task of the clinician to foster the motivation that the patient shows.[11]

In practice, drop out from clinical contact may require different responses depending upon the context. Indeed, drop out may range from (a) failure to take up a first assessment appointment or to return for a second, to (b) a unplanned rupture in a process of established therapy which has been going on for a long time. In the case of early drop out, it may be appropriate to construe it variously as anything from failure of courage to failure of appropriate tuning of clinical response. In the case of later breakdown of therapy, it may be anything from a crisis in the therapeutic relationship to bad manners. The clinician involved needs to think of what has gone wrong and act accordingly. Usually this will involve continuing to be available and to offer to resume contact at least for a while. However, of course, in practice, at some point it will usually be necessary to bring such ready availability to an end. Even then, where possible, the door should not be entirely closed.

DISSOCIATION AND COMPLICATION

Dissociation is a clinical phenomenon which may complicate or even disrupt a therapeutic career. The term is used to denote the mechanism thought to underlie a number of puzzling and apparently disparate behaviours and experiences from inappropriate affect through depersonalisation and functional amnesia to so-called dissociative identity disorder or multiple personality. The common thread is a failure of integration of the mental functions manifest in consciousness, memory, identity and perception. Some phenomena which might be explained in this way are not uncommon in eating-disordered patients (Vanderlinden & Vanderycken, 1997). Most such states are transient and readily manageable. The therapeutic alliance is not threatened and can be maintained. However, major difficulty arises when dissociative states are either so severe or so long-lasting as to disrupt or defeat normal interaction and communication.

There seems to be a link between dissociation and psychological trauma. Indeed, such states are arguably the only psychological conditions where, at least as a working hypothesis, it may be legitimate to infer preceding trauma from current state.[12] Often patients with marked dissociative states have been severely abused either sexually or physically. The dissociation may be thought of as a reaction, perhaps a defence, against the enormity of what has happened to the sufferer. However, it is important to bear in mind that a woman of 28 who was severely and repeatedly abused when she was, say, 9 will hardly ever have spent the whole intervening 19 years in a state of evident and troublesome dissociation. The present state will have been triggered by more recent events and sometimes by the very therapeutic attempt within which it is recognised. The inference should be, therefore, that something is overwhelming the patient's capacity for integration *now* even if that something has to do with current memories of traumas in the distant past. Memories occur in a context and have one foot in the present. The past is unchangeable and so it is the present component that must be worked with.

If a severe dissociative state becomes manifest, it is important to try to produce an explanatory hypothesis. Such a hypothesis or 'story' can be used to inform management but the clinician should be wary of too much certainty. The patient may well be in a highly suggestible state and therapist and patient can ride off together into a jointly constructed fantasy world unless care is taken to avoid this happening. It seems likely that at least some cases of dissociative identity disorder (multiple personality disorder) arise in this way.

Notable dissociation may well be a sign that the patient is being overwhelmed and that it is time for the therapy to slow down or become grounded again in the here and now. Even apparently banal statements about where the patient is and the professional nature of the relationship with the therapist may be helpful. The alternative plan of pushing the exploration of memories and seeking to relive past traumas may seem fascinating and be tempting for the unwary therapist. However, it seems to help the patient rarely if at all and may do harm. Gross dissociation should be taken as a sign to cool it. If the patient is highly distressed or disturbed, she may need to be cared for, perhaps even in hospital, but the therapeutic breakthrough which may seem to be tantalisingly close is usually a mirage. The clinician should ponder but not push. When the patient is once again grounded and integrated, the therapy can continue and may sometimes be informed by what has happened during the time of dissociation.[13]

CHRONICITY

Some people suffer from anorexia nervosa or bulimia nervosa over many years. For some of these, their illness is experienced as a battle that does not change much over these years. Their disorder and the fears and emotions which are associated with it remain a continuing struggle and dilemma. They can imagine recovery and continue to hope to escape but somehow do not. Most long-term sufferers from bulimia nervosa at normal weight seem to fall into this group. For others, life gets built around and alongside the disorder which is experienced as a constant – something that is there and is unlikely to change. Such people have come to accept their disorder as a limitation or even as a way of life. Indeed sometimes, the whole identity of the sufferers seems to have become bound up with their state. They spend little time on the thought of recovery, except perhaps as an impossible dream. Many long-term sufferers from anorexia nervosa have developed these characteristics. Both groups – and clearly there are many long-term sufferers who fall neatly into neither group – may be described as chronic in the sense of having a long-lasting disorder. However, some would wish to reserve the term for the latter group. It is certainly that group who need particular and special thought with regard to what they may best be offered. The first group may well be able to benefit from interventions similar to those sufferers with a much shorter history of disorder. However, to offer treatments which are predicated upon the possibility of recovery to the second group – the truly 'chronic' – is usually to risk missing the point viewed from their perspective. The clinician may feel that recovery is a feasible and desirable goal but it may not seem that way to the sufferer. As ever, exploring how she does feel is an essential prerequisite to finding a way forward.

The fact that a sufferer has had a prolonged illness does not necessarily mean that either she or the clinicians who have tried to help her have done something wrong. Nobody may be to blame. However, the situation is likely to be complicated for both by the experience of unsuccessful treatment. Something of the complexity of such situations may be illustrated by revisiting yet again the fictional story of Faith – this time adapted to be a story of chronicity.

What Might Happen to Faith after a Further Ten Years or So

Fifteen years after the onset of her anorexia nervosa, Faith has built up a complicated career as a sufferer. Her story is a sad one. For a couple of years after her first admission to hospital, Faith avoided contact with specialist services for her eating disorder. She lived at home and attended a local further education college in order to finish her A levels. She did so although her grades were not as good as she had hoped they would be and, furthermore, she took the examinations a year late because of her illness and the hospital admission. The next year she was turned down by the universities of her choice because of her illness. She decided to delay for a further year. Her sister got her a part-time job at a shop, but most of the time she stayed at home. She spent a lot of time with her father. When he had another heart attack and his health deteriorated further, she gave up her job to look after him full time, so that her mother could continue to work. However, their relationship was not easy. He worried about her, nagged her to accept help and expressed his frustration that she refused. However, they found some common ground in a sense that they had both been thwarted in their ambitions by illness. With just a touch of bitterness, he reminded her that, in contrast to him, she could still achieve hers. Faith said that she had to look after him although, of course, that was not the whole reason why she did not seek to recover. It frightened her to think about it and her anorectic thinking was very powerful. They began to have frequent rows and when her father had a third heart attack and died, she blamed herself. In the next few months her condition deteriorated further and her weight fell to below 30 kg for the first time. Her mother and sister were distraught and had complicatedly mixed feelings about Faith's condition. They were worried and dreaded losing another family member but felt frustrated with her refusal to seek help. Secretly they were angry with her because they could not help feeling that, in some way, her disorder was self-inflicted. When she fainted in the street, they called the doctor and supported him when he insisted on calling in the local psychiatrist whom Faith had seen before. This time Faith was admitted to hospital compulsorily under a section of the Mental Health Act. She stayed in the local psychiatric hospital for a couple of weeks before being transferred to a general hospital and then on to a specialist unit 80 miles away where she stayed for six months. At that hospital she battled against the staff but gained some weight. However, she also began inducing vomiting as a way of thwarting the full effects of the requirement to eat and gain weight. At 45 kg she was made an informal patient but discharged herself against advice two weeks later. Out of hospital, she rapidly lost most of the weight that she had gained, partly by the continuing use of vomiting. Once again she became entrenched in a way of life which involved trying to keep her weight at about 35 kg. Now without her father at home she found herself in frequent conflict with her mother who was desperate that something be done to help her. Her mother became involved with a self-help organisation which provided her with a good deal of support. Over the years she became something of a campaigner for better services for people with eating disorders and became very well informed about aspects of the disorder. Both of their lives now revolved around anorexia nervosa. However, Faith herself remained at best ambivalent about change and was often actively antagonistic to her mother's attempts to get her into treatment. At times these took the form of admission to hospital in crisis. In all she had five further admissions, three of them compulsory. These admissions increasingly had the characteristic of being battles or competitions in which Faith would angrily defy the clinicians to cure her. On one occasion, when she was 25, she became very ill physically when her electrolytes were badly disrupted by her vomiting and nearly died. However, she pulled through although later she often said that she wished that she had died. Often she saw little purpose in her life and experienced moments of frustration and anger with herself and the world. At the age of 30 she moved out of her mother's home into a flat of her own. She asserted her right to live her own life whatever its dangers and once wrote an anonymous letter to the press to this effect in response to one of her mother's articles protesting at the lack of expert help for people with anorexia nervosa. She has not had any further *jobs or pursued any formal courses of study. Each day she follows a programme of walks and spends a long time choosing and preparing the small amount of food she eats. Once each week she has tea with her mother and then vomits. However, over the last year, egged on by her nephew Fiona's son, she has acquired a computer and spends a lot of time on the Internet. She likes to communicate with people in French- and German-speaking countries to practise her languages. She now rarely thinks about trying to recover from her anorexia nervosa although her mother still thinks about little else. Faith continues to avoid doctors. At the age of 32, she tripped and fell over, breaking her arm. When treated at the hospital, she was noted to be osteoporotic. She weighed 31 kg. Once again, she came under renewed pressure from her mother and from the family doctor to seek help for her eating disorder.*

The nature of chronicity has received relatively little study. Once again, experience, speculation and opinion have to provide the main basis for ways of thinking about the issues involved. It seems that for some sufferers from anorexia nervosa, the disorder starts to dominate their thinking, at least as far as can be discerned by others. This seems especially to be the case with chronic anorexia nervosa of the pure restricting type. Their thinking has an obsessional quality and any change to an established pattern seems to demand a great deal of them. They give the feeling that they are stuck because the very nature of their thinking is sticky. Others give the impression that they are less stuck than trapped or cornered by their anorectic dilemmas. And for these sufferers, it may be that repeated treatment experiences in which battling has been a feature has contributed to their sense of being cornered. It is tempting to think that their chronicity may in part be iatrogenic. If this is true then the remedy would be increased attention to 'the brokerage of responsibility' at every stage. In the earlier stages of an illness, this could contribute to the prevention of chronicity. When the sufferer already has a long career as a patient, attention to such issues may need to be careful, considered and even exaggerated. If the sufferer is feeling cornered because of past experiences, then the clinician needs to live down his own past behaviour or that of his predecessors if the sufferer is to trust and make appropriate use of any new therapeutic effort on offer. Sometimes this may involve simply keeping things under review at occasional meetings over months or even years.

EATING DISORDERS AND TERMINAL CARE

There has recently been some discussion of whether there might be any place for hospices or other forms of palliative and terminal care in the management of the severest cases of anorexia nervosa (O'Neill, Crowther & Sampson, 1994; Ramsay & Treasure, 1996; Vanderycken, 1998; Williams, Pieri, Sims, Russon & Alison, 1998). The argument in favour cites the fact that anorexia nervosa can be a chronic disorder associated with much suffering and a fatal outcome and that the full range of services, including hospice care, should be available to enable the incurable to die with dignity and the minimum of suffering. Cases have been recorded in which such a course has been followed (O'Neill, Crowther & Sampson, 1994). Indeed, there is at least one case reported from the Netherlands where the Dutch euthanasia procedure was followed (Spreeuwenberg & Kastelein, 1992; Vanderycken, 1998).

Such proposals tend to provoke strong feelings and substantial debate. The majority view seems to be that the use of hospice care for those suffering from anorexia nervosa is misguided. Expert palliative care may be indicated where the physical complications of the disorder themselves constitute an irrecoverable source of pain and suffering, but cases where the physical state becomes not only irrecoverable but terminal must be extremely rare, if they occur at all.[14] The point would seem to be that although some cases of anorexia nervosa may well be *incurable* in the sense that 'everything has been tried' and no further definable treatment intervention can be predicted to lead to improvement, no case can be thought of as *irrecoverable* in the sense that the disorder itself could not improve. There is simply no reason why a change of mind may not lead to a radical change in outlook. Anorexia nervosa in its physical manifestations is still underpinned by malnutrition, which is psychologically driven. Even were this psychologically definable problem found to be based in turn in some physically definable abnormality, the core physical disorder is still potentially reversible. Osteoporosis, alone amongst the common chronic complications of anorexia nervosa, is not predictably reversed by improvement in nutrition. Furthermore, the disorder is full of surprises. It cannot be said of any sufferer with absolute certainty that she has no chance of improvement or even recovery. A sufferer with collapsed vertebrae and associated pain should not be denied expert pain relief and other appropriate care. However, even the worst case is in a different position to an individual with terminal cancer. If the sufferer has set her face against life and is hopeless about her own future, her state resembles more closely that of the depressed patient who makes a similar judgement. She may either be feeling cornered in the way which was discussed before or she may be morbidly depressed or both. Either way hospice care with its implicit agreement with her own assessment of her state is no more indicated than would be the case for the person suffering from an affective disorder.

NOTES

1. The reader should bear in mind that what follows is essentially an account of my opinion on these matters. Other experienced clinicians may have somewhat different views. Furthermore, this is the kind of area where opinion is always likely to be based upon experience rather than upon research or more formal evidence. This is regrettable since, in my view, issues around the management of mixed feelings are central to the whole business of helping people with eating disorders.

2. Such reactions may sometimes be best understood in terms of the psychodynamic concept of countertransference. By this, I do not mean to suggest that the clinician's thoughts, feelings and actions necessarily reflect formative relationships from his or her distant past, although that is possible. It may simply be, for instance, that having some responsibility for a 'child' in danger – even a grown-up one – may provoke thoughts of his or her own child or childhood. The professional clinician may come to feel like a worried parent. This may be associated with all sorts of cajoling, bribing or finger wagging, which may have their place in dealing with a naughty toddler but serve only to complicate the desperately grown-up dilemma of the adult patient. The clinician may fear that his competence or his concern is likely to be questioned. Has he done everything that could be done? The frustrations of the situation may provoke irritation or a determination not to be beaten. Even if the clinician avoids direct anger with the patient, the anorexia nervosa itself may be reified and turned into the enemy in a battle that must be won at all costs. Metaphors of war abound. Indeed, the reader may note such language creeping into this book from time to time. Note the next paragraph in the main text.

3. In my own practice, if battles are developing when the patient is in hospital the first recourse is, of course, to discussion. However, if the problems continue we would usually say to the patient that we don't want to fight and that progress is possible only if everyone is working on balance towards the same ends. (The patient would, explicitly and after due thought, have opted in to the process of hospital treatment in the first place and so any battling represents a change of mind or failure of nerve on her part. – See Chapter 7.) We would suggest that the patient might need a bit of time to think about what she really wants to do at the moment. Perhaps it is not the right time to try to change. We then ask her to leave but tell her that we would keep her bed open for her for perhaps 48 hours and that she could return at any time during this period if she felt that she wanted to try again. We sometimes call this 'chucking out therapy' and it is carried out with an emotional tone which reflects realism and regret rather than anger. In

many cases it allows the sufferer the space to decide again that she really does want to push herself through all of the difficulties of trying to recover. It obliges her to take responsibility for her own dilemma again rather than kidding herself that by agreeing to hospital treatment she is giving it to us. Our idea in asking a patient to leave is not to punish her but rather to help her to avoid a false and potentially damaging resolution of her mixed feelings – and also, of course, to let ourselves off the hook of the difficulties to which such a false resolution leads. Many patients, indeed most, who are so 'chucked out' return within the specified time usually with a fresh resolve. If the patient does not return within the specified time, we would offer her an outpatient appointment to discuss the situation and the next stage.

4. The kind of controversy which I am discussing here arises almost exclusively in relation to anorexia nervosa rather than the other eating disorders. Thus, although people with bulimia nervosa may on occasion be subject to compulsory admission, this is hardly ever because of the bulimia as such but is rather because of suicidal behaviour or other issues which may be construed as aspects of major depression or other comorbidity. The management of such cases may, on occasion, be controversial but their treatment raises only the kind of issues which are not uncommon in other parts of mental health practice. There is little that is special or particular about the dilemmas involved and they will not be discussed further here.

5. To some people this lack of definition seems merely to underline the problematic nature of the whole concept of mental illness. However, definition is rarely an easy matter and some concepts which are unequivocally useful and even central to everyday life defy definition. For instance, have you ever tried to define 'time'? However, a concept may be usable and useful even though it is difficult to define. 'Mental illness' is such a concept, as is 'illness' in general.

6. My own view would be that the treatment of very severe anorexia nervosa under legal compulsion should be confined to specialised centres where such experience can be built up. It should be considered as specialist a business as transplant surgery. Indeed, this could be argued for the inpatient treatment of anorexia nervosa in general and the argument is even more compelling for the kind of patients for whom compulsion is appropriately considered. It is all too easy to imagine a scenario in which a clinician inexperienced in handling anorexia nervosa uses compulsion too soon and then constructs a situation where the patient is detained but continues to battle against a nursing team who are uncomfortable with the difficult and unfamiliar task which has been foisted upon them. Sometimes the process is repeated many times. Thus, it seems to me, are constructed some of

the extreme emergencies which then present to specialist centres as almost 'impossible' cases.

7. In England and Wales, there have been test cases which have established that such feeding may be considered to be medical treatment and lawful in appropriate circumstances. The relevant judgements rejected the argument that the delivery of nutrition could not be considered treatment (Lanceley & Travers, 1993; Dyer 1994). The whole issue of compulsion has been interestingly debated in a recent pamphlet by Janet Treasure and Rosalind Ramsay (Treasure & Ramsay, 1998).

8. My own practice has been to avoid compulsion and to try to sweat it out with the patient even in quite extreme situations. On balance, I feel that this is nearly always the best thing to do, even though it may seem risky and others might judge that I am failing to intervene when I should. I certainly have no objection in principle to the compulsory treatment of the mentally ill. Indeed, I have detained patients with anorexia nervosa, not for the treatment of that disorder but rather as a way of managing comorbid disorder such as severe depression with suicidal behaviour or risk. However, my own practice has been mainly within a local service which takes only a few patients referred from afar. There are centres which specialise in taking much more than their fair share of very severely ill patients and which serve a wide catchment area in this way. Often these patients will have been dealt with by other clinicians – sometimes several – and almost by definition those patients who become tertiary referrals will have done poorly. Many are likely to feel frightened and cornered in just the kind of way that I have tried to outline. It is not surprising that sometimes the clinicians who take over their care in the midst of a crisis judge that compulsion is the best course.

9. There are many ways of trying to promote a setting in which emotionally difficult issues can be discussed. In my experience humour can be valuable. It can help to promote an atmosphere in which comments – both positive and negative – about feelings and actions can be given and taken seriously but without unnecessary earnestness. It is also a way of acknowledging one's own difficulties or gaffs without making too much of a meal of them. Furthermore, humour may rattle up and down hierarchies and get around roles and preconceptions. Teams under stress often develop a shared sense of humour – sometimes so-called 'black' humour – which serves to help them to hold together although it may sometimes be a source of embarrassment should it be exposed to the outside world. Context is all. Of course, care is required both in the sense of being careful and in the sense of being caring. Humour is one way of dealing with risky

issues but it can go wrong and can be cruel. The joker needs to be able to flip into seriousness and repair if it seems that any damage has been done. However, on balance, when it comes naturally, humour seems often to be an important lubricant of a well-working team.

10. I rather like the image of someone caught up in the midst of a thorn bush. It will hurt to escape and will take courage to do so. And such courage is good. A friend beside the bush may advise, cheer and move the odd branch but the escapee has to do the work, feel the pain and effect the escape. If the bystander tries to pull the trapped person free by force it will usually cause similar pain, frighten the trapped person and probably get them even more stuck. That is cruelty and is bad. I guess that the kind of collusion discussed above is like providing company, emotional support and perhaps a bit of painkiller but leaving the person trapped in the bush.

11. Of course, the typical therapeutic relationship is unusual in the way that it seems to demand a high level of trust and intimacy of disclosure in the context of a meeting between strangers. Furthermore, the disclosure and trust is asymmetrical, in that this demand is upon the patient but not upon the clinician. It is perhaps surprising that so many troubled people can and do manage this. That they do is importantly related to the whole social context of clinical practice and the sense of safety and predictability which this may provide. Such issues are inherent in the codes and mores of professionalism. Sometimes such codes are felt to be too stuffy or restrictive – perhaps too unnatural – but we forget at our peril that they contribute to our ability to ask our patients to do what is not at all natural or easy, and to share with us those things that are most painful or embarrassing to them. In our unthinking moments of self-congratulation we may tell ourselves that it is our extraordinary skill, empathy or even our niceness that makes the chief contribution to this ability to help people to open up to us. I think that we should allow ourselves such thoughts only in small doses when we are at an especially low ebb. At other times we should remember the potency of our roles and be thankful for what they give us. Indeed, it may be that an important component of our skill may be avoiding complicating or jeopardising this potency that comes to us with our role. It is chastening to recall that there are circumstances in which people are more willing to disclose difficulties to a computer than they are to a human being.

12. I have argued above that this is always a mistake. Indeed, even in the case of dissociative states, the clinician should be wary of being too confident about inferring prior trauma and certainly should not make assumptions as to its nature.

13. This advice is personal and based upon clinical experience rather than evidence. Some clinicians would be more active in dealing with notable dissociation occurring in the therapy of an eating-disordered patient. They take a bolder or perhaps braver approach than that which I advocate. In particular, some would use hypnosis. Readers can find a sensible and knowledgeable account of such an approach in Vanderlinden and Vanderycken (1997).

14. I subscribe to this majority view. Furthermore, I have personally never come across a case where the option of hospice care seemed even worthy of consideration. However, I have come across a case where it had been considered seriously by others, although by the time I was involved, the young woman in question had a BMI of 17 and was physically stable and without notable complications. She went on to leave hospital and fared no worse than many other people who have had a severe anorectic illness. Would the outcome have been different if she had indeed been moved to a hospice when she was very ill?

11

THE ORGANISATION OF SERVICES FOR PEOPLE WITH EATING DISORDERS

The preceding chapters have discussed how individual clinicians or teams of clinicians may seek to help individual sufferers. However, all such efforts occur in a context. If the sufferer and the professional are to get together, they must find each other and almost always the professional must be paid. The encounter occurs in the setting of some kind of organised service. This may be a part of a general service or practice or one which is especially focused on providing for people with eating disorders. This chapter will discuss the issues arising from the organisation of services for people with eating disorders. It will discuss the processes by which the treatment encounter may come about and some of the problems – some inevitable and some avoidable – that may occur in the organisations that seek to make treatment available.

FILTERS ON THE PATHWAY TO CARE

Chapter 2 introduced the idea of filters on the pathway to care. In any community there will be people who suffer from eating disorders. A variable proportion of them will find their way through the filters to competent professionals. Such professionals may be in short supply but even when this is not the case, the process of getting clinician and sufferer together can be somewhat hit or miss. It should be the function of service organisation to facilitate this process. Different types of organisation have different advantages and different snags. However, in every case the sufferer – or someone acting on her behalf – must construe her state as one for which it is appropriate for her to seek professional help. It should be in the interests of all concerned for the population at large – and amongst them those who suffer from eating disorders – to be informed appropriately about the nature of the disorders and what can be done about them. Without such education, the ideas about eating disorders which are prevalent in a community – even amongst some health care professionals – may at times be unhelpful. For instance, the disorders may be thought of as little more than the fashionable fads of silly girls or as a dreadful scourge for which draconian interventions are required. Either belief may be an obstacle to appropriate care and treatment for the average sufferer.

SEEKING HELP

The next step in the filtering process will differ, depending upon the overall organisation of health care. There are two broad types. In the first, the would-be patient is able to approach any practitioner, however specialised, directly. In the second, the patient is obliged to seek first the advice of a generalist – usually a general medical practitioner – who acts as a filter or gatekeeper for more specialist services.

When services are organised with direct access to specialists, the patient may experience difficulties in knowing which practitioner to approach. She is facing her own unique problem and, at least at first, will not have had prior experience of which professional, or even perhaps which type of professional, is most appropriate for her needs. She may seek advice but again she may not know whose advice is most trustworthy. In such a 'free market', explicit or implicit claims to expertise are not always to be trusted and eating disorders is not a field in which the unwary can easily tell who has a sound claim to expertise and who has not. Often the evident claims of those who offer help may be in inverse proportion to their actual qualification and credibility. But how is she to know? Even deciding the specialty to which her ideal helper should belong may not be obvious. Should she go for a general internal physician, an endocrinologist, a psychiatrist, a clinical psychologist, some sort of psychotherapist or what? Should she go to several practitioners with different bits of her problem? Furthermore, even with a choice that is in principle 'free', there may be major constraints arising from issues of cost, geography and simple availability. Few sufferers have the luxury – and the burden – of an entirely uncomplicated choice. Of course, the components of the sufferer's personal view of her problem and her ambivalence – fear, embarrassment and so on – may also influence the direction in which she turns for help. Sometimes a sufferer who is wary of attention to the emotional aspects of the condition may opt to seek the help of an internal physician whom she expects not to emphasise these. Conversely, someone who dreads physical change may think that a psychotherapist may not push too much for weight gain and so on.

When health services are organised around some sort of gatekeeping generalist, the sufferer seeking help is confronted with a different set of issues. How things go will depend upon how approachable, competent and knowledgeable is the person who occupies this key role. At best, the sufferer may find all of the help that she needs from that clinician. For instance, a good family doctor may well be able in some instances to make a sufferer feel safe enough to make progress or even to get out of her disorder altogether. Furthermore, the primary care team associated with that doctor may have individuals within it who have the skills to deliver the help that is necessary without referral to secondary services. This may be a matter of luck and happenstance or it may be because the team has sought to develop a rational first intervention for eating disorder – for instance, through the use of guided self-help (Fairburn & Carter, 1997). However, if referral to some kind of secondary care is needed then, in the best of circumstances, the primary care physician or whoever will know a lot about what is available and be able to refer the sufferer to an appropriate service or clinician. The sufferer has access to the generalist's knowledge of the kind of help that is likely to be useful and where it may be found locally. Of course, her own views should influence the final decision about referral but she does not have the full burden of an unaided choice which could, at worst, be little better than guesswork. At best she has someone in her corner to advise her and guide her through what can be a jungle of potential helpers. However, when the system does not work well, the sufferer may experience the gatekeeper as an obstacle. He may be unsympathetic to her request for any help for her problem or the help that he offers or facilitates may not be congenial or appropriate. His prejudices may be added to her ambivalence to produce a real mess. Furthermore, in this kind of system, there may in practice be an additional filter. The gatekeeper in primary care may refer the sufferer to a specialist within a secondary service, but that 'specialist' may mean someone in the mental health field who is nevertheless a *generalist* psychiatrist, psychologist or whatever. That practitioner, as in the case of the primary care team, may well be able to offer appropriate help but sometimes it may be that a further referral is required to someone who is a true specialist in the treatment of eating disorders.

Either of the two broad systems for accessing health care can work well. However, when they do not, the sufferer may experience the first as a lottery and the second as an obstacle course. To the practitioners working within them, the two systems also present different problems.

OFFERING HELP

The practitioner working within either kind of system is likely to be keen to provide what is best for his patients – and of course for himself. Fortunately these two aims may well seem to coincide in most cases. However, it is often the case that the first kind of system – what might be called the 'free market' system – tends to go along with a sense that each practitioner or service is at least potentially in competition with others. The clinician or service hopes to attract patients, and patients bring with them the financial resources to sustain or improve the service. The clinician is likely to be keen to maximise the effectiveness and acceptability of the service to the individual patient, subject only to the ability of the patient – or more likely some third party – to afford to pay for the treatment. This is what might be called the traditional and uncomplicated clinician–patient relationship. By contrast, many gatekeeper systems often involve the provision of a service for a population defined either geographically as in many directly state-funded systems or by membership of a some kind of collective such as a health maintenance organisation. Within such a system, the clinician will need to think not only about effectiveness and acceptability but also about efficiency and the best use of limited resources in meeting the needs not only of the individual patient but also of all similar and potential patients in the population from which she comes. Of course, in either system, the resources available for the treatment of a patient are likely to have some limit. Indeed, both in state-funded and insurance-based systems the influence of those who directly foot the bill is increasing.

THIRD PARTIES

Those who fund health care, whether they be states or insurance companies, have an interest in providing for the populations for which they are responsible, and must also seek to do so within a limited budget. To the clinician and to the individual patient, the second imperative can sometimes seem to be much the more powerful. In controlling their budgets, third parties tend to seek to limit what is available or offered by clinicians to patients. They are not uncommonly experienced as being tight fisted or heavy handed in doing so. In principle, of course, patient, clinician and the provider of third party funding all have a common interest in treatment that is both effective and economical. In practice it may not feel that way.

    In discussing the overall organisation of services, it may be best to focus upon the question of how help can be most rationally and efficiently provided for a population. This is likely to be addressed most directly by clinicians and others planning the provision of services within a state-funded system. However, the issues involved in such planning are likely to impinge indirectly upon practice within most health care systems regardless of their type.[1]

NEED AND DEMAND

A naive view of service provision would look first at the level of particular morbidity in a population and at the best available treatments for the condition in question. Then, by dint of some simple calculation, the planner would work out what is needed to provide the optimal treatment for all of those who suffer from the disorder in question in that population. Such an approach would take into account that no treatment is universally effective or acceptable and that the needs of some sufferers are complicated. Nevertheless, this kind of calculus could provide an estimate of what might be called maximum rational need. Also, for some conditions – say the immediate orthopaedic consequences of severe road traffic accidents – it presumably approximates to actual need and to demand. This, however, is unlikely to be the case for the eating disorders.

Need and demand may become disconnected in two broad ways. Need may exceed demand because sufferers are reluctant to access services, do not know that they are available or become somehow clogged in the filters on the pathways to them. All of these are likely to apply to people suffering from eating disorders for reasons that have been discussed elsewhere. There is a good deal of evidence that a substantial proportion – even a majority – of people suffering from eating disorders do not find their way to services (van Hoeken, Lucas & Hoek, 1998). Theoretical need does indeed exceed actual demand. A mismatch of this kind may present both practical and ethical problems for service planners and providers. For the provider, there may be a fear of being swamped by too much demand. For the planner, there must be a real temptation to limit provision to the level of demand rather than need, especially if those with unmet needs are unobtrusive and quiet. Arguably, this is unethical if the unmet need is known and effective interventions are available. However, those who have to provide for all health needs on a limited budget may perhaps be forgiven if they provide first for those whose needs are most evident or about whom the most noise is made. The champions of the eating disordered have a continuing role in reminding both purchasers and providers of their needs.

There is also a complex relationship between provision and demand. If a service is available and known to be good by those who might use it or refer others to it, the demand for it arising from its catchment population is likely be much higher than from a similar population where no such service exists. Good services tend to convert hidden needs into evident demands.[2]

In principle, demand may exceed need where sufferers seek more treatment than is required or treatments that are ineffective. In the field of eating disorders this is rarely a problem in absolute terms although a hard-pressed service may find that at times it may need to question whether it is providing for the less ill or less responsive at the expense of the more ill or more responsive. Debates which pursue such questions are likely to be difficult and inconclusive. Actual practice often contains many dilemmas and imponderables. Nevertheless, such questions are worth asking every now and then.

There are so many factors that may influence actual demand that predicting numbers is necessarily an imprecise business. However, as a 'guesstimate', a service for a defined population in a 'western' country would do well to plan for around 20 referrals of eating disordered adults per 100,000 total population per year. There might well be more, but a service should not plan for less if it is aiming for something like comprehensive provision.

OPTIMAL PROVISION AND COMPREHENSIVE PROVISION

In providing for the needs of a population, it would seem sensible that the provision should aim to be both optimal for the individual sufferer and comprehensive for the population served. However, even in the best of circumstances, these two aims may sometimes conflict. The most obvious conflict may be around money and resources but this is not the only issue. Another conflict may be between mounting a service which is generalist and local against one that is specialist but based away from the sufferer's community. Furthermore, a service which is able to do one thing well – say provide good, accessible, long-term psychotherapy – may not be able to do something else – say provide inpatient treatment of very severe and life-threatening anorexia nervosa. This would be fine if it were not the case that some individuals have the need for both kinds of intervention.

Where service provision is clearly divided between those who purchase services for individuals or populations and those who actually provide such services, different principles apply to the purchasers and the providers. Purchasers need to aim to provide access to a comprehensive range of services for their people. In contrast, providers of clinical service may or may not offer to provide such a comprehensive range. They should be clear about what they can and, more importantly, what they *cannot* provide. If the service offered is not comprehensive then the purchaser can in principle seek what is missing from other providers. In practice, of course, there may still be many problems even when each party is clear in their expectations. However, if clarity is lacking then there may be room for an unholy alliance based upon a collusive fudge of the issues. Thus, for instance, purchasers may choose to believe that they have made adequate provision for eating disorders if they make an arrangement with a distant hospital with a special inpatient programme which, however, provides nothing for the bulk of sufferers for whom such care is inappropriate. The clinicians at the hospital, on the other hand, may not choose to emphasise what they cannot provide but rather to waffle on about an outreach programme which amounts only to some follow-up for severe cases. Each side seems to gain from the fudge in the short term but the patients and potential patients lose out. The reverse case would be where a community service glosses over the fact that they are quite unable to provide for the few very severe cases even though they can deal adequately with the many. They may implicitly claim that early intervention will abolish any need for inpatient treatment even though there is little or no evidence that this is the case. Such unhappy covering over of gaps in provision may also occur of course in systems where the split between purchaser and provider is not emphasised or is functionally absent. Furthermore, even when all parties are honest and straightforward, the sufferer whose needs are complex and varied may find herself experiencing considerable lack of coherence and even discontinuity of her care when different bits are provided by different agencies.

A COMPREHENSIVE SERVICE

The previous chapters on treatment have discussed the elements which together could constitute a comprehensive service for people with eating disorders. Boxes 11.1 and 11.2 summarise these for anorexia nervosa and bulimia nervosa, respectively. Broadly speaking, both require the availability of appropriate clinicians who are able to assess, monitor and treat patients mainly as outpatients. Assessment needs to be multidimensional, involving the psychological, the social and the physical. Teams consisting of people with different skills may be involved. However, at its heart, the enterprise of recovery for the patient is a personal one and it is usually best if therapy too is a personal matter involving one or a few key individual clinicians. Such people need to carry a personal case load. (As a 'guesstimate', a comprehensive specialist secondary service for adults with eating disorders should aim for a minimum of one such clinician for each 100,000 total population served. This is such a neat figure that it reveals its approximate nature. However, as a rule of thumb, it is not perhaps too far out.) In practice, clinicians drawn from a variety of professions – medicine, nursing, clinical psychology – can with suitable training, support and a measure of flexibility fulfil the role of therapist and case manager for most patients. Each individual clinician will need to know when to ask for the involvement of others. In particular, there is a need to know when and how to invoke the more intensive forms of management, such as hospital admission. The availability of such intensive care for the minority who need it is an essential component of a comprehensive service. The optimal service will facilitate the provision of such additional team-based management whilst minimising disruption to the personal therapy which is likely both to precede and follow it.

Ideally, treatment should not be a relay race but a journey with a consistent guide. This is especially so for the treatment of anorexia nervosa because therapy tends to be prolonged. It also needs to be tailored to the particular patient even though elements may be 'off the peg'. Furthermore, it is more likely to involve consideration of the need for inpatient treatment. The more varied the elements involved in a treatment career, the more important is it that there should be some consistency in at least one of the clinicians involved. Service organisation should recognise this need. It should also recognise that the treatment of anorexia nervosa is usually a long and labour-intensive business. For instance, a cohort of local

---

Box 11.1   Summary of Service for Anorexia Nervosa

A comprehensive service for those suffering from anorexia nervosa should be able to provide, or at least ensure the provision of, the following:

- Assessment which includes the psychological, the social and the physical.
- Long-term therapeutic relationship with a clinician with suitable psychotherapeutic skills.
- Availability of more intensive care when necessary through admission to hospital and/or special day care, ideally without disruption of the therapeutic relationship.
- Ability to treat and manage psychiatric comorbidity.
- Ability to treat and manage physical comorbidity and monitor complications.
- Involvement of families and others as appropriate.
- Follow up.
- Good communication and links with other services or agencies as appropriate.

patients in Leicester had on average 32 sessions over two years if they were never admitted and 107 sessions over four years if they were amongst the third who did go into hospital at some stage of the treatment (Palmer, Gatward, Black & Park, 2000).

A full service for anorexia nervosa requires not only the availability of different forms of clinical management but also a cadre of skilled and flexible therapists and case managers who can work with the patient in a variety of modes. The whole needs to be organised in a context in which the sometimes pressing physical aspects of care can be monitored and addressed.

By contrast, the treatment of bulimia nervosa is often time limited, at least in relation to the phase of initial active therapy. Furthermore, there are arguments in favour of it being less 'bespoke' and more uniform and delivered in accord with a preplanned programme (Fairburn, 1997b). This is certainly the case with the form of cognitive-behavioural therapy (CBT) for which there is the most evidence of efficacy. The therapists involved need to have training in the particular treatment and to work in a context where a more flexible response can be invoked for the special case and for those who have gone through first line therapies without much benefit. The concept of stepped care is popular and seems rational (Fairburn & Peveler, 1990). Within a model of stepped care for bulimia nervosa, sufferers are first offered lesser interventions such a guided self-help and a psychoeducational group. Full CBT, or whatever is the mainline treatment, is reserved for those who do not respond adequately. For those who do not respond to the main treatment there may be a further step to another therapy. Such stepped care seems to be a good idea although there is little evidence about how effective it is in everyday practice. Being able to predict which sufferers require which treatment would be better than stepped care, but the data are not there to do this reliably at present. However, clinicians will often act upon their judgement for better or worse and fast track some patients directly to the later steps of their system.

A full service for bulimia nervosa needs either a similar flexibility to that which was outlined for anorexia nervosa or a well-organised system of stepped care. Either can be organisationally demanding. Furthermore, even when treatments are predominantly time limited and 'programme led', the overall service and the process of assessment and reassessment needs to have a user friendly, human face if the sufferer is to feel that she is being understood and well looked after. As with anorexia nervosa there is a need for a mechanism to deal with physical issues. However, the need for admission is likely to be much less.

Only a comprehensive service can, in principle, provide a seamless service. However, a comprehensive service needs to be big, and must also serve a sizeable population. This means that for some of its potential

---

Box 11.2   Summary of Service for Bulimia Nervosa

A comprehensive service for those suffering from bulimia nervosa should be able to provide, or at least ensure the provision of, the following:

- Assessment which includes the psychological, the social and the physical.

- Short-term psychotherapy of a kind for which there is evidence of efficacy in bulimia nervosa.

- Other interventions including guided self-help, psychoeducational groups and/or drug therapy could be offered as initial therapies.

- Additional therapies for those patients who do not respond to the short-term therapy.

- Special or more prolonged therapy for complicated cases, especially those with other damaging behaviours and/or personality disorders.

- Ability to treat and manage psychiatric comorbidity if necessary by admission.

- Ability to treat and manage physical comorbidity and monitor complications.

- Involvement of families and others as appropriate.

- Reassessment and follow up as appropriate.

- Good communication and links with other services or agencies as appropriate.

---

patients it may not be local. Experience would suggest that all elements of a comprehensive service can be justified if the total population served is approaching a million. If it is much smaller, the number of candidates for the rarer but necessary forms of management, especially inpatient treatment, falls below the level where provision is easy or economical. For instance, if we assume that each year between 30 and 50 people with anorexia nervosa are expected to present to an adult service from a population of 1 million, and at most a third of these required admission, then the inpatient facility would have perhaps 10 to 15 new patients in a year. This would be enough to justify a special programme. A population of 250,000 would give rise to perhaps three or four such patients each year and it would be difficult to sustain a critical mass and an appropriate culture in an inpatient unit with this kind if throughput. These 'guesstimate' figures are for adults – that is, sufferers over 16. Child and adolescent services for people below this age are likely to need a catchment area of several million to justify a specialist inpatient service for anorexia nervosa. The need for beds for adult bulimia sufferers is likely to be smaller than for anorexia and, furthermore, when such patients are admitted it is usually because of crises which resemble those of other psychiatric patients. Their needs in such crises are not very 'special' and they can often be appropriately managed on a one-off basis without any special programme.

A service which is truly comprehensive and able to respond to all of the eating disorders would need to combine the characteristics outlined above and be flexible in responding to the more unusual problems such as those discussed in Chapter 9. The dilemma of rare skills and specialism versus local provision and ready access has no entirely satisfactory solution except perhaps in big cities where large populations exist in small spaces. Too much aggregation and specialism may leave the local generalists with less confidence and skill in dealing with people with eating disorders than they might otherwise have. Too little may mean that patients get a poor deal. It may be possible to reduce these problems somewhat by organising services in the form of a 'hub and spoke' model. Within such an arrangement, the 'hub' is the centre which contains the more specialised facilities which are needed by the few, such as inpatient or day patient provision together with the coordinating and organising centre of the service. The spokes are the localities which, however, have a permanent and defined relationship with the hub. Indeed, it may be that all of the professionals are employed at and by the hub and simply spend part of their time working within the spokes. Be that as it may, these professionals form an ongoing link between the local and the central which can ameliorate some of the difficulties that could otherwise arise.

Specialist services need to take care of their boundaries and of their relationships with their conceptual and geographical neighbours. Patients do not always present in neat ways which conform to our preconceptions. Good neighbours can work together and sort out border disputes. When this is not the case, the unusual patient may lose out and be the subject of neglect or rejection referrals. Complex and difficult cases such as the young woman with a history of abuse and neglect in childhood, a borderline personality disorder, drug and alcohol problems, recurrent self-harm and severe bulimia nervosa may rattle around services in a bizarre game of clinical pass the parcel unless all concerned can come to some decision as who should respond. In such circumstances guidelines and acceptance criteria, although much loved by managers, are a poor substitute for good working relationships between clinicians.

ORGANISATIONS OF SUFFERERS AND THEIR FAMILIES

In many places there are organisations led by sufferers and their families which seek to provide a variety of benefits for their members and other sufferers. Most provide information and support which is delivered through literature, meetings and telephone help lines. Some seek to provide more focused help as a complement to, or sometimes as a substitute for, professional treatment. Their relationships with professional services range from the cool through the ambivalent to the supportive. Likewise, their form ranges from the local and ephemeral to the national and well established. The best provide a very important voice for sufferers and their families and a major antidote for the sense of isolation which they can often feel.

In the United Kingdom, a national organisation called the Eating Disorders Association (EDA) was formed in 1989 through the coming together of smaller groups. It provides a wide variety of services through its national and local activities. It has come to have some influence and seeks to act as a pressure group for the improvement of professional services as well as a source of support and information. There is a real need for such advocacy. It has a professional membership as well as being an organisation for sufferers and families. Professionals too can sometimes feel isolated.

TRAINING AND SUPERVISION

Clinicians working with eating-disordered people need training and supervision. Some of the necessary knowledge, skills and attitudes will have come from their basic professional training. Different professionals will be likely to bring different attributes. For instance, the doctor should know more than most about physical issues and drugs. Furthermore, if he is a psychiatrist he will be comfortable in assessing and dealing with major mental disorder and suicidal risk. The psychologist may have more training in cognitive behavioural therapy, the dietician in nutrition and the nurse in supportive counselling or whatever. However, membership of any one profession does not of itself predict all of the features which are desirable in the clinician who is equipped to deal with a case load of eating-disordered people. In general, services cannot rely upon being able to recruit fully competent and confident people. Most services have to grow their own clinicians. However, doing so can have major benefits for the service as a whole.

Becoming a good clinician in the field of eating disorders requires the acquisition of some particular knowledge and some special skills but most of all there is the issue of confidence. That needs to be grown and developed through experience, training and the opportunity to reflect upon clinical practice with others. Eating disorder services need to foster such opportunities. Individual practitioners may gain from going on particular courses to learn, for instance, particular therapeutic techniques such as CBT for bulimia nervosa. However, many may need their general therapeutic skills nurtured and sustained by ongoing clinical supervision. Everyone benefits from working in an atmosphere which manages to combine – at least most of the time – warm collegial support for the individual with an acceptance that critical scrutiny is necessary if progress is to be made. Service organisation needs to address these issues of formal training, ongoing supervision and the promotion of a good atmosphere.

Unfortunately there is, at the time of writing at least in the UK, something of a dearth of good courses and training opportunities which prepare clinicians for work with eating-disordered people. Even formal training in particular focused therapies is in short supply and those that are on offer are sometimes of uncertain relevance and provenance. There are plenty of one-day meetings on this or that and lots of conferences but although these have their value they are rarely to be thought of as *training* experiences except in the widest sense. It is to be hoped that good cross-professional training courses will be developed to grow and sustain the clinicians who will grow and sustain adequate services.

Provision of clinical supervision within services is important but also associated with potential difficulty. Indeed the word 'supervision' has a number of associated meanings. One meaning arises from the world of dynamic psychotherapy where therapists are encouraged to have a regular opportunity to discuss their therapeutic relationships with an experienced third party, the supervisor. This serves a number of purposes, including the addressing of the issues of transference and countertransference so that they become tools of, rather than impediments to, therapy. Such supervision is essential for those in training. It may be less crucial but is still advantageous for the experienced and the fully trained. This sense of the word 'supervision' overlaps with the sense which is used more widely in relation to other therapies and forms of clinical practice where the overseeing and didactic elements of supervision may be more emphasised. The whole business can sometimes become tangled up with issues of status and hierarchy. Then people may become sensitive about who can supervise whom. These can become issues which touch upon personal and professional sensitivities. The range of issues which may be involved and their particularity makes it unwise or impossible to suggest definite solutions for general use. A wide variety of arrangements may work well. However, a service and the people within it who do not have regular opportunities to scrutinise their work with patients in a setting which feels safe and supportive but allows robust scrutiny are likely to be missing out. Their patients may miss out too.

RESPONSIBILITY

A related issue is that of clinical responsibility. This, too, is an ambiguous term and can also be a sensitive one on occasion. However, as with supervision and the like, some sort of workable arrangement needs to be in operation within a service if it is to operate well.

Throughout this book there has been an emphasis upon the need for the eating-disordered patient to take appropriate responsibility for her own recovery. However, the clinician who would help her has necessary responsibilities too. There are things about which he is – or should be – more knowledgeable than the patient. For instance, he is likely to know more about the risk of osteoporosis as a persistent consequence of malnutrition. As a more complicated example, he may have an importantly different view from the patient on the experiences which arise from stringent eating restraint. The patient may interpret these as signs of personal weakness or greed. The clinician has another perspective derived from the wider study of other people. This different slant is potentially helpful to the sufferer. Furthermore, the clinician knows the type of treatment that has helped people in similar situations. The clinician, therefore, has some useful knowledge and thereby a degree of sapiential authority. The clinician has a responsibility to try to help the patient by sharing such knowledge and using such authority where and when his judgement dictates. The aim should be to empower the patient by allowing her judgements about herself to be appropriately informed. However, the contact between clinician and patient is a personal one and the clinician cannot – or should not – simply bomb the patient with expertise or opinion. Likewise, the clinician has to use judgement in deciding when and how to offer advice, treatment or other intervention. Doing what might sometimes be the right thing in the wrong way or at the wrong time may be disastrous. These things are a matter of judgement and such judgements are the essence of professionalism, and the professional is, of course, responsible and accountable for them. So much is clear. However, the nature of the problem and the context in which help is offered and responsibility exercised may complicate these issues.

The treatment of an eating-disordered patient is likely to include problems which fall into different domains which may be central to the competence of different professions and different professionals. Eating disorders are, of their nature, both psychological and physical. Their features vary through a wide spectrum of kinds. This spectrum ranges from those features which are private, subjective and open only to empathetic understanding (such as the sufferer's self-concept), to those which are in principle behaviourally manifest (such as self-induced vomiting) and then on through evident bodily problems (such as extreme low weight) to physical issues which may be discovered only upon investigation (such as cardiac changes secondary to electrolyte disturbance). Even this array leaves out the family, interpersonal and social context of the disorder. This complexity of problem tends to promote a complexity of suitable response and sometimes the need for a number of professionals to share responsibility for that response even within a unitary eating-disorders service. Each profession and each professional may have sensitivities about which part of the responsibility is 'theirs'. None of us can be guaranteed to be always rational and never proprietorial or even childish about such issues, particularly when the heat is on and we are anxious.

The context of service provision may involve referral from another professional who retains involvement, as in the case of a primary care physician or general practitioner. Furthermore, the individual sufferer may, in addition, be appropriately in touch with more than one clinical or other helping agency. Lastly, the sufferer may in some sense occupy the sick role, for instance having time off work or be claiming benefits because of her disorder. Or sometimes, she may be declining to construe herself as sick even when others think that this would be sensible. She may be ambivalent about the whole business of seeking help even when her state is extreme.

Amidst this thicket of issues the clarity of responsibility which is present within the simple archetype of the professional relationship outlined above may tend to get blurred. This will not normally hinder in practice the progress of treatment and care. However, sometimes it may. Furthermore, we live in litigious times and, when things go wrong, muddled lines of responsibility and accountability may be exposed. Legal processes tend to require and sometimes artificially contrive black and white judgements even where the prevailing colour is grey. Managerial structures in agencies which provide clinical services may be sued, along with the individual professional, and may thus require the anticipation of such processes in every case – hence the current fashion for elaborate systems of policies, guidelines and risk management documents. Once again there is no one prescription for how services should address these issues, but addressed in some way they must be. 'Good communication' is often the favoured medicine and it is certainly an essential ingredient of any remedy. However, some sort of broad principles are best agreed ahead of the inevitable problems which will sooner or later test a system. When arrangements are complex some sort of superordinate responsibility is required. However, it is best to avoid endless pyramidal systems where responsibility and accountability pass up hierarchies away from the those who have real contact with the sufferer. These systems are less flexible, less reliable and more likely to become persecutory than those where the buck stops with a real clinician who can see the patient.

AUDIT, RESEARCH AND DEVELOPMENT

Services for people with eating disorders are nearly always busy. There is rarely a shortage of patients and nearly always a shortage of time and resources. Nevertheless, services should try to examine what they are doing and, indeed, what they are *not* doing but perhaps should be doing. Time should be found for audit of the treatment process and assessment of its outcomes. Audit works when it is 'real' in the sense that those involved in the service care about the issue being audited.[3] The topics need to be issues which are important and about which there is genuine concern. If the venture is a truly shared exercise rather than an imposed ritual, the process is unlikely to be threatening and the results will be believable and acceptable. Then the audit cycle can lead to real insight and sometimes to genuine improvement in practice.

Routine measures undertaken at regular intervals through the careers of patients can add a great deal to the impressions of the clinician about the progress or otherwise of an individual patient. Such data on all patients of a service aggregated together can be invaluable. Furthermore, they are increasingly being demanded by managers and purchasers of health care – and also by patients and their families (Black & Young, 1998). Even 'quick and easy' measures such as self-report questionnaires like the Eating Disorders Inventory (EDI) (Garner, 1991) can add something to the story.

Research, too, is sometimes viewed as a luxury. It is not. At the very least, eating disorders services should be the critical consumers of research findings. They cannot afford to be otherwise when our ignorance and limited success in helping people is as it is. Clinicians and managers who run services should try to promote an atmosphere and circumstance in which the digestion of research is valued. Journal clubs and journal subscriptions are worth while, as are attendance at research-based conferences. In discussing training above, attendance at such conferences was mentioned in a rather dismissive way. Indeed, such meetings rarely provide focused *training* but what they may promote, along with some new knowledge, is the appropriate mix of enthusiasm and critical thinking which sustains good practice and does not allow it to stagnate.[4] Taking part in research and joining the 'invisible college' of people who contribute to the literature is even more valuable in this respect. Research does not have to be 'big' to be useful.

MONEY, IMAGE AND ADVOCACY

Lastly, there is money. In almost all services, the resource available to do the job feels as though it is too little. Sometimes the limiting scarcity is of people or facilities even where the money would be potentially available, but it is usually a lack of money that is the obstacle. This is a big issue and a little paragraph. There is no answer to the problem here. In practice there usually has to be many partial answers and much wheeling and dealing. However, those who run or hope to run services for people with eating disorders should not be backward in fighting for their share of whatever resources are available and looking for more. The very first paragraph of this book made mention of the ambivalent attitude to eating disorders which is widespread in the general public and in many of our professional colleagues. Those who control the purse strings of our health care systems are drawn from both groups. Eating disorders have an image problem. These disorders are not appropriately thought of as either rare and extraordinary or trivial and silly. They are a significant public health problem for our societies and the source of suffering and sometimes premature death to individuals. Those of us who are involved professionally in the field need to be advocates in the cause of improving what are, much too often, the inadequate and poorly informed responses of health services to these disorders.

NOTES

1. As a child of the British National Health Service, I am inclined to the belief that health services which are funded directly through taxation are more likely to serve the needs of populations efficiently, economically and equitably than is the case with other systems. However, I am not blind to their problems which, in practice, are many. Nevertheless, because, at their best, they require thought about the needs of whole populations, much of the rest of this chapter will tend to refer to this type of service except where otherwise stated. Readers working within other systems may sometimes find themselves needing to translate the discussion into terms more relevant to their context.

2. I call this the 'Field of Dreams' phenomenon after the movie in which Kevin Costner hears voices telling him to build a baseball field on his farm. The voices keep whispering 'If you build it they will come'. In the film, this refers to the ghosts of famous ball players who emerge from between the rows of corn. However, the message applies to those who would create new services for people with eating disorders. This may be encouraging to clinicians wishing to provide a service or set up a practice in a place with little apparent demand. However, to planners who are strapped for cash it raises the spectre of an escalating demand from the many if something good is provided for the few whose needs are already evident.

3. Too often audit is undertaken because 'they' say that it is the thing to do. Likewise, the idea of 'Quality' has been put about as if it were a new concept which never occurred to anyone before about ten years ago. Time and effort can be diverted from quality practice – with a small q – to feed paper exercises in the name of 'Quality'. Such exercises tend to be trivial or trendy, or both. In my experience they do not usually produce anything of worth. To the question 'Who is responsible for quality?', the answer should be 'We all are and always have been'. That having been said, it is not always easy to persuade oneself and one's colleagues to spend valuable time in formal audit, reassessment and the like. I am as guilty as the next person in this respect and for years in the Service in which I work we had extensive standard assessments of all of our patients when they first came along, but much less in the way of standard assessments of their subsequent course or outcome.

4. When we seem to be in need of encouragement or things are going wrong, I sometimes say to myself and my colleagues that we should congratulate ourselves upon being one of the best eating disorder services in the business – this is arguable, but we do need cheering up sometimes – but that nevertheless we are not that good at treating eating disorders and need to get better. One function of research and, in particular, of research conferences is to disseminate new ideas and findings. Another is to provide reassurance that others are also floundering about, and finding difficult, the same things that we do.

REFERENCES

Abed, R T (1998) The sexual competition hypothesis for eating disorders. *British Journal of Medical Psychology*, **71**, 525–547.

Abdu, R A, Garritano, D & Culver, O (1987) Acute gastric necrosis in anorexia nervosa and bulimia: two case reports. *Archives of Surgery*, **122**, 830–832.

Abrams, K, Allen, L & Gray, J (1993) Disordered eating attitudes and behaviors, psychological adjustment and ethnic identity: comparison of black and white female college students. *International Journal of Eating Disorders*, **14**, 49–57.

Agras, W S, Dorian, B, Kirkley, B G, Arnow, B & Bachman, J (1987) Imipramine in the treatment of bulimia: a double-blind controlled study. *International Journal of Eating Disorders*, **6**, 29–38.

Agras, W S, Schneider J A, Arnow B, Raeburn S D & Telch C F (1989) Cognitive-behavioural treatment with and without exposure plus response prevention in the treatment of bulimia nervosa: a reply to Leitenberg and Rosen. *Journal of Consulting and Clinical Psychology*, **57**, 778–779.

Agras, W S, Telch, C F, Arnow, B, Eldredge, K, Henderson, J & Marnell M, (1995) Does interpersonal therapy help patients with binge eating disorder who fail to respond to cognitive-behavioral therapy? *Journal of Consulting and Clinical Psychology*, **63**, 356–360.

Agras, W S, Walsh, B T, Wilson, G T & Fairburn, C G (1999) A multisite comparison of cognitive behavioural therapy (CBT) and interpersonal therapy (IPT) in the treatment of bulimia nervosa. Paper presented at Eating Disorders 99; Fourth London International Conference on Eating Disorders, April 1999.

Andersen, A E (1995) Eating disorders in males. In: Brownell, K D & Fairburn C G (Editors) *Eating Disorders and Obesity: A Comprehensive Handbook*. Guilford Press, New York and London.

APA, (1980) *Diagnostic and Statistical Manual of Mental Disorders* (3rd edition). American Psychiatric Association, Washington, DC.

APA, (1987) *Diagnostic and Statistical Manual of Mental Disorders* (3rd edition – revised). American Psychiatric Association, Washington, DC.

APA, (1994) *Diagnostic and Statistical Manual of Mental Disorders* (4th edition). American Psychiatric Association, Washington, DC.

Attia, E, Haiman, C, Walsh, B T & Flater, S R (1998) Does fluoxetine augment the inpatient treatment of anorexia nervosa? *American Journal of Psychiatry*, **155**, 548–551.

Baran, S A, Weltzin, T E & Kaye, W H (1995) Low discharge weight and outcome in anorexia nervosa. *American Journal of Psychiatry*, **152**, 1070–1072.

Beck, A T, Rush, A J, Shaw, B F & Emery, G (1979) *Cognitive Therapy of Depression*. Guilford Press, New York.

Beumont, P J, George, G G & Smart D E (1976) 'Dieters' and 'vomiters and purgers' in anorexia nervosa. *Psychological Medicine*, **6**, 617–622.

Beumont, P J & Large, M (1991) Hypophosphataemia, delirium and cardiac arrhythmia in anorexia nervosa. *Medical Journal of Australia*, **155**, 519–522.

Birmingham, C L, Alotham, A F & Goldner, E M (1996) Anorexia nervosa: refeeding and hypophosphataemia. *International Journal of Eating Disorders*, **20**, 211–213.

Birmingham, C L, Goldner, E M & Bakan, R (1994) Controlled trial of zinc supplementation in anorexia nervosa. *International Journal of Eating Disorders*, **15**, 251–255.

Black, D W & Young M (1998) Setting up an eating disorders service. *European Eating Disorders Review*, **6**, 225–228.

Bliss, E L & Branch, C H (1960) *Anorexia Nervosa: Its History, Psychology and Biology*. Hoeber, New York.

Blouin, J, Schnarre, K, Carter, J, Blouin, A, Tener, L, Zuro, C & Barlow, J (1995) Factors affecting dropout rate from cognitive-behavioral group treatment for bulimia nervosa. *International Journal of Eating Disorders*, **17**, 323–329.

Bowlby, J (1988) *A Secure Base: Clinical Applications of Attachment Theory*. Tavistock/Routledge, London.

Browne, A & Finkelhor, D (1986) Impact of child sexual abuse: a review of the research. *Psychological Bulletin*, **99**, 66–77.

Brownell, K D (1995) Eating disorders in athlete. In: Brownell, K & Fairburn, C (Editors) *Eating Disorders and Obesity: A Comprehensive Handbook*. Guilford Press, New York and London.

Brownell, K & Fairburn, C (editors) (1995) *Eating Disorders and Obesity: A Comprehensive Handbook*. Guilford Press, New York and London.

Bruch,H (1973) *Eating Disorders: Obesity, Anorexia Nervosa and the Person Within*. Basic Books, New York

Bruch H (1978) *The Golden Cage: the Enigma of Anorexia Nervosa*. Harvard University Press, Cambridge, Mass.

Brumberg, J J (1988) *Fasting Girls: The Emergence of Anorexia Nervosa as a Modern Disease*. Harvard University Press, Cambridge, Mass.

Bryant-Waugh, R & Kaminski Z (1993) Eating disorders in children: an overview. In Lask, B & Bryant-Waugh, R (Editors) *Childhood Onset Anorexia Nervosa and Related Eating Disorders*. Psychology Press, Hove.

Bulik, C M, Sullivan, P F, Carter, F A & Joyce, P R (1996) Lifetime anxiety disorders in women with bulimia nervosa. *Comprehensive Psychiatry*, **37**, 368–374.

Bulik, C M, Sullivan, P F, Carter, F A, McIntosh, V V & Joyce, P R (1998) The role of exposure with response prevention in the cognitive-behavioural therapy for bulimia nervosa. *Psychological Medicine*, **28**, 611–623.

Button, E (1993) *Eating Disorders: Personal Construct Therapy and Change*. John Wiley & Sons, Chichester.

Button, E J, Sonuga-Barke, E J S, Davies, J & Thompson, M (1996) A prospective study of self-esteem in the prediction of eating problems in adolescent schoolgirls: questionnaire findings. *British Journal of Clinical Psychology*, **35**, 193–203.

Cachelin, F M, Striegal-Moore, R H, Elder, K A, Pike, K M, Wilfley, D E & Fairburn, C G (1999) Natural course of a community sample of binge eating disorder. *International Journal of Eating Disorders*, **25**, 45–54.

Carter, F A & Bulik, C M (1994) Exposure treatments for bulimia nervosa: procedure, efficacy and mechanisms. *Advances in Behaviour Research and Therapy*, **16**, 77–129.

Carter, J C & Fairburn, C G (1998) Cognitive-behavioural self-help for binge eating disorder: a controlled effectiveness study. *Journal of Consulting and Clinical Psychology*, **66**, 616–623.

Cash, T F & Deagle, E A (1997) The nature and extent of body-image disturbance in anorexia nervosa and bulimia nervosa: a meta-analysis. *International Journal of Eating Disorders*, **22**, 107–125.

Casper, R C, Eckert, E D, Halmi, K A, Goldberg, S C & Davis, J M (1980) Bulimia: its incidence and clinical importance in patients with anorexia nervosa. *Archives of General Psychiatry*, **37**, 1030–1034.

Channon, S, de Silva, P, Hemsley, D & Perkins, R (1989) A controlled trial of cognitive behavioral and behavioral treatment for anorexia nervosa. *Behaviour Research and Therapy*, **27**, 529–535.

Clinton, D N (1996) Why do eating disordered patients drop out? *Psychotherapy and Psychosomatics*, **65**, 29–35.

Cochrane, C E, Brewerton, T D, Wilson, D B & Hodges, E L (1993) Alexithymia in eating disorders. *International Journal of Eating Disorders*, **14**, 219–222.

Collier, D A, Sham, P C, Arranz, M J, Hu, X & Treasure, J (1999) Commentary on 'Understanding the genetic predisposition to anorexia nervosa'. *European Eating Disorders Review*, **7**, 96–102.

Collings, S & King, M (1994) Ten-year follow-up of 50 patients with bulimia nervosa. *British Journal of Psychiatry*, **164**, 80–87.

Connan, F (1998) Machismo nervosa; an ominous variant of bulimia nervosa. *European Eating Disorders Review*, **6**, 154–159.

Connan, F & Treasure, J L (1998) Stress, eating and neurobiology. In: Hoek, H W, Treasure, J L & Katzman, M A (Editors) *Neurobiology in the Treatment of Eating Disorders*. John Wiley & Sons, Chichester and New York.

Cooper, P J (1995) Bulimia nervosa and binge eating; a guide to recovery Robinson; London In: Hoek, H W, Treasure, J L & Katzman, M A (Editors) *Neurobiology in the Treatment of Eating Disorders*. John Wiley & Sons, Chichester and New York.

Cooper, P J (1995) Eating disorders and their relationship to mood and anxiety disorders. In: Brownell, K D & Fairburn, C G (Editors) *Eating Disorders and Obesity: A Comprehensive Handbook*. Guilford Press, New York and London.

Cooper, P J & Fairburn, C G (1986) The depressive symptoms of bulimia nervosa. *British Journal of Psychiatry*, **148**, 268–274.

Cooper, P J, Coker, S & Fleming, C (1996) An evaluation of the efficacy of cognitive behavioural self-help for bulimia nervosa. *Journal of Psychosomatic Research*, **40**, 281–287.

Cooke, R A, Chambers, J B, Singh, R, Todd, G J, Smeeton, N C, Treasure, J & Treasure, T (1994) QT interval in anorexia nervosa. *British Heart Journal*, **72**, 69–73.

Copeland, P M & Herzog, D B (1987) Menstrual abnormalities. In: Hudson, J & Pope, H G J (Editors) *The Psychobiology of Bulimia*. American Psychiatric Association, Washington, DC.

Crisp, A H (1967) Anorexia nervosa. *Hospital Medicine*, **1**, 713–718.

Crisp, A H (1980) *Anorexia Nervosa: Let Me Be*. Academic Press, London.

Crisp, A H, Norton, K, Gowers, S, Halek, C, Bowyer, C, Yeldham, D, Levett, G & Bhat, A (1991) A controlled study of the effect of therapies aimed at adolescent and family psychopathology in anorexia nervosa. *British Journal of Psychiatry*, **159**, 325–333.

Crisp, A H (1997) Anorexia nervosa as a flight from growth: assessment and treatment based on the model. In: Garner, D M & Garfinkel, P E (Editors) *Handbook of Treatment for Eating Disorders* (second edition). Guilford Press, New York and London.

Dare, C & Eisler, I (1995) Family therapy. In: Garner, D M & Garfinkel, P E (Editors) *Handbook of Treatment for Eating Disorders* (second edition). Guilford Press, New York and London.

Dare, C & Eisler, I (1997) Family therapy for anorexia nervosa. In: Garner, D M & Garfinkel, P E (Editors) *Handbook of Treatment for Eating Disorders* (second edition). Guilford Press, New York and London.

Dennis, A B & Sansome, R A (1991) The clinical stages of treatment for eating disorder patients with borderline personality disorder. In: Johnson, C L (Editor) *Psychodynamic Treatment of Anorexia Nervosa and Bulimia.* Guilford Press, New York.

de Zwaan, M (1997) Status and utility of a new diagnostic category: binge eating disorder. *European Eating Disorders Review,* **5,** 226–240.

Dolan, R J, Mitchell, J & Wakeling, A (1988) Structural brain changes in patients with anorexia nervosa. *Psychological Medicine,* **18,** 349–353.

Dyer, C (1994) Judge allows force feeding of mentally competent patient. *British Medical Journal,* **309,** 291–292.

Eckert, E D, Halmi, K A, Marchi, P, Grove, W & Crosby, R (1995) Ten-year follow-up of anorexia nervosa: clinical course and outcome. *Psychological Medicine,* **25,** 143–156.

Eisler, I (1995) Family models of eating disorders. In: Szmukler, G, Dare, C & Treasure, J (Editors) *Handbook of Eating Disorders: Theory, Treatment and Research.* John Wiley & Sons, Chichester.

Eisler, I, Dare, C, Russell, G F M, Szmukler, G, le Grange, D & Dodge, E (1997) Family and individual therapy in anorexia nervosa. *Archives of General Psychiatry,* **54,** 1025–1030.

Ellison, Z R & Foong, J (1998) Neuroimaging in eating disorders. In: Hoek, H W, Treasure, J L & Katzman, M A (Editors) *Neurobiology in the Treatment of Eating Disorders.* John Wiley & Sons, Chichester and New York.

Emborg, C (1999) Mortality and causes of death in eating disorders in Denmark 1970–1993: a case register study. *International Journal of Eating Disorders,* **25,** 243–251

Fairburn, C G (1981) A cognitive behavioural approach to the management of bulimia. *Psychological Medicine,* **11,** 707–711.

Fairburn, C G (1995a) Physiology of anorexia nervosa. In: Brownell, K D & Fairburn, C G (Editors) *Eating Disorders and Obesity: A Comprehensive Handbook.* Guilford Press, New York and London.

Fairburn, C G (1995b) *Overcoming Binge Eating.* Guilford Press, New York.

Fairburn, C G (1997a) Interpersonal psychotherapy for bulimia nervosa In: Garner, D M & Garfinkel, P E (Editors) *Handbook of Treatment for Eating Disorders* (second edition). Guilford Press, New York and London.

Fairburn, C G (1997b) Towards evidence-based and cost-effective treatment for bulimia nervosa. *European Eating Disorders Review,* **5,** 145–148.

Fairburn, C G & Beglin, S J (1990) Studies of the epidemiology of bulimia nervosa. *American Journal of Psychiatry,* **147,** 401–408.

Fairburn, C G & Beglin, S J (1994) Assessment of eating disorders: interview or self report questionnaire? *International Journal of Eating Disorders,* **16,** 363–370.

Fairburn, C G & Carter, J C (1997) Self-help and guided self-help for binge eating problems. In: Garner, D M & Garfinkel, P E (Editors) *Handbook of Treatment for Eating Disorders* (second edition). Guilford Press, New York and London.

Fairburn, C G & Cooper, Z (1993) The Eating Disorders Examination (12th edition). In: Fairburn, C G & Wilson, G T (editors) *Binge Eating; Nature, Assessment and Treatment.* Guilford Press, New York and London.

Fairburn, C G, Cooper, Z, Doll, H A & Welch, S L (1999) Risk factors for anorexia nervosa: three integrated case comparisons. *Archives of General Psychiatry,* **56,** 468–476.

Fairburn, C G, Doll, H A, Welch, S L, Hay, P J, Davies, B A & O'Connor, M E (1998) Risk factors for binge eating disorder: a community based case-control study. *Archives of General Psychiatry*, **55**, 425–432.

Fairburn, C G & Peveler, R C (1990) Bulimia nervosa and the stepped care approach to management. *Gut*, **31**, 1220–1222.

Fairburn, C G, Jones, R, Peveler, R C, Carr, S J, Solomon, R A, O'Connor, M E, Burton, J & Hope, R A (1991) Three psychological treatments for bulimia nervosa. *Archives of General Psychiatry*, **48**, 463–469.

Fairburn, C G, Jones, R, Peveler, R C, Hope, R A & O'Connor, M E (1993) Psychotherapy and bulimia nervosa: the longer term effects of interpersonal psychotherapy, behaviour therapy and cognitive-behaviour therapy. *Archives of General Psychiatry*, **50**, 419–428.

Fairburn, C G, Marcus, M D & Wilson, G T (1993) Cognitive-Behavioural Therapy for binge eating and bulimia nervosa: a comprehensive treatment manual. In: Fairburn, C G & Wilson, G T (Editors) *Binge Eating; Nature, Assessment and Treatment*. Guilford Press, New York and London.

Fairburn, C G, Norman, P A, Welch, S L, O'Connor, M E, Doll, H A & Peveler, R C (1995) A prospective study of outcome in bulimia nervosa and the long-term effects of three psychological treatments. *Archives of General Psychiatry*, **52**, 304–312.

Fairburn, C G, Welch, S L, Doll, H A, Davies, B A & O'Connor, M E (1997) Risk factors for bulimia nervosa: a community based case-control study. *Archives of General Psychiatry*, **54**, 509–517.

Ferguson, J M & Damluji, N F (1988) Anorexia nervosa and schizophrenia. *International Journal of Eating Disorders*, **7**, 343–352.

Fettes, P A & Peters, J M (1992) A meta-analysis of group treatments for bulimia nervosa. *International Journal of Eating Disorders*, **11**, 97–110.

Fichter, M M, Elton, M, Engel, K, Meyer, A-E, Mall, H & Poustka, F (1991) Structured Interview for Anorexia and Bulimia Nervosa (SIAB): development of a new instrument for the assessment of eating disorders. *International Journal of Eating Disorders*, **10**, 571–592.

Fichter, M M, Herpertz, S, Quadflieg, N & Herperttz-Dahlmann, B (1998) Structured Interview for Anorexia and Bulimic Disorders for DSM-IV and ICD-10: updated (third) revision. *International Journal of Eating Disorders*, **24**, 227–249.

Fichter, M M & Quadflieg, N (1997) Six-year course of bulimia nervosa. *International Journal of Eating Disorders*, **22**, 361–384.

Fluoxetine Bulimia Nervosa Collaborative Study Group (1992) Fluoxetine in the treatment of bulimia nervosa: a multi-center placebo-controlled double-blind trial. *Archives of General Psychiatry*, **49**, 139–147.

Fombonne, E (1995) Anorexia nervosa; no evidence of an increase. *British Journal of Psychiatry*, **166**, 464–471.

Fosson, A, de Bruyn, R & Thomas, S (1996) Physical aspects. In: Lask, B & Bryant-Waugh, R (Editors) *Childhood Onset Anorexia Nervosa and Related Eating Disorders*. Psychology Press, Hove.

Fosson, A, Knibbs, J, Bryant-Waugh, R & Lask, B (1987) Early onset anorexia nervosa. *Archives of Disease in Childhood*, **62**, 114–118.

Freeman, C P L (1992) Day-patient treatment for anorexia nervosa. *British Review of Anorexia nervosa and Bulimia*, **6**, 2–8.

Frisch, R E & McArthur, J (1974) Menstrual cycles: fatness as a determinant of minimum weight for height necessary for their maintenance and onset. *Science*, **185**, 941–951.

Fullerton, D T, Wonderlich, S A & Gosnell, B A (1995) Clinical characteristics of eating disorder patients who report sexual or physical abuse. *International Journal of Eating Disorders*, **17**, 243–249.

van Furth, E F (1998) The treatment of anorexia nervosa. In: Hoek, H W, Treasure, J L & Katzman, M A (Editors) *Neurobiology in the Treatment of Eating Disorders*. John Wiley & Sons, Chichester and New York.

Gard, M C E & Freeman, C P L (1996) The dismantling of a myth: a review of eating disorders and socioeconomic status. *International Journal of Eating Disorders*, **20**, 1–12.

Garfinkel, P E & Walsh, B T (1997) Drug therapies. In: Garner, D M & Garfinkel, P E (Editors) *Handbook of Treatment for Eating Disorders* (second edition). Guilford Press, New York and London.

Garner, D M (1991) *Eating Disorders Inventory – 2: Psychological Assessment Resources*, Odessa, FL.

Garner. D M (1997) Psychoeducational principles in treatment In: Garner, D M & Garfinkel, P E (Editors) *Handbook of Treatment for Eating Disorders* (second edition). Guilford Press, New York and London.

Garner, D M & Garfinkel, P E (1979) The Eating Attitudes Test: an index of the symptoms of anorexia nervosa. *Psychological Medicine*, **9**, 273–279.

Garner, D M & Garfinkel, P E (Editors) *Handbook of Treatment for Eating Disorders* (second edition). Guilford Press, New York and London.

Garner, D M, Garfinkel, P E, Schwartz, D M & Thompson, M M (1980) Cultural expectations of thinness in women. *Psychological Reports*, **47**, 483–491.

Garner, D M, Olmsted, M P, Bohr, Y & Garfinkel, P E (1982) The Eating Attitudes Test; psychometric features and clinical correlates. *Psychological Medicine*, **12**, 871–878.

Garner, D M, Olmsted, M P & Polivy, J (1983) Development and validation of a multidimensional Eating Disorders Inventory for anorexia nervosa and bulimia. *International Journal of Eating Disorders*, **2**, 15–34.

Garner, D M, Vitousek, K M & Pike, K M (1997) Cognitive-behavioral therapy in anorexia nervosa. In: Garner, D M & Garfinkel, P E (Editors) *Handbook of Treatment for Eating Disorders* (second edition). Guilford Press, New York and London.

Garner, D M & Wooley, S C (1991) Confronting the failure of behavioural and dietary treatments of obesity. *Clinical Psychology Review*, **11**, 729–780.

Gerlingoff, M, Backmund, H & Franzen, U (1998) Evaluation of a day treatment programme for eating disorders. *European Eating Disorders Review*, **6**, 96–106.

Gillberg, I C, Rastam, M & Gillberg, C (1995) Anorexia nervosa 6 years after onset: Part I, Personality disorders. *Comprehensive Psychiatry*, **36**, 61–69.

Glendinning, L & Phillips, M (1996) Nursing management. In: Lask, B & Bryant-Waugh, R (Editors) *Childhood Onset Anorexia Nervosa and Related Eating Disorders*. Psychology Press, Hove.

Goldberg, D M and Huxley, P (1980) *Mental Illness in the Community: The Pathway to Psychiatric Care*. Tavistock, London.

Goldstein, D J, Wilson, M G, Ascroft, R C & Al-Banna, M (1999) Effectiveness of fluoxetine therapy in bulimia nervosa regardless of comorbid depression. *International Journal of Eating Disorders*, **25**, 19–27.

Goldstein, D J, Wilson, M G, Thompson, V L, Potvin, J H & Rampey, A H (1995) Long-term fluoxetine treatment of bulimia nervosa (Fluoxetine Bulimia Nervosa Research Group). *British Journal of Psychiatry*, **166**, 660–666.

Goodwin, G M, Fairburn, C G & Cowen, P J (1987) Dieting changes serotonergic function in women, not men: implications for the aetiology of anorexia nervosa. *Psychological Medicine*, **17**, 839–842.

Gowers, S G & Crisp, A H (1990) Anorexia nervosa in an 80 year-old woman. *British Journal of Psychiatry*, **157**, 754–757.

Gowers, S G, North, C D, Byram, V & Weaver, A B (1996) Life event precipitants of adolescent anorexia nervosa. *Journal of Child Psychology, Psychiatry and Allied Disciplines*, **37**, 469–477.

Gowers, S, Norton, K, Halek, C & Crisp, A H (1994) Outcome of outpatient psychotherapy in a random allocation treatment study of anorexia nervosa. *International Journal of Eating Disorders*, **15**, 165–177.

le Grange, D, Eisler, I, Dare, C & Russsell, G F M (1992) Evaluation of family therapy in anorexia nervosa. *International Journal of Eating Disorders*, **12**, 347–357.

Gray, J, Ford, K & Kelly, L (1987) The prevalence of bulimia in a black college population. *International Journal of Eating Disorders*, **6**, 733–740.

Gull, W W (1874) Anorexia nervosa (apepsia hysterica, anorexia hysterica). *Transactions of the Clinical Society of London*, **7**, 22–28.

Habermas, T (1989) The psychiatric history of anorexia nervosa and bulimia nervosa: weight concerns and bulimic symptoms in early case reports. *International Journal of Eating Disorders*, **8**, 259–273.

Habermas, T (1992) Further evidence on early case descriptions of anorexia nervosa and bulimia nervosa. *International Journal of Eating Disorders*, **11**, 351–359.

Halmi, K A, Eckert, E, LaDu, T J & Cohen, J (1986) Anorexia nervosa: treatment efficacy of cyproheptidine and amitriptyline. *Archives of General Psychiatry*, **43**, 177–181.

Halmi, K A, Eckert, E, Marchi, P, Sampugnaro, V, Apple, R & Cohen, J (1991) Comorbidity of psychiatric diagnoses in anorexia nervosa. *Archives of General Psychiatry*, **48**, 712–718.

Hamilton, L, Brooks-Gunn, J & Warren, M (1985) Sociocultural influences on eating disorders in professional female ballet dancers. *International Journal of Eating Disorders*, **4**, 465–477.

Hay, P (1998) The epidemiology of eating disorder behaviours: an Australian community-based survey. *International Journal of Eating Disorders*, **23**, 371–382.

Henderson, M & Freeman, C P L (1987) A self-rating scale for bulimia: the 'BITE'. *British Journal of Psychiatry*, **150**, 18–24.

Herman, C P & Polivy, J (1984) A boundary model for the regulation of eating. In: Stunkard, A J & Stellar, E (Editors) *Eating and its Disorders*. Raven Press, New York.

Herzog, D B (1995) Psychodynamic psychotherapy for anorexia nervosa. In: Brownell, K D & Fairburn, C G (Editors) *Eating Disorders and Obesity: A Comprehensive Handbook*. Guilford Press, New York and London.

Herzog, D B, Keller, M B & Lavori, P W (1988) Outcome in anorexia nervosa and bulimia nervosa. *Journal of Nervous and Mental Disease*, **176**, 131–143.

Herzog, D B, Keller, M B, Lavori, P W, Kenny, G M & Sacks, N R (1992) The prevalence of personality disorders in 210 women with eating disorders. *Journal of Clinical Psychiatry*, **53**, 147–152.

Herzog, W, Deter, H-C & Vanderycken, W (Editors) (1992) *The Course of Eating Disorders: Long Term Follow-Up Studies of Anorexia and Bulimia Nervosa*. Springer-Verlag, Berlin.

Higgitt, A & Fonagy, P (1993) Psychotherapy in borderline and narcissistic personality disorder. In: Tyrer, P & Stein, G (Editors) *Personality Disorder Reviewed*. Gaskell, London.

Higgs, J F, Goodyer, I M & Birch, J (1989) Anorexia nervosa and food refusal emotional disorder. *Archives of Disease in Childhood*, **64**, 346–351.

Hill, A J (1993) Pre-adolescent dieting: implications for eating disorders. *International Review of Psychiatry*, **5**, 87–100.

Hill, A J & Pallin, V (1999) Dieting awareness and low self worth: related issues in 8 year-old girls. *International Journal of Eating Disorders*, **24**, 405–413.

Hoek, H W (1993) Review of the epidemiological studies of eating disorders. *International Review of Psychiatry*, **5**, 61–74.

Hoek, H W, Bartelds, A I M, Bosveld, J J F, van der Graf, Y, Limpens, V E L, Maiwald, M & Spaaij, C J K (1995) Impact of urbanisation on detection rates of eating disorders, *American Journal of Psychiatry*, **152**, 1272–1278.

Hoek, H W, van Harten, P N, van Hoeken, D & Susser, E (1998) Lack of relation between culture and anorexia nervosa – results of an incidence study on Curacao. *New England Journal of Medicine*, **338**, 1231–1232.

van Hoeken, D, Lucas, A R & Hoek, H W (1998) Epidemiology. In: Hoek, H W, Treasure, J L & Katzman, M A (Editors) *Neurobiology in the Treatment of Eating Disorders*. John Wiley & Sons, Chichester and New York.

Holden, N L (1990) Is anorexia nervosa an obsessive-compulsive disorder? *British Journal of Psychiatry*, **157**, 1–5.

Holmes J, (1997) Attachment, autonomy, intimacy: some clinical implications of attachment theory. *British Journal of Medical Psychology*, **70**, 231–248.

Holland, A J, Sicotte, N & Treasure, J (1988) Anorexia nervosa: evidence for a genetic basis. *Journal of Psychosomatic Research*, **32**, 561–571.

Hsu, L K G (1988) The outcome of anorexia nervosa: a reappraisal. *Psychological Medicine*, **18**, 807–812.

Hsu, L K G (1995) Outcome of bulimia nervosa. In: Brownell, K D & Fairburn, C G (Editors) *Eating Disorders and Obesity: A Comprehensive Handbook*. Guilford Press, New York and London.

Hsu, L K G (1997) Can dieting cause an eating disorder? *Psychological Medicine*, **27**, 509–513.

Hsu, L K G, Kaye, W H & Weltzin, T (1993) Are eating disorders related to obsessive compulsive disorders? *International Journal of Eating Disorders*, **14**, 305–318.

Hurley, J B, Palmer, R L & Stretch, D (1990) The specificity of the Eating Disorders Inventory: a reappraisal. *International Journal of Eating Disorders*, **9**, 419–424.

Johnson, C (Editor) (1991) *Psychodynamic Treatment of Anorexia Nervosa and Bulimia*. Guilford Press, New York.

Johnson, C (1995) Psychodynamic treatment of bulimia nervosa. In: Brownell, K D & Fairburn, C G (Editors) *Eating Disorders and Obesity: A Comprehensive Handbook*. Guilford Press, New York and London.

Joughin, N A, Crisp, A H, Gowers, S G & Bhat, A V (1991) The clinical features of late onset anorexia nervosa. *Postgraduate Medical Journal*, **67**, 973–977.

Kaplan, A S & Olmsted, M P (1997) Partial hospitalization. In: Garner, D M & Garfinkel, P E (Editors) *Handbook of Treatment for Eating Disorders (second edition)*. Guilford Press, New York and London.

Katzman, M A (1997) Getting the difference right: it's power not gender that matters. *European Eating Disorders Review*, **5**, 71–74.

Katzman, M A & Lee, S (1997) Beyond body image: the integration of feminist and transcultural theories in the understanding of self starvation. *International Journal of Eating Disorders*, **22**, 385–394.

Kaye, W H (1995) Neurotransmitters and anorexia nervosa. In: Brownell, K D & Fairburn, C G (Editors) *Eating Disorders and Obesity: A Comprehensive Handbook*. Guilford Press, New York and London.

Kaye, W H, Greeno, C G, Moss, H, Fernstrom, J, Fernstrom, M, Lilenfeld, L R, Weltzin, T & Mann, J J (1998) Alterations in serotonin activity and psychiatric symptoms after recovery from bulimia nervosa. *Archives of General Psychiatry*, **55**, 927–935.

Keel, P K & Mitchell, J E (1997) Outcome of bulimia nervosa. *American Journal of Psychiatry*, **154**, 313–321.

Keel, P K, Mitchell, J E, Miller, K B, Davis, T L & Crow, S J (1999) Long-term outcome of bulimia nervosa. *Archives of General Psychiatry*, **56**, 63–69.

Keller, M, Herzog, D, Lavori, P, Bradburn, I & Mahoney, E (1992) The natural history of bulimia nervosa: extraordinarily high rates of chronicity, relapse, recurrence and psychosocial morbidity. *International Journal of Eating Disorders*, **12**, 1–10.

Kendler, K S, MacLean, C, Neale, M, Kessler, R, Heath, A & Eaves, L (1991) The genetic epidemiology of bulimia nervosa. *American Journal of Psychiatry*, **148**, 1627–1637.

Kendler, K S, Walters, E E, Neale, M, Kessler, R C, Heath, A C & Eaves, L J (1995) The structure of the genetic and environmental risk factors for six major psychiatric in women. *Archives of General Psychiatry*, **52**, 372–383.

Kerberg, O, Selzer, M, Koenigberg, H W, Carr, A & Applebaum, A (1989) *Psychodynamic Psychotherapy of Borderline Patients*. Basic Books, New York.

Keys, A, Brozek, J, Henschel, A, Mickelson, O & Taylor, H L (1950) *The Biology of Human Starvation*. University of Minnesota Press, Minneapolis.

King, M & Mezey, G (1987) Eating behaviour in male racing jockeys. *Psychological Medicine*, **17**, 249–253.

Kisely, S (1999) Psychotherapy for severe personality disorder: exploring the limits of evidence based purchasing. *British Medical Journal*, **318**, 1410–1412.

Klerman, G L, Weissman, M M, Rounsaville, B J & Chevron, E S (1984) *Interpersonal Psychotherapy of Depression*. Basic Books, New York.

Killen, J D, Taylor, C B, Hayward, C, Wilson, D M, Haydel, K F, Hammer, L D, Simmonds, B, Robinson, T N, Litt, I, Vardy, A & Kraemer, H (1994) Pursuit of thinness and onset of eating disorder symptoms in a community sample of adolescent girls: a three year prospective analysis. *International Journal of Eating Disorders*, **16**, 227–238.

Killick, S & Allen, C (1997) Shifting the balance. *European Eating Disorders Review*, **5**, 33–41.

Kingston, K, Szmukler, G, Andrewes, D, Tress, B & Desmond, P (1996) Neuropsychological and structural brain changes in anorexia nervosa before and after refeeding. *Psychological Medicine*, **26**, 15–28.

Lacey, J H (1983) Bulimia nervosa, binge eating and psychogenic vomiting: a controlled treatment study and long term outcome. *British Medical Journal*, **286**, 1609–1613.

Lacey, J H (1992) Long-term follow-up of bulimic patients treated in integrated behavioural and psychodynamic treatment programmes. In: Herzog, W, Deter, H-C & Vanderycken, W (Editors) *The Course of Eating Disorders: Long Term Follow-Up Studies of Anorexia and Bulimia Nervosa*. Springer-Verlag, Berlin.

Lacey, J H (1995) Inpatient treatment of multi-impulsive bulimia nervosa In: Brownell, K D & Fairburn, C G (Editors) *Eating Disorders and Obesity: A Comprehensive Handbook*. Guilford Press, New York and London.

Lacey, J H & Dolan, B (1988) Bulimia in British Blacks and Asians: a catchment area study. *British Journal of Psychiatry*, **152**, 73–79.

Lacey, J H & Evans, C D H (1986) The impulsivist; a multi-impulsive personality disorder. *British Journal of Addiction*, **81**, 641–649.

Lacey, J H & Gibson, E (1985) Does laxative abuse control body weight? A comparative study of purging and vomiting bulimics. *Journal of Human Nutrition (Applied Nutrition)*, **39A**, 36

Lacey, J H & Read, T R C (1993) Multi-impulsive bulimia: description of an inpatient eclectic treatment programme and a pilot follow-up study of its efficacy. *European Eating Disorders Review* **1**, 22–31.

Laessle, R G (1990) Affective disorders and bulimic syndromes. In: Fichter, M M (Editor) *Bulimia Nervosa: Basic Research, Diagnosis and Therapy*. John Wiley & Sons, Chichester.

Lanceley, C & Travers, R (1993) Anorexia nervosa; forced feeding and the law (letter). *British Journal of Psychiatry*, **163**, 835.

Lasegue, E C (1874) De l'anorexie hysterique. *Archives Generales de Medicine*, **21**, 385–403.

Lask, B (1996) Family therapy and family counselling. In: Lask, B & Bryant-Waugh, R (Editors) *Childhood Onset Anorexia Nervosa and Related Eating Disorders*. Psychology Press, Hove.

Lask, B & Bryant-Waugh, R (Editors) (1996) *Childhood Onset Anorexia Nervosa and Related Eating Disorders*. Psychology Press, Hove.

Lask, B & Fosson, A (1996) Physical treatments. In: Lask, B & Bryant-Waugh, R (Editors) *Childhood Onset Anorexia Nervosa and Related Eating Disorders*. Psychology Press, Hove.

Lee S, Ho, T P & Hsu, L K G (1993) Fat phobic and non-fat phobic anorexia nervosa – a comparative study of 70 Chinese patients in Hong Kong. *Psychological Medicine*, **23**, 999–1017.

Leitenberg, H, Rosen, J C, Gross, J, Nudelman, S & Vara, L (1988) Exposure plus response prevention treatment of bulimia nervosa. *Journal of Consulting and Clinical Psychology*, **56**, 535–541.

Levine, M D & Marcus, M D (1998) The treatment of binge eating disorder. In: Hoek, H W, Treasure, J L & Katzman, M A (Editors) *Neurobiology in the Treatment of Eating Disorders*. John Wiley & Sons, Chichester and New York.

Linehan, M M (1993) *Cognitive-Behavioral Treatment of Borderline Personality Disorder*. Guilford Press, New York and London.

Linehan, M M, Armstrong, H E, Suarez, A, Allman, D & Heard, H L (1991) Cognitive-behavioral treatment of chronically parasuicidal borderline patients. *Archives of General Psychiatry*, **48**, 1060–1064.

Lilenfeld, L R & Kaye, W H (1998) Genetic studies of anorexia and bulimia nervosa. In: Hoek, H W, Treasure, J L & Katzman, M A (Editors) *Neurobiology in the Treatment of Eating Disorders*. John Wiley & Sons, Chichester and New York.

Lucas, A R, Beard, C M, O'Fallon, W M & Kurland, L T (1991) 50-year trends in the incidence of anorexia nervosa in Rochester, Minnesota: a population-based study. *American Journal of Psychiatry*, **148**, 917–922.

Marcus, M D (1995) Binge eating and obesity. In: Brownell, K D & Fairburn, C G (Editors) *Eating Disorders and Obesity: A Comprehensive Handbook*. Guilford Press, New York and London.

Marcus, M D (1997) Adapting treatment for patients with binge-eating disorder. In: Garner, D M & Garfinkel, P E (Editors) *Handbook of Treatment for Eating Disorders* (second edition). Guilford Press, New York and London.

Marcus, M D, Smith, D, Santelli, R & Kaye, W (1992) Characteriszation of eating disordered behaviour in obese binge eaters. *International Journal of Eating Disorders*, **12**, 249–255.

Marcus, M D, Wing, R R & Fairburn, C G (1995) Cognitive treatment of binge eating versus behavioural weight control in the treatment of binge eating disorder. *Annals of Behavioral Medicine*, **17**, S090.

Masson, J M (1984) *Freud: the Assault on Truth*. Faber & Faber, London.

Matsunaga, H, Kriike, N, Iwasaki, Y, Mitaya, A, Yamagi, S & Kaye, W H (1999) Clinical characteristics in patients with anorexia nervosa and obsessive-compulsive disorder. *Psychological Medicine*, **29**, 407–414.

Mayer, L E S & Walsh, B T (1998) Pharmacotherapy of eating disorders. In: Hoek, H W, Treasure, J L & Katzman, M A (Editors) *Neurobiology in the Treatment of Eating Disorders*. John Wiley & Sons, Chichester and New York.

McLoughlin, D M, Spargo, E, Wassif, W S, Newham, D J, Peters, T J, Lantos, P L & Russell, G F M (1998) Structural and functional changes in skeletal muscle in anorexia nervosa. *Acta Neuropathologica*, **96**, 632–640.

McCluskey, S E, Lacey, J H & Pearce, J M (1992) Binge eating and polycystic ovaries (letter). *Lancet*, **340**, 723.

McManus, F & Waller, G (1995) A functional analysis of binge-eating. *Clinical Psychology Review*, **15**, 845–865.

Meyer, C, Waller, G & Waters, A (1998) Emotional states and bulimic psychopathology. In: Hoek, H W, Treasure, J L & Katzman, M A (editors) *Neurobiology in the Treatment of Eating Disorders*. John Wiley & Sons, Chichester and New York.

Merrill, C, Mines, R & Starkey, R (1987) The premature dropout in the group treatment of bulimia nervosa. *International Journal of Eating Disorders*, **6**, 293–300.

Miller, W R & Rollnick, S (1991) *Motivational Interviewing: Preparing People for Change Addictive Behaviours*. Guilford Press, New York and London.

Milosevic, A (1999) Eating disorders – a dentist's perspective. *European Eating Disorders Review*, **7**, 103–110.

Mitchell, J E (1995) Medical complications of bulimia nervosa. In: Brownell, K D & Fairburn, C G (Editors) *Eating Disorders and Obesity: A Comprehensive Handbook*. Guilford Press, New York and London.

Mitchell, J E, Pyle, R L, Eckert, E D, Hatsukami, D & Lentz, R (1983) Electrolyte and other physiological abnormalities in patients with bulimia. *Psychological Medicine*, **13**, 273–278.

Mitchell, J E, Seim, H C, Colon, E & Pomeroy, C (1987) Medical complications and medical management of bulimia. *Annals of Internal Medicine*, **107**, 71–77.

Mount Sinai (1965) Evolution of psychosomatic concepts – anorexia nervosa: a paradigm. *The International Psycho-Analytic Library*, No. 65. Hogarth Press, London.

Mumford, D B, Whitehouse, A M & Platts, M (1991) Sociocultural correlates of eating disorders among Asian schoolgirls in Bradford. *British Journal of Psychiatry*, **158**, 222–228.

Mussell, M P, Mitchell, J E, Weller, C L, Raymond, N C, Crow, S J & Crosby, R D (1995) Onset of binge eating, dieting, obesity and mood disorders among subjects seeking treatment for binge eating disorder. *International Journal of Eating Disorders* **17**, 395–410.

Mussell, M P, Mitchell, J E, Fenna, C J, Crosby, R D, Miller, J P and Hoberman, H M (1997) A comparison of binge eating and dieting in the development of bulimia nervosa, *International Journal of Eating Disorders*, **21**, 353–360.

Nasser, M (1997) *Culture and Weight Consciousness*. Routledge, London.

Nathan, J S & Allison, D B (1998) Psychological and physical assessment of persons with eating disorders. In: Hoek, H K, Treasure, J L & Katzman, M A (Editors) *Neurobiology in the Treatment of Eating Disorders*. John Wiley & Sons, Chichester and New York.

Neilsen, S & Molbek, A G (1998) Eating disorders and type I diabetes: overview and summing-up. *European Eating Disorders Review*, **6**, 4–26.

Neilsen, S, Moller-Madsen, S, Isager, T, Jorgensen, J, Pagsberg, K & Theander, S (1998) Standardised mortality in eating disorders – a quantitative summary of previously published and new evidence. *Journal of Psychosomatic Research*, **44**, 413–434.

Newton, R, Freeman, C, Hannan, W & Cowen, S (1993) Osteoporosis and normal weight bulimia nervosa – which patients are at risk? *Journal of Psychosomatic Research*, **37**, 239–247.

Olmsted, M P, Davis, R, Garner, D M, Rockert, W, Irvine, M J & Eagle, M (1991) Efficacy of a brief group psychoeducational intervention for bulimia nervosa. *Behaviour Research and Therapy*, **29**, 71–83.

Olmsted, M P & Kaplan, A S (1995) Psychoeducation in the treatment of the eating disorders. In: Brownell, K D & Fairburn, C G (Editors) *Eating Disorders and Obesity: A Comprehensive Handbook*. Guilford Press, New York and London.

O'Neill, Crowther T & Sampson, G (1994) Anorexia nervosa: palliative care of terminal psychiatric disease. *American Journal of Hospice and Palliative Care*, **11**, 36–38.

Opplinger, R A, Landry, G L, Foster, S W & Lambercht, A C (1993) Bulimic behaviors among interscholastic wrestlers: a statewide survey. *Pediatrics*, **91**, 826–831.

Owen, J B (1998) Models of eating disturbance in animals. In: Hoek, H W, Treasure, J L & Katzman, M A (Editors) *Neurobiology in the Treatment of Eating Disorders*. John Wiley & Sons, Chichester and New York.

Palmer, R L (1989) The Spring Story: a way of talking about clinical eating disorder. *British Review of Anorexia Nervosa and Bulimia*, **4**, 33–41.

Palmer, R L (1993) Weight concern should not be a necessary criterion for the eating disorders; a polemic. *International Journal of Eating Disorders*, **14**, 459–465.

Palmer, R L (1995) Sexual abuse and eating disorders In: Brownell, K D & Fairburn, C G (Editors) *Eating Disorders and Obesity: A Comprehensive Handbook*. Guilford Press, New York and London.

Palmer, R L (1998) Culture, constitution, motivation and the mysterious rise of bulimia nervosa. *European Eating Disorders Review*, **6**, 81–84.

Palmer, R L, Christie, M, Cordle, C, Davies, D & Kenrick, J (1987) The Clinical Eating Disorders Rating Instrument (CEDRI); a preliminary description. *International Journal of Eating Disorders*, **6**, 9–16.

Palmer, R L, Gatward, N, Black, S & Park, S (2000) Anorexia nervosa: service consumption and outcome of local patients in the Leicester Service. *Psychiatric Bulletin* (in press).

Palmer, R L & Oppenheimer, R (1992) Childhood sexual experiences with adults: a comparison of women with eating disorders and those with other diagnoses. *International Journal of Eating Disorders*, **12**, 359–364.

Palmer, R L, Robertson, D N, Cain, M & Black, S (1996) The Clinical Eating Disorders Rating Instrument (CEDRI): Evidence for validity in practice. *European Eating Disorders Review*, **4**, 149–156.

Parry-Jones, B (1991) Historical terminology of eating disorders. *Psychological Medicine*, **21**, 21–28.

Parry-Jones, B & Parry-Jones, W L (1995) History of bulimia and bulimia nervosa. In: Brownell, K D & Fairburn, C G (Editors) *Eating Disorders and Obesity: A Comprehensive Handbook*. Guilford Press, New York and London.

Patchell, R A, Fellows, H A & Humphries, L L (1994) Neurological complications of anorexia nervosa. *Acta Neurologica Scandinavica*, **89**, 111–116.

Patton, G C (1988) Mortality in eating disorders. *Psychological Medicine*, **18**, 947–951.

Patton, G C, Johnson-Sabine, E, Wood, K, Mann, A H & Wakeling, A (1990) Abnormal eating attitudes in London schoolgirls – a prospective epidemiological study. *Psychological Medicine*, **20**, 383–394.

Patton, G C, Wood, K & Johnson-Sabine, E (1986) Physical illness: a risk factor in anorexia nervosa. *British Journal of Psychiatry*, **149**, 756–759.

Patton, G C, Selzer, R, Coffey, C, Carlin, J B & White, R (1999) Onset of adolescent eating disorders: population based cohort study over 3 years. *British Medical Journal*, **318**, 765–768.

Peveler, R C (1995) Eating disorders and diabetes. In: Brownell, K D & Fairburn, C G (Editors) *Eating Disorders and Obesity: A Comprehensive Handbook*. Guilford Press, New York and London.

Peveler, R C & Fairburn, C G (1989) Anorexia nervosa in association with diabetes mellitus – a cognitive behavioural approach to treatment. *Behaviour Research and Therapy*, **27**, 95–99.

Peveler, R C & Fairburn, C G (1992) The treatment of bulimia nervosa in patients with diabetes mellitus. *International Journal of Eating Disorders*, **11**, 45–53.

Pieri, L F & Campbell, D A (1999) Understanding the genetic predisposition to anorexia nervosa. *European Eating Disorders Review*, **7**, 84–95.

Piran, N & Kaplan, A S (Editors) (1990) *A Day Hospital Group Treatment Program for Anorexia Nervosa and Bulimia Nervosa*. Brunner Mazel, New York,

Pirke, K M (1995) Physiology of bulimia nervosa. In: Brownell, K D & Fairburn, C G (Editors) *Eating Disorders and Obesity: A Comprehensive Handbook*. Guilford Press, New York and London.

Polivy, J & Federoff, I (1997) Group Psychotherapy. In: Garner, D M & Garfinkel, P E (Editors) *Handbook of Treatment for Eating Disorders (second edition)*. Guilford Press, New York and London.

Polivy, J & Herman, C P (1995) Dieting and its relation to eating disorder. In: Brownell, K D & Fairburn, C G (Editors) *Eating Disorders and Obesity: A Comprehensive Handbook*. Guilford Press, New York and London.

Pope, H G, Hudson, J I, Nixon, R A & Herridge, P L (1986) The epidemiology of ipecac abuse. *New England Journal of Medicine*, **313**, 1457–1459.

Prochaska, J O & DiClementi, C C (1986) Towards a comprehensive model of change. In: Miller W R & Heather N (Editors) *Treating Addictive Behaviours: Processes of Change*. Plenum Press, New York.

Prochaska, J O & DiClementi, C C (1992) The transtheoretical model of change. In: Norcross, J C & Goldfried, M R (Editors) *Handbook of Psychotherapy Integration*. Basic Books, New York.

Ramsay, R, Ward, A, Treasure, J & Russell, G F M (1999) Compulsory treatment in anorexia nervosa: short term benefits and long-term mortality. *British Journal of Psychiatry*, **175**, 147–153.

Rastam, M (1992) Anorexia nervosa in 51 Swedish children and adolescents: premorbid problems and comorbidity. *Journal of the American Academy of Child and Adolescent Psychiatry*, **31**, 819–829.

Rastam, M & Gillberg, C (1991) The family background in anorexia nervosa: a population based study. *Journal of the American Academy of Child and Adolescent Psychiatry*, **30**, 283–289.

Rastam, M & Gillberg, C (1992) Background factors in anorexia nervosa: a controlled study of 51 teenage cases including a population sample. *European Child and Adolescent Psychiatry*, **1**, 54–65.

Rastam, M, Gillberg, C, Gillberg, I C & Johansson, M (1997) Alexithymia in anorexia nervosa: a controlled study using the 20-item Toronto alexithymia scale. *Acta Psychiatrica Scandinavica*, **95**, 385–388.

Ratan, D, Ghandi, D & Palmer, R L (1998) Eating disorders in British Asians. *International Journal of Eating Disorders*, **24**, 101–105.

Ratnasutiya, R H, Eisler, I, Szmukler, G I & Russell, G F M (1991) Anorexia nervosa: outcome and prognostic factors after 20 years. *British Journal of Psychiatry*, **158**, 495–502.

Raymond, N, Mussell, M, Mitchell, J E, Crosby, R & de Zwaan, M (1995) An age matched comparison of subjects with binge eating disorder and bulimia nervosa. *International Journal of Eating Disorders*, **18**, 135–143.

Rigotti, N A, Neer, R M, Skates, S J, Herzog, D B & Nussbaum, S R (1991) The clinical course of osteoporosis in anorexia nervosa: a longitudinal study of cortical bone mass. *Journal of the American Medical Association*, **265**, 1133–1138.

Rintala, M & Mustajoki, P (1992) Could mannequins menstruate? *British Medical Journal*, **305**, 1575–1576.

Robin, A L, Siegal, P T, Koepke, T, Moye, A W & Tice, S (1994) Family therapy versus individual therapy for adolescent females with anorexia nervosa. *Journal of Developmental and Behavioral Pediatrics*, **15**, 111–116.

Robinson, P H, Clarke, M & Barrett, J (1988) Determinants of delayed gastric emptying in anorexia nervosa. *Gut*, **29**, 458–464.

Rosen, J C & Leitenberg, H (1985) Exposure plus response prevention treatment of bulimia. In: Garner, D M & Garfinkel, P E (Editors) *Handbook for Psychotherapy of Anorexia Nervosa and Bulimia*. Guilford Press, New York.

Rossiter, E M, Agras, W S, Telch, C F & Schneider, A (1993) Cluster B personality disorder characteristics predict outcome in the treatment of bulimia nervosa. *International Journal of Eating Disorders*, **13**, 349–358.

Roy-Byrne, P, Lee-Brenner, K & Yager, J (1984) Group therapy for bulimia. *International Journal of Eating Disorders*, **3**, 97–116.

Russell, G F M (1970) Anorexia nervosa: its identity as an illness and its treatment In: Price, J H (Editor) *Modern Trends in Psychological Medicine* (Volume 2). Butterworth, London.

Russell, G F M (1979) Bulimia nervosa: an ominous variant of anorexia nervosa? *Psychological Medicine*, **9**, 429–448.

Russell, G F M (1995) Anorexia nervosa through time. In: Szmuckler, G, Dare, C & Treasure, J (Editors) *Handbook of Eating Disorders: Theory, Treatment and Research*. John Wiley & Sons, Chichester and New York.

Russell, G F M (1997) The history of bulimia nervosa. In: Garner, D M & Garfinkel, P E (Editors) *Handbook of Treatment for Eating Disorders* (second edition). Guilford Press, New York and London.

Russell, G F M, Szmukler, G I, Dare, C & Eisler, I (1987) An evaluation of family therapy in anorexia nervosa and bulimia nervosa. *Archives of General Psychiatry*, **44**, 1047–1056.

Rutherford, J, McGuffin, P, Katz, R J & Murray, R M (1993) Genetic influences on eating attitudes in a normal female twin population. *Psychological Medicine*, **23**, 425–436.

Sabine, E J, Yonance, A, Farrington, A J, Barratt, K & Wakeling, A (1983) Bulimia nervosa: a placebo controlled double-blind therapeutic trial of mianserine. *British Journal of Clinical Pharmacology*, **15**, 195S–202S.

Santonaso, P, Ferrara, S & Favaro, A (1999) Differences between binge eating disorder and nonpurging bulimia nervosa. *International Journal of Eating Disorders*, **25**, 215–218.

Schmidt, U (1998) Treatment of bulimia nervosa. In: Hoek, H W, Treasure, J L & Katzman, M A (Editors) *Neurobiology in the Treatment of Eating Disorders.* John Wiley & Sons, Chichester and New York.

Schmidt, U, Jiwany, A & Treasure, J (1993) A controlled study of alexithymia in eating disorders. *Comprehensive Psychiatry*, **34**, 54–58.

Schmidt, U, Humfress, H & Treasure, J (1997) The role of general family environment and sexual and physical abuse in the origins of eating disorders. *European Eating Disorders Review*, **5**, 184–207.

Schmidt, U, Tiller, J, Blanchard, M, Andrews, B & Treasure, J (1997) Is there a specific trauma associated with anorexia nervosa? *Psychological Medicine*, **27**, 523–530.

Schmidt, U, Tiller, J & Treasure, J (1993) Setting the scene for eating disorders: childhood care, classification and course of illness, *Psychological Medicine*, **23**, 663–672.

Schmidt, U & Treasure, J (1993) *Getting Better Bit(e) by Bit(e).* Lawrence Erlbaum Associates, London.

Schneider, J & Agras, W (1987) Bulimia in males: a matched comparison with females. *International Journal of Eating Disorders*, **6**, 235–242.

Schwartz, R, Barrett, M J & Saba, G (1985) Family therapy for bulimia. In: Garner, D & Garfinkel, P (Editors) *Handbook of Psychotherapy for Anorexia and Bulimia.* Guilford Press, New York.

Selvini-Palazzoli, M (1974) *Self-starvation: From the Intrapsychic to the Transpersonal Approach.* Chaucer, London.

Serfaty, M & McCluskey, S (1998) Compulsory treatment of anorexia nervosa and the moribund patient. *European Eating Disorders Review*, **6**, 27–37.

Serpell, L & Treasure, J (1997) Osteoporosis – a serious health risk in chronic anorexia nervosa. *European Eating Disorders Review*, **5**, 149–157.

Sharpe, C W & Freeman, C P L (1993) The medical complications of anorexia nervosa. *British Journal of Psychiatry*, **162**, 452–462.

Silverman, J A (1995) History of anorexia nervosa. In: Brownell, K D & Fairburn, C G (Editors) *Eating Disorders and Obesity: A Comprehensive Handbook.* Guilford Press, New York and London.

Silverman, J A (1997) Anorexia nervosa: historical perspective on treatment. In: Garner, D M & Garfinkel, P E (Editors) *Handbook of Treatment for Eating Disorders* (second edition). Guilford Press, New York and London.

Smeets, M A M (1997) The rise and fall of body size estimation in anorexia nervosa: a review and reconceptualisation. *European Eating Disorders Review*, **5**, 75–95.

Spitzer, R L, Devlin, M J, Walsh, B T, Hasin, D, Wing, R, Marcus, M D, Stunkard, A J, Wadden, T, Yanovski, S, Agras, S, Mitchell, J and Nonas, C (1992) Binge eating disorder: a multi-site field trial of the diagnostic criteria. *International Journal of Eating Disorders*, **11**, 191–203.

Soundy, T J, Lucas, A R, Suman, V J & Melton, L J (1995) Bulimia nervosa in Rochester, Minnesota from 1980 to 1990. *Psychological Medicine*, **25**, 1065–1071.

Spitzer, R L, Marcus, M D, Walsh, B T, Hasin, D, Wing, R, Stunkard, A, Wadden, T, Yanovski, S, Agras, S, Mitchell, J & Nonas (1992) Binge eating disorder: a multi-site field trial of the diagnostic criteria. *International Journal of Eating Disorders*, **11**, 191–203.

Spitzer, R L, Yanovski, S, Wadden, T, Wing, R, Marcus, M D, Stunkard, A J, Devlin, M, Mitchell, J, Hasin, D & Horne, R (1993) Binge eating disorder: its further validation in a multi-site study. *International Journal of Eating Disorders*, **13**, 137–153.

Spreeuwenberg, C & Kastelein, W R (1992) Hulp bij zelfdoding anorexia nervosa-patient (Help with self-killing of anorexia nervosa patient). *Medisch Contact*, **17**, 541–543.

Steiger, H & Stotland, S (1996) Prospective study of outcome of bulimia as a function of axis II comorbidity: long term response on eating and psychiatric symptoms. *International Journal of Eating Disorders*, **20**, 149–161.

Stein, S, Chaloub, N & Hodes, M (1998) Very early-onset bulimia nervosa: report of two cases. *International Journal of Eating Disorders*, **24**, 323–327.

Steinhausen, H-C, Rauss-Mason, C & Seidel, R (1991) Follow-up studies of anorexia nervosa. *Psychological Medicine*, **21**, 447–451.

Stevenson, J & Meares, R (1992) An outcome study of psychotherapy for patients with borderline personality disorder. *American Journal of Psychiatry*, **149**, 358–362.

Striegal-Moore, R H (1995) A feminist perspective on the etiology of eating disorders. In: Brownell, K D & Fairburn, C G (Editors) *Eating Disorders and Obesity: A Comprehensive Handbook*. Guilford Press, New York and London.

Stunkard, A J (1993) A history of binge eating. In: Fairburn, C G & Wilson, G T (Editors) *Binge Eating: Nature, Assessment and Treatment*. Guilford Press, New York and London.

Strober, M (1995) Family-genetic perspectives on anorexia nervosa and bulimia nervosa. In: Brownell, K D & Fairburn, C G (Editors) *Eating Disorders and Obesity: A Comprehensive Handbook*. Guilford Press, New York and London.

Strober, M, Freeman, R & Morrell, W (1997) The long term course of severe anorexia nervosa in adolescents: survival analysis of recovery, relapse, and outcome predictors over 10–15 years in a prospective study. *International Journal of Eating Disorders*, **22**, 339–360.

Stunkard, A J & Sobal, J (1995) Psychosocial consequences of obesity. In: Brownell, K D & Fairburn, C G (Editors) *Eating Disorders and Obesity: A Comprehensive Handbook*. Guilford Press, New York and London.

Sullivan, P F (1995) Mortality in anorexia nervosa. *American Journal of Psychiatry*, **152**, 1073–1074,

Sullivan, P F, Bulik, C M & Kendler, K S (1998) The epidemiology and classification of bulimia nervosa. *Psychological Medicine*, **28**, 599–610.

Swift, W J, Andrew, D & Barlage, N E (1986) The relationship between affective disorder and eating disorders: a review of the literature. *American Journal of Psychiatry*, **143**, 290–299.

Szmukler, G I, Andrewes, D, Kingston, K, Chen, L, Stargatt, R & Stanley, R (1992) Neuropsychological impairment in anorexia nervosa before and after refeeding. *Journal of Clinical and Experimental Neuropsychology*, **14**, 347–352.

Szmukler, G, Dare, C & Treasure, J (Editors) (1995) *Handbook of Eating Disorders: Theory, Treatment and Research*. John Wiley & Sons, Chichester and New York.

Szmukler, G I, Eisler, I, Gillies, C & Hayward, M (1985a) The implications of anorexia nervosa in a ballet school. *Journal of Psychiatric Research*, **19**, 177–181.

Szmukler, G I, Eisler, I, Russell, G F M & Dare, C (1985b) Anorexia nervosa, parental 'expressed emotion' and dropping out of treatment. *British Journal of Psychiatry*, **147**, 265–271.

Szmukler, G I, McCance, C, McCrone, L & Hunter, D (1986) Anorexia nervosa: a psychiatric case register study from Aberdeen. *Psychological Medicine*, **16**, 49–58.

Szmukler, G I, Young, G P, Miller, G, Lichtenstein, M & Binns, D S (1995) A controlled trial of cisapride in anorexia nervosa. *International Journal of Eating Disorders*, **17**, 345–357.

Theander, S (1985) Outcome and prognosis in anorexia nervosa and bulimia: some results of previous investigations compared with those of a Swedish long-term study. *Journal of Psychiatric Research*, **19**, 493–508.

Thompson, J, Palmer, R L & Petersen, S (1988) Is there a physiological component to counterregulation? *International Journal of Eating Disorders*, **7**, 307–319.

Touyz, S W, Beumont, P J V, Glaun, D, Phillips, T & Cowie, I (1984) A comparison of lenient and strict operant conditioning programs in refeeding patients with anorexia nervosa. *British Journal of Psychiatry*, **144**, 517–520.

Treasure, J & Campbell, I (1994) The case for biology in anorexia nervosa. *Psychological Medicine*, **24**, 3–8.

Treasure, J & Kordy, H (1998) Evidence based care of eating disorders: beware the glitter of the randomised controlled trial. *European Eating Disorders Review*, **6**, 85–95.

Treasure, J & Ramsay, R (1998) Hard to swallow: compulsory treatment in eating disorders. Maudsley Discussion Paper No. 3.

Treasure, J, Schmidt, U, Troop, N, Tiller, J, Todd, G, Keilen, M & Dodge, E (1994) First step in managing bulimia nervosa: controlled trial of a therapeutic manual. *British Medical Journal*, **308**, 686–689.

Treasure, J, Todd, G, Brolly, M, Tiller, J, Nehmed, A & Denman, F (1995) A pilot study of a randomised trial of cognitive analytic therapy versus educational behavioural therapy for adult anorexia nervosa. *Behaviour Research and Therapy*, **33**, 363–367.

Treasure, J & Ward, A (1997) A practical guide to the use of motivational interviewing in anorexia nervosa. *European Eating Disorders Review*, **5**, 102–114.

Troop, N A, Holbrey, A, Trowler, R & Treasure, J L (1994) Ways of coping in women with eating disorders. *Journal of Nervous and Mental Disease*, **182**, 535–540.

Turnbull, S, Ward, A, Treasure, J, Jick, H & Derby, L (1996) The demand for eating disorder care: an epidemiological study using the General Practice Research Database. *British Journal of Psychiatry*, **169**, 705–712.

Tuschen, B & Bents, H (1995) Intensive brief inpatient treatment of bulimia nervosa. In: Brownell, K D & Fairburn, C G (Editors) *Eating Disorders and Obesity: A Comprehensive Handbook*. Guilford Press, New York and London.

Vanderlinden, J & Vanderycken, W (1997) *Trauma, Dissociation and Impulse Control in Eating Disorders*. Brunner/Mazel, Bristol, Pennsylvania.

Vanderycken, W (1994) Emergence of bulimia nervosa as a separate diagnostic entity: review of the literature from 1960 to 1979. *International Journal of Eating Disorders*, **16**, 105–116.

Vanderycken, W (1998) Whose competence should we question? *European Eating Disorders Review*, **6**, 1–3.

Vanderycken, W & van Deth, R (1990) A tribute to Lasegue's description of anorexia nervosa (1873), with completion of its English translation. *British Journal of Psychiatry*, **157**, 902–908.

Vanderycken, W & van Deth, R (1994) *From Fasting Saints to Anorexic Girls: The History of Self Starvation*. Athlone Press, London.

Vanderycken, W & Pierloot, R (1983) Drop-out during in-patient treatment of anorexia nervosa: a clinical study of 133 patients. *British Journal of Medical Psychology*, **56**, 145–156.

van Hanswijck de Jonge, P & van Furth, E (1999) Eating disorders in models: fact or fiction? *European Eating Disorders Review* (in press).

Vitousek, K (1995) Cognitive-behavioural therapy for anorexia nervosa. In: Brownell, K D & Fairburn, C G (Editors) *Eating Disorders and Obesity: A Comprehensive Handbook*. Guilford Press, New York and London.

Wadden, T A, Foster, G D & Letizia, K A (1992) Response of obese binge eaters to treatment by behavioral therapy combined with very low calorie diet. *Journal of Consulting and Clinical Psychology*, **60**, 808–811.

Waller, G (1997) Drop-out and failure to engage in individual outpatient cognitive behavioural therapy for bulimic disorders. *International Journal of Eating Disorders*, **22**, 35–41.

Walsh, B T (1995) Pharmacotherapy of eating disorders. In: Brownell, K D & Fairburn, C G (Editors) *Eating Disorders and Obesity: A Comprehensive Handbook*. Guilford Press, New York and London.

Walsh, B T & Garner, D M (1997) Diagnostic Issues. In: Garner, D M & Garfinkel, P E (Editors) *Handbook of Treatment for Eating Disorders* (second edition). Guilford Press, New York and London.

Walsh, B T, Hadigan, C M, Devlin, M J, Gladis, M, & Roose, S P (1991) Long-term outcome of antidepressant treatment of bulimia nervosa. *American Journal of Psychiatry*, **148**, 1206–1212.

Webster, J & Palmer, R L (2000) The childhood and family background of women with clinical eating disorders: a comparison with women with major depression and women without psychiatric disorder. *Psychological Medicine*, **30**, 57–60.

Welch, S L, Doll, H A & Fairburn, C G (1997) Life events and the onset of bulimia nervosa; a controlled study. *Psychological Medicine*, **27**, 515–522.

Welch, S L & Fairburn, C G (1994) Sexual abuse and bulimia nervosa: three integrated case-control comparisons. *American Journal of Psychiatry*, **151**, 402–407.

Whittal, M C, Agras, W S & Gould, R A (1999) Bulimia nervosa: a meta-analysis of psychosocial treatments and pharmacological treatments. *Behavior Therapy*, **30**, 117–135.

Wilfley, D E, Agras, W S, Telch, C F, Rossiter, E M, Schneider, J A, Cole, A G, Sifford, L, & Raeburn, S D (1996) Group cognitive-behavioural therapy and group interpersonal psychotherapy for the non-purging bulimic individual: a controlled comparison. *Journal of Consulting and Clinical Psychology*, **61**, 296–305.

Williams, C J, Pieri, L, Sims, A, Russon, L & Alison, D (1998) Controversies in management Does palliative care have a role in treatment of anorexia nervosa? *British Medical Journal*, **317**, 195–197.

Williams, P & King, M (1987) The 'epidemic' of anorexia nervosa: another medical myth? *Lancet*, **1**, 205–207.

Williamson, I (1999) Why are gay men a high risk group for eating disorders? *European Eating Disorders Review*, **7**, 1–4.

Wilson, G T (1993) Assessment of binge eating. In: Fairburn, C G & Wilson, G T (Editors) *Binge Eating; Nature, Assessment and Treatment*. Guilford Press, New York and London.

Wilson, G T (1995) Eating disorders and addictive disorders. In: Brownell, K D & Fairburn, C G (Editors) *Eating Disorders and Obesity: A Comprehensive Handbook*. Guilford Press, New York and London.

Wilson, G T (1996a) Treatment of bulimia nervosa: when CBT fails. *Behaviour Research and Therapy*, **34**, 197–212.

Wilson, G T (1996b) Manual-based treatments: the clinical application of research findings. *Behaviour Research and Therapy*, **34**, 295–315.

Wilson, G T (1999) Treatment of bulimia nervosa: the next decade. *European Eating Disorders Review*, **7**, 77–83.

Wilson, G T, Eldridge, K L, Smith, D & Niles, B (1991) Cognitive-behavioural treatment with and without response prevention for bulimia. *Behaviour Research and Therapy*, **29**, 575–583.

Wilson, G T, Fairburn, C G & Agras, W S (1997) Cognitive-Behavioural Therapy for bulimia nervosa. In: Garner, D M & Garfinkel, P E (Editors) *Handbook of Treatment for Eating Disorders* (second edition). Guilford Press, New York and London.

Winston, A P, Jamieson, C P, Madira, W, Gatward, N M & Palmer, R L (1999) The prevalence of thiamine deficiency in anorexia nervosa. *International Journal of Eating Disorders* (in press).

Wiseman, C V, Gray, J J, Mosimann, J E & Ahrems, A H (1992) Cultural expectations of thinness in women; an update. *International Journal of Eating Disorders*, **11**, 85–89.

Wonderlich, S A (1995) Personality and eating disorders. In: Brownell, K D & Fairburn, C G (editors) *Eating Disorders and Obesity: A Comprehensive Handbook.* Guilford Press, New York and London.

Wonderlich, S A, Brewerton, T D, Jocic, Z, Dansky, B S & Abbott, D W (1997) Relationship of childhood sexual abuse and eating disorders. *Journal of the Academy of Child and Adolescent Psychiatry*, **36**, 1107–1115.

Wonderlich, S A, Fullerton, D, Swift, W J and Klein, M H (1994) Five year outcome from eating disorders: relevance of personality disorders. *International Journal of Eating Disorders*, **15**, 233–244.

Wonderlich, S A, Wilsnack, R W, Wilsnack, S C & Harris, T R (1996) Childhood sexual abuse and bulimic behavior in a nationally representative sample. *American Journal of Public Health*, **86**, 1082–1086.

Wooley, S C (1995) Feminist influences on the treatment of eating disorders. In: Brownell, K D & Fairburn, C G (Editors) *Eating Disorders and Obesity: A Comprehensive Handbook.* Guilford Press, New York and London.

World Health Organisation (1992) *The ICD-10 Classification of Mental and Behavioural Disorders: Clinical Descriptions and Diagnostic Guidelines.* WHO, Geneva.

INDEX